SPEAKING VOLUMES

Women, Reading, and Speech in the Age of Austen

Speaking Volumes

WOMEN, READING, AND SPEECH
IN THE AGE OF AUSTEN

Patricia Howell Michaelson

STANFORD UNIVERSITY PRESS
Stanford, California 2002

Stanford University Press
Stanford, California
© 2002 by the Board of Trustees of the
Leland Stanford Junior University

Printed in the United States of America
on acid-free, archival-quality paper

Library of Congress Cataloging-in-Publication Data
Michaelson, Patricia Howell
Speaking volumes : women, reading, and speech in the age of
Austen / Patricia Howell Michaelson.
p. cm.
Includes bibliographical references (p.) and index.
ISBN 0-8047-4075-5 (acid-free paper)
1. English fiction—Women authors—History and criticism.
2. Women—Books and reading—England—History—19th
century.   3. Women—Books and reading—England—
History—18th century.   4. Women and literature—England—
History—19th century.   5. Women and literature—England—
History—18th century.   6. Austen, Jane, 1775–1817—
Criticism and interpretation.   7. Austen, Jane, 1775–1817—
Contemporaries.   8. Language and languages—Sex differences.
9. Language and culture—England.   10. Oral interpretation—
History.   11. Reader-response criticism.
12. Speech in literature.   I. Title.

PR8a68.W6 M53 2002
823'7099287—dc21   2001048428

Original Printing 2002

Last figure below indicates year of this printing:
11   10   09   08   07   06   05   04   03   02

Typeset by BookMatters in 10.5/12.5 Bembo

for Joel

Acknowledgments

A portion of Chapter 5 was previously published in "Reading *Pride and Prejudice*," *Eighteenth-Century Fiction* 3 (1990), 65–76; I am grateful to the editors for permission to reprint.

A few passages in Chapters 1 and 4 were previously published in "Women in the Reading Circle," *Eighteenth-Century Life* 13 (1989), 59–69.

Chapter 2 borrows some material from "Religious Bases of Eighteenth-Century Feminism: Mary Wollstonecraft and the Quakers," *Women's Studies* 22 (1993), 281–95, copyright OPA N.V., reprinted with permission from Gordon and Breach Publishers.

Contents

Illustrations

Preface

This project originated, as many do, in a personal experience. While not exactly a "Janeite," by the time I was in my early twenties, I felt I knew *Pride and Prejudice* pretty much by heart. But then, one summer, a friend and I read it aloud to each other, and I was astonished at how different—and how much better—this text was than the one I had read so many times to myself. Every sentence had barbs that I had skimmed over. Surely, I thought, this novel was meant to be read aloud. And once I made that leap, I started collecting evidence of all kinds of oral readings in the late eighteenth century. However, the project soon moved out from the original formalist question (In what ways was this novel written to take advantage of oral performance?) to one that turned toward the reader (What happened to the reader when she performed a text?), and from there it was only a short hop to the relationship of reading and speech in the late eighteenth century.

Though I come to this topic from a base in British literary studies, my argument must be seen as situated both there and in gender studies conceived more broadly. In emphasizing the continuing oral qualities in and oral performance of text, I argue against the tradition that links "the rise of the novel" firmly to print culture and to silent, solitary reading. And in insisting that women constructed complex characters in speech—characters in which gender may or may not be the most salient quality—I argue against the unfortunate tendency of both eighteenth- and twentieth-century language theorists to define "woman's language" as a coherent sociolect.

xiii

Two brief notes on my own language. First: literary scholars use various terms for the time period of concern in this book, roughly Jane Austen's lifetime (1775–1817). Those who emphasize change within the period tend to call this age "Romantic." Others, like myself, feel that that term overemphasizes one kind of literature within the period and neglects works (like Austen's) that have little in common with Romanticism proper. These scholars include the period in the "long" eighteenth century; I will imply that term even when I omit the adjective. Second, in a work concerned with constructing identity in speech, I have taken the liberty of following the current practice of my own speech community, the Quakers, even where that conflicts with scholarly norms. In particular, although Quaker speech has dropped some of the singularities described in Chapter 2, we still avoid the use of honorific or hereditary titles. Where this may cause confusion (Stanhope for Chesterfield, for example), I have given the title in parentheses and cross-referenced it in the index.

This project has benefited from the support of many friends and colleagues. My colleagues at the University of Texas at Dallas, especially Michael Wilson and Jerry Soliday, have been unstinting in their willingness to listen and gracious in sharing their considerable wisdom. Nancy Tuana's advice and example and Elke Matijevich's hospitality (and birding skills!) have been inspiring. I am grateful to Dean Dennis Kratz for financial support. Colleagues in eighteenth-century studies have generously read portions of the text and made many suggestions for improvement; they include Paula Backscheider, Barbara Benedict, Michèle Cohen, Claudia Johnson, Clive Jones, Shelley King, Lawrence E. Klein, Carol Percy, and Eddie Warren. Their knowledge, judgment, and gifts of time are much appreciated. Robert DeMaria Jr., John O'Neill, and Peter Rabinowitz gave needed encouragement at crucial moments. In these hard times for academic presses, I thank Stanford University Press for continuing the tradition of scholarship and hope that its trust and labor are rewarded. Thanks are also due to my faith community, the Atlanta Monthly Meeting of the Religious Society of Friends; to my siblings, nieces, and nephew; and especially to my husband, Joel Bowman, whose love sustains me. This book is dedicated to him.

SPEAKING VOLUMES

Women, Reading, and Speech in the Age of Austen

Introduction

Speaking Volumes is an interdisciplinary study of English women and language in the late eighteenth and early nineteenth centuries, and especially of the connections that contemporaries made between speech and reading. The ambiguity of my title is meant to capture that connection: do women speak volumes, or do volumes speak? The first formulation points to the ancient stereotype of the loquacious woman, a stereotype that still resonated in the eighteenth century, as indeed it does to some extent today. By invoking this stereotype, I concede its importance in the discursive practices of the period. However, the task of this book is more celebratory: it is first to recapture, insofar as possible, the linguistic practices of individual women, and second, to understand how literature could assist women in developing multifaceted linguistic identities. Eighteenth-century (male) language theorists posited "woman" as a single, unified class of speakers; *Speaking Volumes* explores the ways women could construct complex characters in speech. Using a wide range of evidence from language texts, schoolbooks, diaries and letters, conduct books, and works of literature (most prominently, the novels of Jane Austen), I show how women of the eighteenth century used the stereotype strategically, while insisting implicitly that their gender identity was not always the most salient one.

In shifting from generalized discourse to individual language use, I give up the kinds of large claims that some historians find so tempting. But my gesture parallels the recent turn among feminist linguists away from the broad generalizations about women's language that characterized the pioneering work in the field, toward the specific and complex ways in which language is actually used. In a recent review article, Deborah Cameron argues that it is time to shift our attention from "woman's language" (a mode of speech) to "the language used by women" (who may use many modes); she describes this as a shift from a symbolic category to an empirical one.[1] At the same time, the two remain linked insofar as individual women utilize symbolic "woman's language" in constituting themselves as gendered beings. It is the point at which the symbolic and the empirical meet that is the focus here.

As Cameron's essay indicates, the field of language and gender has matured to the extent that it now incorporates many theoretical positions and its own self-critique. But to my knowledge, this is the first book to examine the speech of women of the past. Most recent work in feminist linguistics begins with the close examination of transcribed "natural" conversations; for obvious reasons, this limits its scope to the present. As a literary and cultural historian, I do not claim that *Speaking Volumes* uses the methods of the social sciences. However, insofar as this kind of sociolinguistics focuses on the close analysis of individual usage, it both parallels the activities of close reading and legitimizes the use of a historical record that may be spotty or incomplete.

As a historical work, *Speaking Volumes* necessarily relies on written representations of speech. I argue below that the representational nature of textual evidence is, in itself, meaningful. But more important, I make the historical argument that in this period, text and speech were conceived of as closely intertwined—hence the second meaning of my title. While scholars of eighteenth-century literature have emphasized the burgeoning of print culture in the period, *Speaking Volumes* points rather to the continuing importance of the spoken word in eighteenth-century rhetorical theory and to the ways literature was conceived of in terms of oral performance. At the end of the book, I argue for reconceiving fiction like that of Jane Austen as an avenue for the development of women's skill in speech.

Speaking Volumes thus participates in two quite different scholarly conversations. To that on language and gender, it aims to add a historical dimension that has so far been lacking. In that on eighteenth-century literature, it moves our understanding of the cultural practice of reading in entirely new directions. Mindful that my reader may be familiar with only one of these conversations—and because this project entails obvious methodological problems that must be addressed—I intend this Introduction to be truly introductory, taking more time than is perhaps usual to situate my argument.

Feminism, Voice, and Silence

Let me begin by exploring the third meaning of my title: the allusion to the paradoxical commonplace "Her silence spoke volumes." In 1965, Tillie Olsen published "Silences in Literature," an essay that would frame one of the defining metaphors of contemporary feminism: that of voice. Olsen wrote of the external factors that hinder authors' production: the "unnatural" silences caused by censorship, by lack of access to education, by lack of time and the freedom to focus on oneself when one must work and raise children. Although she pointedly included men in her discussion, Olsen's essay in large part recapitulated the ideas Virginia Woolf had expressed about women writers in *A Room of One's Own*. But Olsen's key term—*silence*—crystallized those ideas so memorably that metaphors of silence became a shorthand for women's oppression in now-classic texts like Adrienne Rich's *On Lies, Secrets, and Silence* and Audre Lorde's "The Transformation of Silence into Language and Action." The converse of silence, not "sound" or "noise" but "voice," came to express both self-definition and authority. Carol Gilligan's *In a Different Voice* used the metaphor to celebrate the patterns of moral development that she saw as common to American women, patterns that had been excluded from the dominant paradigm. Mary Field Belenky and the coauthors of *Women's Ways of Knowing* were struck by how many of the women they interviewed used metaphors of voice and silence, in contrast to the visual metaphors traditional in male-dominated science and philosophy. For their subjects, having no voice meant being ignored, meant letting others define them; those with a voice spoke for themselves and were heeded. Susan Sniader Lanser put it thus: "Despite compelling interrogations of 'voice' as a humanist fiction, for the collectively and personally silenced the term has become a trope of identity and power: as Luce Irigaray suggests, to find a voice (*voix*) is to find a way (*voie*)."[2]

But for all its evocative power, the metaphor of voice has, I believe, become ossified in ways that have negative consequences. These are of two kinds: the hidden costs of the metaphor itself, and the way the very success of the metaphor has obscured other meanings of silence and voice. To take the latter first: in ordinary language use, silence is by no means always negative, nor voice positive; both silence and voice are employed by competent speakers. Moreover, this dominant metaphor has encouraged us to pity, ignore, or discount the many generations of women for whom silence represented a potentially useful strategy. Feminist historians have used the metaphor as they undertook the project of recovery and have positioned themselves as listening to the voices of the past. The current study participates in this project. But allowing women to speak in their own way—especially women of the past—must include understanding their use of silence.

In its crudest form, the metaphor of voice and silence assumes that voice *is equivalent* to authority and silence *is equivalent* either to apathetic passivity or, more usually, to being silenced by an oppressor. Passive silence is registered in the AIDS activists' "silence = death," in which silence is a refusal to get involved, indeed a complicity in evils against which one should speak out. Passive silence is denial. As the title of her essay indicates, for Audre Lorde silence is the lack of language and of action. Silence corrupts the individual and harms the group: "you're never really a whole person if you remain silent, because there's always that one little piece inside you that wants to be spoken out" (42); "it is not difference which immobilizes us, but silence. And there are so many silences to be broken" (44).

If Lorde presents silence as a bad choice that should and can be altered, for other feminists "silence" is used interchangeably with "being silenced." This usage emphasizes a power relationship in which women are forced into the weaker position. An early use of this metaphor was the concept of "mutedness," developed by anthropologists Edwin and Shirley Ardener. Because anthropologists had spoken mostly with men, they argued, women's lives were described not only in men's words rather than their own, but through male systems of perception. "Mutedness" was thus the opposite of self-definition.[3] The silencing is much more coercive in the work of early feminist linguists like Dale Spender, who argued that virtually all language was based on male systems of perception, so that women were forced to speak in a male idiom or be silent. More recently, the work of Marsha Houston and Cheris Kramarae continues this trend: "There are myriad ways of silencing women or of ensuring that we do not say anything untoward. One way is simply to exclude women from certain public forums. . . . In our personal lives also the power to silence another is not simply the power to *prevent* her talk; it is also the power to *shape and control* her talk, to restrict the things that she may talk about and the ways she is permitted to express them, to permit her to speak, but to suppress her authentic voice."[4]

The metaphor of silence and voice has worked powerfully in articulating for women both a serious problem and a clear solution. But its emphasis on expressing oneself leans on an individualism that may be unexamined as a core value. Mary Crawford discusses aspects of the metaphor as riding on "the assertiveness bandwagon." Beginning in the 1970s, women were told that their lack of assertiveness interfered with self-actualization but that reeducation was relatively easy. Assertiveness training focused on linguistic behaviors that disrupted women's presumed attentiveness to offering support or maintaining relationships; women were taught not to give justifications for their statements, not to respond to their "opponent," to reiterate rather than to become engaged. Women given assertiveness training were taught to ignore what the other person said—to refuse to interact in the terms suggested by the other. Crawford stresses the dependence of assertiveness on stereotypically male norms: "In the assertiveness training movement, the ethic of human interdependence and connectedness was muted by the emphasis on individual rights, and autonomy was held up as the model of mental health."[5] Moreover, she argues that assertiveness, in stressing self-expression over communication, violates "natural language" rules of cooperation. For example, assertiveness training urges the violation of customary responses to indirectness. But indirectness has useful functions (primarily, the saving of face), and speakers who seem to be incapable of indirectness are in some sense incompetent (69–74). In other words, the metaphor of voice, as it has been widely used by feminists, not only participates in the stereotypical male norms that are precisely what is at issue, but also misrepresents the nature of conversational interaction.

Recent studies by linguists criticize the binary opposition of speech and silence. In ordinary use, speech and silence fall along a continuum; both are a part of conversation. And while silence is a measurable physical phenomenon, the meaning of silence varies widely in different cultures and, within any given culture, in different situations.[6] For example, it is easy to see that a given period of silence might be "normal" in Sweden, but not in Italy, or that a person speaking a set number of words might be considered taciturn in the south, voluble in the north. And apart from quantifying norms is the question of what silence means. Among Western Apaches, for example, silence "is used when meeting strangers. It is through not speaking to a newly met person that strangers create a feeling of interpersonal relationship." The Amish also use silence differently than do other Western cultures: "by the reduction of the amount of ceremonial talk . . . the community's silence manifests its unity with the absolute."[7]

Even within a single culture, silence has different meanings in different contexts. The feminist metaphor of silence, as discussed above, insists that silence is either a chosen or an imposed passivity. But in many circumstances silence constitutes a powerful action, often an exertion of power.[8] Many have noted that in psychoanalytic situations, for example, it is the silent analyst who is the person in control; the patient reveals himself by groping for words. Michel Foucault highlights the situation of the interrogated prisoner, for whom silence is the most powerful possible resistance. Less dramatically, as Adam Jaworski points out, silence may be a successful strategy during an argument, for it may effect the goal of keeping the door open for further communication (24).

For women, especially women of the past, speech and silence in ordinary conversation have not had the meanings assigned to them by the dominant metaphor. Women's speech has rarely been a sign of authority; on the contrary, it has been vilified as the cackling of hens or, where women have tried to claim authority, as an outrage perpetrated by a virago. When speech is so interpreted, silence may well be the best strategic choice. In our thinking about women and language, it is time to replace metaphors equating voice and silence with power and submission, in favor of imagining a range of strategies possible in any specific linguistic encounter, and a range of motivations guiding our strategic choices. Indeed, speaking and silence should not be seen solely as a power game that everyone tries to win. A silent listener may be the more social partner, by making room for an other. In addition, we must distinguish between one person's silence while another speaks and true, total silence. Few things are as truly collaborative as shared silence: it requires the simultaneous participation of everyone present. Metaphors that focus on dominance take an overly narrow view of what happens in linguistic interaction.

Finally, the metaphor of silence and voice has tended to categorize women unrealistically as either victims or heroines. This is not to deny that some women have been victimized, nor that others have spoken out courageously. But equating courage with speech tends to make us unsympathetic to women in cultures where speech is valued differently or, indeed, where it is not possible. It may cause us to denigrate or ignore women from other cultures or (the subject here) women of the past.

Linguistic Approaches to Gender

If the feminist metaphorical use of *silence* and *voice* hinders our understanding of women of the past, a more linguistic approach may serve us better. This project has been profoundly influenced by the work on language and gender that has appeared in the past twenty-odd years, especially in that branch of sociolinguistics that focuses on the ethnography of speaking. That is, I am less interested here in the sexism "built into" our language, like the so-called generic masculine or the tendency of words referring to women (like *mistress*) to become degraded in meaning. Rather, my interest is in language use and how language constructs a social identity.

Until recently, work on language and gender has presupposed that both those categories are fixed: that language use is a fairly accurate index of gender or, to put it crudely, that women just speak differently from men. The now-classic feminist linguistic works of the 1970s and 1980s differ, however, according to their emphasis on "dominance" or "difference." Studies on dominance explore the power relations expressed in conversation. Beginning with Robin Lakoff's *Language and Woman's Place,* work in this area has focused on the linguistic elements that tend to weaken women's status. Women, it is argued, adopt low-status positions by hesitating, by using hedges ("sort of," "a bit"), or by adding tag questions ("don't you think?") that ask for approval—all elements that resist claiming an authoritative position. Men not only tend not to "weaken" their own statements, but also tend to dominate the conversation, holding the floor longer and being more willing to interrupt or perform other face-threatening acts. On the other hand, linguists emphasizing "difference," like Deborah Tannen, celebrate the facilitative role that women play. These scholars see women's questions not as signs of weakness, but rather as ways of engaging the conversational partner and maintaining relationships. Women are the ones who perform the "conversational work."[9]

As the field of language and gender has matured, scholars have criticized both of these approaches for reproducing the very stereotypes that have harmed women in the past. Both approaches imagine a homogeneous category "woman," in opposition to a homogeneous category "man." And both posit (in their crudest forms) a one-to-one relationship between linguistic elements and their cultural meanings. But the link between language and gender resists such simple description. As Deborah Cameron puts it, "the relationship between using a certain kind of language and constructing a certain kind of gender identity is almost always an indirect or mediated one. In the succinct formulation of Elinor Ochs, 'few features of language directly and exclusively index gender.'"[10] As I argued above, linguistic elements like silence may have many meanings, depending on the specific context in which they are used; Deborah Tannen points out that even interruptions may be considered signs of solidarity rather than of rudeness in a "high-involvement" speech community like that of New York Jews. And Sara Mills argues that we cannot absolutely conflate gender and power, though they obviously often overlap. The features that linguists have labeled "weak" (false starts, hesitations) and "strong" (interrupting and other face-threatening acts) may be used strategically by either men or women; conversely, a given linguistic element like hesitation may have multiple meanings. Mills argues "that discourse competence comes only from a combination of cooperative and competitive strategies. . . . One speech style for all encounters marks discourse incompetence."[11]

The other term, *gender,* must also be qualified. Not only does the category "women" include others besides the Anglo middle-class women who were the tacit subjects of early work on language and gender; it also must incorporate the range of identities that every individual woman asserts as she speaks. We can extend Mills's skepticism about a neat opposition between male and female language to question the exaggerated privileging of gender as a category in linguistic scholarship. Differences among speakers might be described according to any number of categories; it is a cultural artifact that we have been so attentive to gender differences.[12] Miriam Meyerhoff highlights the multiplicity of social identities we all claim; gender identity might be the most salient in a given context, but it might not be. In any interaction, the speaker may express solidarity with an other by using linguistic features that mark occupational status, for example, or regional identity. Meyerhoff summarizes with the following points:

1. Speakers possess many different identities, some personal, some group (or social).
2. Identities vary in their salience in different communicative events, but all of a speaker's different identities are always present and are all available to the speaker in every communicative event.
3. Identities vary in salience depending on numerous non-linguistic variables: topic, interlocutor, affective goals of the speaker.
4. A speaker's identification with different identities has the potential to change during the life cycle.[13]

At the same time, however, the stakes for the study of language and gender have been raised: in the years since so many areas of scholarship have taken the "linguistic turn," language (or discourse) is viewed ever more strongly as constitutive of social identity. Gender identity, however that is defined, is largely "performed" linguistically. Recently, feminist linguists have begun to utilize the postmodern concept of "performativity" articulated by Judith Butler and others, which understands gender neither as something inborn nor as something learned once and for all, but rather as something constantly practiced as we perform acts that are recognized as implying or constituting gender. This concept has several appealing features for linguists and for the present study. Most important, it captures the ongoing construction of character through language use, recognizing the importance of the hundreds of messages we create each day. In addition, it strives to balance the social norms imposed upon us and the agency with which we choose to follow or subvert those norms. Finally, the notion of performativity seems particularly apt for work on the eighteenth century, a period in which (as many have argued) modern notions of subjectivity—like the authentic self—were developing but had not yet become naturalized.[14]

The field of language and gender today, then, makes stronger but much more complex claims than it did twenty years ago. Its insights will serve to help separate the eighteenth-century discourse on "woman's language" (which as we will see had the homogenizing tendency of the earliest work on dominance and difference, as well as anticipating some of its claims) from the varied language use of individual women speaking in specific contexts. Since eighteenth-century women were excluded from most forms of public speech, the focus here will be on private conversation and on how women developed strategies that enabled them both to achieve their local goals within the conversation and to construct identities that went beyond the stereotype.

Language and Gender and the Past

While leaning heavily on recent work in feminist linguistics, this project breaks new ground in attempting to apply that field's concerns to the past. In so doing, it crosses disciplinary boundaries in ways that may seem problematic. Contemporary linguistics favors the spoken language and the methods of social science: experimental situations or controlled observation. Fields within linguistics that do address the past, of course, use written evidence, but they then limit their claims to matters of vocabulary or grammar; they do not attempt to describe language use in conversational interaction. A historical project like mine faces the obvious challenge of evidence: eighteenth-century speech has not survived except in written representations. Thus some linguistic features are entirely lost to us: pronunciation, facial expressions, or pauses may be described in the surviving documents but are not represented directly. For all the descriptions we read, we simply don't know what the squeaky "masquerade voice" sounded like. In addition, representations of speech tend to clean up the spoken word. Anyone who has seen a transcript of a real-life conversation knows how unlike literary dialogue it is: an accurate transcript shows speakers making grammatical errors, switching directions in midsentence, using fragments, and so on. Features like the hedges or interruptions that have been important to feminist linguists are apt to be dropped from the historical record.[15]

We are in a bind: written representations of conversations are inaccurate, but they are all we have. One way out of this bind is to clarify what is knowable and what isn't. It is *not* possible to reconstruct transcripts of his-

torical conversations using written evidence. Many linguists have contrasted
the lexical and syntactic differences between spoken and written language:
in general, written language uses a larger vocabulary and more complex
structures. (The dichotomy is not absolute; for example, a formal oral presentation may use more complex language than a casual letter.)[16] We can
probably assume, but can never know, that these differences were also features of eighteenth-century language use. But in any case, one cannot work
backward from a written document to the speech it represents.

However, the focus of this book is not on lexical and syntactic features
of language, but rather on conversational interaction and on the linguistic
construction of identity. These, I suggest, are not so different in written and
spoken language. They depend on the shared knowledge of social norms,
which are expressed implicitly in fictional conversations as well as in real
ones, in writing as well as in speech. And while spoken interactions follow
somewhat different rules than do literary dialogue and other written representations (for example, rituals of greeting and leave-taking are rarely represented in novels), I would argue that they are no less "constructed."[17] That
is, the performance of gender in speech can be as intentional or as uncon-
scious as the creation of character by an author. Many features studied by
feminist linguists survive in written representations and will be significant
for this study. They include interactive questions, such as who holds the
floor, whose topics are pursued, how confrontational or polite the speakers
are, as well as the strategies women use to support or challenge their conventional gender identity. Ethnographers of communication define "communicative competence" as "the knowledge of what is and what is not
appropriate to say in any specific cultural context," according to one's position within a speech community.[18] For women of the late eighteenth century, the limits of appropriate speech were codified in strict social rules that
can be inferred by the historian.

Eighteenth-century authors were very well aware of the rules governing conversational interactions. In this project, I rely on an eclectic array of
sources, including conversation manuals, treatises by language theorists,
schoolbooks, conduct books, diaries and letters, and literary texts. I assume
throughout that these sources both reflect and teach the social norms at
stake. Furthermore, the norms can usefully be described in the terms not
only of the eighteenth century but also of our own time. In number 126 of
Johnson's *Rambler*, for instance, "Generosa" complains that women are
treated as fools when they ask questions:

> I enquired yesterday of a gentleman eminent for astronomical skill, what
> made the day long in summer, and short in winter; and was told that nature

protracted the days in summer, lest ladies should want time to walk in the park; and the nights in winter, lest they should not have hours sufficient to spend at the card-table.

I hope you do not doubt but that I heard such information with just contempt, and I desire you to discover to this great master of ridicule, that I was far from wanting any intelligence which he could have given me. I asked the question with no other intention than to set him free from the necessity of silence, and gave him an opportunity of mingling on equal terms with a polite assembly from which, however uneasy, he could not then escape, by a kind introduction of the only subject on which I believed him able to speak with propriety.[19]

This is an obvious example of what Pamela M. Fishman called "conversational work," the facilitative role that is expected of women: by asking an elementary question, Generosa pretends to be ignorant so as to make a male speaker more comfortable. The conversational role that Fishman identified in modern women speakers was probably also played by women of the past.[20]

While we can never recreate a transcript of a real-life eighteenth-century conversation, we can at least examine the ways in which conversations were reported and the significance of various representational strategies. That is, how does a particular representation, a specific invocation of the social norms, serve the author's purposes? In an unusual example, three representations have survived of a conversation between Samuel Johnson and Mary Knowles. The conversation took place on April 15, 1778, toward the end of a dinner party at the home of the bookseller Charles Dilly, which was attended by six or seven people.

The earliest surviving version still postdates the conversation by seven years: it is in a 1785 letter from Anna Seward (the poet, who was present) and reveals her dislike of Johnson. Seward's version, unlike the other two, is for a specific audience (a woman friend) and is framed by a sympathetic history of Jenny Harry, who converted to Quakerism at age eighteen and was disowned by her father and by friends like Johnson; Jenny has asked Knowles (a Quaker) to plead her case. The gist of the ensuing conversation is that Johnson believes that propriety forbids a young woman to reject the religion in which she was raised. But the representation highlights the authority of Knowles's speech. Knowles consistently sets the agenda, speaks in longer segments and more coherently; Johnson, on the other hand, merely responds to her agenda, uses "lower" diction, and speaks in puffs of anger. Where she argues theology and urges kindness toward others, Johnson is self-centered. The opening interchange is typical:

"I am to ask thy indulgence, Doctor, towards a gentle female to whom thou usedst to be kind, and who is uneasy in the loss of that kindness. Jenny Harry weeps at the consciousness that thou wilt not speak to her."

"Madam, I hate the odious wench, and desire you will not talk to me about her."[21]

Similarly, a bit further on, Knowles speaks in theological terms, Johnson only about himself:

"Ah! Doctor, we cannot rationally suppose that the Deity will not pardon a defect in judgment (supposing it should prove one) in that breast where the consideration of serving him, according to its idea, in spirit and truth, has been a preferable inducement to that of worldly interest."

"Madam, I pretend not to set bounds to the mercy of the Deity; but I hate the wench, and shall ever hate her. I hate all impudence; but the impudence of a chit's apostasy I *nauseate*." (101)

Throughout, Johnson seems out of control, responding only in anger. Even Boswell, in this version, recognizes Knowles's authority: "I never saw this mighty lion so chafed before," he says (103). Seward's account is highly feminist not only in its sense, but in its representation of conversational interaction. Indeed, Seward attributes Jenny Harry's original conversion to the power of Mary Knowles's speech: "She speaks with clear and graceful eloquence on every subject. Her antagonists were shallow theologists, and opposed only idle and pointless raillery to deep and long-studied reasoning on the precepts of Scripture, uttered in persuasive accents, and clothed with all the beauty of language" (98).

The next version of this encounter was published in the *Gentleman's* and in the *Lady's Magazine* in 1791, and according to Boswell it was written by Knowles herself. This version presents little context and is introduced simply as "An interesting Dialogue between the late Dr. Johnson, and Mrs. Knowles the Quaker." Here, the topic is less focused on Jenny Harry and more on Johnson's ignorance of Quakerism; and Johnson's personal attacks are aimed less at Jenny than at Knowles. It begins thus:

Mrs. K. Thy friend Jenny H—— desires her kind respects to thee, doctor.
Dr. J. To *me!*—tell me not of her! I hate the odious wench for her apostasy: and it is you, madam, who have seduced her from the Christian religion.
Mrs. K. This is a heavy charge indeed. I must beg leave to be heard in my own defence: and I intreat the attention of the present learned and candid company, desiring they will judge how far I am able to clear myself of so cruel an accusation.
Dr. J. (Much disturbed at this unexpected challenge, said) You are a woman, and I give you quarter.

Mrs. K. I will not take quarter. There is no sex in souls; and in the present case I fear not even Dr. Johnson himself.[22]

Throughout this version, Knowles speaks in long paragraphs, while Johnson responds with a sentence or two. Where she produces numerous arguments about Quaker thec ogy, he merely repeats his assertion that Quakers are not Christian. Again, Johnson speaks in angry bursts: "Pshaw! pshaw!—an accountable creature!—girls accountable creatures!" (489).

My point is not really that a remarkable woman could best Johnson in conversation. Rather, it is that the norms governing conversational interaction in the eighteenth century are remarkably similar to those of our time, and that these survive (if implicitly) in any representation. The power relations are revealed in terms familiar to feminist linguistics: Who proposes topics? whose topics are pursued? who holds the floor? Johnson's reaction is a textbook example of the idea that holding the floor indicates dominance. After Knowles's longest speech, we are told, "the doctor grew very angry, still more so at the space of time the gentlemen insisted on allowing his antagonist wherein to make her defence, and his impatience excited one of the company, in a whisper, to say, 'I never saw this mighty lion so chafed before'" (490).

A third and very different representation appears in Boswell's *Life of Johnson*. Boswell devotes only a single paragraph to Mary Knowles, at the end of a fifteen-page description of the evening's conversation. In this version, significantly, Johnson's contributions are longer and more substantial. For example,

MRS. KNOWLES. "[The New Testament] is clear as to essentials."
JOHNSON. "But not as to controversial points. The heathens were easily converted, because they had nothing to give up; but we ought not, without very strong conviction indeed, to desert the religion in which we have been educated."[23]

Not only has Johnson's language been cleaned up and his points made more reasonably, but the issue of conversion—which in the other versions centered on women's autonomy—is now utterly gender-neutral. Johnson's angry outbursts are merely alluded to ("He then rose again into a passion, and attacked the young proselyte in the severest terms of reproach, so that both the ladies seemed to be much shocked" [299]). Boswell does have a footnote defending his own version, and the editor of the modern scholarly edition pointedly notes that Seward's version is inaccurate. But again, my point is not to reconstruct a transcript of the actual conversation, only to show that the strategies for representing authority in conversation may not have changed very much, and thus that with due care we may work back-ward from the representations to the social norms.

The representations of this conversation illustrate the power relations that have been central to feminist linguistics. A very different kind of discourse competence is portrayed in the *Memoirs* of Harriette Wilson, a notorious Regency demirep. Being short of cash and getting too old to attract rich patrons, Wilson combined the announcement of the forthcoming memoirs with blackmail: those who wished to be omitted from the book could pay Wilson directly. Apparently a number of men did take Wilson's offer, though Arthur Wellesley (first Duke of Wellington) reportedly responded with a curt "Publish and be damned!" The later sections of the *Memoirs* consist largely of rather pitiful descriptions of Wilson's efforts to get Henry Charles Somerset (sixth Duke of Beaufort) to honor his son's promise of a lifetime annuity to Wilson, and of her acquiescence to less and less desirable patrons. But the earlier portions depict Wilson's rise framed largely in dialogue. Walter Scott praised the accuracy of the representations, "in which the style of the speaker, so far as known to me, is exactly imitated."[24] As ever, this is simply not knowable for us. What is remarkable in this text is Wilson's mastery of a wide range of styles, indicating her discourse competence. While the narrative voice is constant, in representations of dialogue Wilson is sensitive to the nuances of dialect and sociolect. For example, in one especially novelistic scene, she rides in a carriage with a lady and her French beau, an Irishman, and other assorted characters, imitating the language of fashion as well as the brogue.

As a supremely competent speaker, Wilson masters a number of styles and uses each strategically. When it is to her advantage, she uses the complex syntax and religious sentiment of courtly language. After seeing one lover's beautiful, deaf wife, for example, she tells him, "If ever our intimacy is discovered, so as not to disturb her peace of mind, on that day we must separate for ever. I can but die, and God, I hope, will have mercy on me . . . : but we are not monsters! therefore, we will never indulge in selfish enjoyments at the expense of misery to any one of our fellow-creatures, much less one who depends on you for all her happiness" (154–55).

Often, that is, Wilson represents herself as a conventional courtly lady. But, perhaps not surprisingly, her favorite context is one in which violating gender stereotypes is encouraged: "I love a masquerade; because a female can never enjoy the same liberty anywhere else. It is delightful to me to be able to wander about in a crowd, making my observations, and conversing with whomsoever I please without being liable to be stared at or remarked upon, and to speak to whom I please, and run away from them the moment I have discovered their stupidity" (462). Throughout the *Memoirs,* Wilson revels in her freedom to control the conversation. She is a master of one-upmanship, winning verbal contests through ritualized insult. When she is bored by one John Ward, she asks whether he keeps a valet and advises him to bring him next time: " 'For what, I pray?' 'Merely to laugh at your jokes,' I rejoined. 'It is such hard work for you, Sir, who have both to cut the jokes and to laugh at them too!'" (111). Another time, Wilson is annoyed when three people crash her box at the theater. She tells her companion, in French, "Let us make ourselves so disagreeable that they will be glad to go," and when he asks how, "'You shall see,' said I, 'although I am going to be very vulgar; but the case is desperate, for it is death to be stuck behind these fat people'" (374). And then, she accomplishes her end by informing the unwanted guests that they may be tainted by being seen with a whore.

In Wilson's representations of language and gender, Arthur Wellesley gets especially harsh treatment—in retaliation, perhaps, for refusing to pay up. Notoriously taciturn, Wellesley speaks here in phrases and grunts. In one scene—later engraved in commercial caricatures—he stands in the rain and calls up to Wilson's bedroom window, where another lover pretends to be a maid.

> "Come down, I say," roared this modern Blue Beard, "and don't keep me here in the rain, you old blockhead."
>
> "Sir," answered Argyle, in a shrill voice, "you must please to call out your name, or I don't dare to come down, robberies are so frequent in London just at this season, and all the sojers, you see, coming home from Spain, that it's quite alarming to poor lone women."
>
> Wellington took off his hat.... "You old idiot, do you know me now?"
>
> "Lord, sir," answered Argyle, anxious to prolong this ridiculous scene, "I can't give no guess; and, do you know, sir, the thieves have stolen a new water-butt out of our airy, not a week since, and my missus is more timbersome than ever!"
>
> "The devil!" vociferated Wellington, who could endure no more, and . . . returned home to his neglected wife and family duties. (231)

Harriette Wilson's *Memoirs,* however suspect as a transcript of actual speech, reveal not only a sensitivity to the power relations so central to feminist linguistics, but also the range of skills required for discourse competence. Wilson clearly knows how to perform gender linguistically; the little scene above is humorous exactly because of its exaggerated use of gender stereotypes. But Wilson, given her status as a courtesan, can highlight for us the very constructedness of gender in language use. She may choose to

1. "The General Out-Generalled, or First Come, First Served" (1825). Wellesley is denied entrance by an aristocrat disguised as a maid, speaking woman's language. An anonymous caricature. (Courtesy of the Library of Congress)

speak "as a woman"—as a good, subservient, modest woman—or she may choose to construct one of many other characters for herself. As a highly novelistic account, Wilson's *Memoirs* cannot tell us how women "really" spoke during the Regency period. But the representational force of her reported conversations is valuable in its own right, in demonstrating how character is constructed in speech.

Reading and Speech

If part of my goal is to engage the concerns of feminist linguistics for the study of the past, it seems odd to have chosen a historical period that scholars characterize largely by its connection to print culture, and to devote so much time to novels—even such marvelous ones as Austen's. Let me turn briefly, then, to the second meaning of my title—volumes that speak—and to the scholarly conversation on the reading of literature in which I situate my work.

Interest in readership developed in the 1970s and 1980s around the work of the "reader-response" critics. One of several challenges to the then-still-dominant New Criticism, reader-response criticism argued that meaning does not lie in "the text itself" (the New Critical mantra) nor in the author's intention (the most traditional orientation), but rather in the interpretive acts performed by readers. Reader-response critics established different points at which they located the balance between interpretive conventions that were shared among authors and readers and more purely subjective reactions to the text, but they all focused their attention on the reader reading in the present. At the same time, however, other scholars were urging a return to historical approaches to literature, noting that reader-response criticism shared with the New Criticism a pointed lack of interest in how texts functioned in their own time. Since then, work on readers in history has burgeoned.[25]

Another possible historiographic narrative would locate the beginnings of work on readership in the work of Walter J. Ong and others. This work posits a binary opposition between thought in oral and in literate cultures; Ong's thesis is captured in the title "Writing Is a Technology That Restructures Thought." For example, he says, oral literature is performed in ways that force it to be situational (responding to its audience) and episodic (or open-ended); writing, in literate cultures, is relatively context-free, and tends to be structured logically. Within this tradition, authors like Elizabeth L. Eisenstein made the further distinction between manuscript and print cultures, describing the ways the invention of the printing press altered the place of writing in society. Ong's work, while admired as pioneering, has been criticized for its "technological determinism" by scholars who emphasize that what is meaningful is not the technology per se, but rather technology's specific cultural uses.[26] In the present context, more troubling still is the either/or nature of the opposition. Central to this book is the notion that, in a literate culture, writing and speech are inseparable.[27]

Within eighteenth-century studies, scholars have pursued both the more technological and the more cultural strains of work on reading. Many have argued that it was in the eighteenth century, hundreds of years after the European invention of the printing press, that print culture finally came into its own. These scholars would point to a dramatic increase in literacy rates—at least as perceived by contemporaries—and an equally dramatic shift away from a system of literary patronage, toward a more fully commercialized mode of supporting literary production. This shift is personified in the figure of Samuel Johnson, who self-consciously rejected the patronage of Philip Dormer Stanhope (fourth Earl of Chesterfield) and whose masterful dictionary relies for its authority on written, not oral, sources.[28]

The focus on the rise of print culture has also led to arguments that new kinds of reading developed in the eighteenth century: that people read more widely, quickly, and superficially than in earlier periods, and that such reading was normally performed silently and alone. This kind of reading, it is asserted, is particularly well suited to the reading of the most interesting new genre of the period: the novel. Moreover, the novel was considered a "low" genre during the period and was particularly associated with women authors and readers. Indeed, for many years, the dominant scholarly paradigm of eighteenth-century reading favored the "woman in the closet," a female reader who shuts herself up in solitude to enjoy the (perhaps erotic) pleasures of the text. Conversely, the practice of silent reading has been seen as having influenced the ways the novel developed.[29]

There is no question that eighteenth-century commentators often railed against the way solitary reading corrupted young women. But we overgeneralize if we look only at this evidence; these statements must be balanced against the many accounts of oral reading in the same period. In *Speaking Volumes,* I will concentrate on these latter accounts. I do this not to deny or belittle the importance of silent, solitary reading, but rather to emphasize the ways in which reading together functioned both to reinforce domestic relationships and to provide practice in the art of speaking. For it is the connections between reading and speech that are really at stake here.[30]

Finally, a word on my attention to the novel rather than literary genres that were arguably equally widely read (or religious writings that were far more widely read), and my favoring of Austen's novels over those of other authors. My bias is obviously partly autobiographical; as I noted in the Preface, my entrée into this project was through the novels of Jane Austen. In addition, since the publication of Nancy Armstrong's *Desire and Domestic Fiction* (1987), scholars have asserted the importance of eighteenth-century novels in socializing women readers, though they disagree broadly on whether reading fiction was emancipatory or whether it reinforced patriarchal norms. These scholars would emphasize reading not as a technology but as a social practice that works to constitute us as members of a society, by leading us to internalize society's values. Armstrong, writing as a Foucauldian and looking first to the conservative conduct-book literature, argued that novels created the very forms of subjectivity and desire that they seemed to reflect. Others would emphasize a wider range of literature, much of which critiques conservative norms, and would allow women readers more agency in the ability to read critically.[31] The view that reading is constitutive of character makes the study of literature more compelling, but the relation between reading and socialization must remain complex.

Speaking Volumes focuses on one aspect of this socialization, the interconnectedness of reading and speech. This will involve both how texts were actualized as speech—that is, how they were performed—and how contemporaries saw reading as a way of practicing authoritative speech. At the end of *Speaking Volumes*, I will argue that novels took the place of conversation manuals in performing this function. I highlight the novels of Austen here and throughout the book both because they beautifully illustrate the discourses on women's speech and because their canonical status makes them more accessible to the modern reader. Without diminishing the appreciation of her unique genius, I assume throughout that Austen, like other women I discuss, is generally representative of her period and participates in its discourses.

Each of my chapters highlights a different kind of oral performance. For two reasons, I have chosen to focus each chapter on one individual woman. The first is practical: because the topic of women, reading, and speech is so broad, and because this is new territory, focusing on individuals helped set reasonable limits. But more important, I am convinced that it is only at the level of the individual that the richness of language use becomes apparent. My aim is not to write biography, but to respect the complexity of historical forces as they touch the individual. Each of my "characters" was affected by the conduct-book norms that we think of as typical in the period, but each also played other roles. In looking at their use of language, we will see their multiple affiliations in their voice and in their silence.

Part I of *Speaking Volumes* contrasts the stereotypes of "woman's language" with the complexities of individual practice. Chapter 1 provides an overview of the discourse on women's speech in the eighteenth century, as written about by language theorists, educators, and conduct-book authors. The reader will not be surprised to find that women's speech was often vilified and that women were lumped together as a single class. This will set up the task for the book, exploring how individual women, faced with this situation, were able to develop the range of linguistic strategies required for discourse competence.

Each of the other chapters looks at the issues of oral performance from a different perspective. Chapter 2 explores the conflict between the norms of polite language and those of one speech community, the Quakers. I show how Amelia Opie, who converted late in life, tried to negotiate this conflict to establish linguistic solidarity with the Quakers while retaining a place in the "polite" world. My goal is to demonstrate that even in very strict speech communities, like the Quakers', real people use language in flexible ways. In Chapter 3, I consider the struggles of Sarah Siddons to bridge the gap between theatrical speech and ordinary language; her identity as a tragic heroine, which granted her a social position unlike that of any earlier actress, was incompatible with the linguistic strategies required in ordinary life. In this chapter, I begin to consider the relation of reading and speech. I argue that the elocutionists' attention to "correct" performance affected the display not only of professionals like Siddons but also of "ordinary" women as represented in works by Burney and Austen.

Part II of *Speaking Volumes* explores eighteenth-century discourses connecting reading and speech. Chapter 4 turns to readers in domestic settings, arguing the dominance of the "patriarchal reader," who chose, interpreted, and censored books for his family; my exemplar here is the Burney family. In this case, the metaphor of "silencing" seems compelling, though I also consider alternatives to the patriarchal norm. I show how family reading participated in both the affectionate and the disciplinary aspects of domesticity. Finally, in Chapter 5 I argue that novels took the place of conversation manuals in educating speakers. I rely here on the novels of Jane Austen, especially *Pride and Prejudice* (whose heroine masters both direct and indirect speech) and *Persuasion* (where Austen seems much more skeptical about the connection of speech and ethos). My emphasis remains, however, on the *reader* of these novels and on how performing novels was understood to help develop skill in speaking.

There is much that remains undone. My "characters" all came from the middle ranks of society, and all lived in or near London; I have not attempted to describe language use by women of other classes or regions. In addition, all of my "characters" were exceptional in their public successes and in the kinds of documentary evidence they left behind. But I hope that these chapters, with all their limitations, suggest how we can bring the concerns of feminist linguistics to bear on the past while offering a contribution to the histories of women, women's literature, and reading.

PART I

Performing Gender in Speech

CHAPTER I

Women and Language
in the Eighteenth Century

Leave the distortion of language to men who cannot embellish it like
yourself—and to women.
—Elizabeth Inchbald, *Remarks for "The British Theatre"*

The most famous woman speaker of the eighteenth century has entered
our language as a term for the foolish misuse of words: *malapropism.* Mrs.
Malaprop is the duenna of Richard Brinsley Sheridan's 1775 comedy *The
Rivals,* who tries to catch a husband for herself as she arranges a match for
her beautiful niece. In the play, she is ridiculed for many things, but most
memorably for her fractured English. Mrs. Malaprop's errors are, consistently, neither regionalisms nor errors of grammar; rather, they result from
her reaching for difficult words. She prides herself on her literary attain-
ment, and a surprising number of her malapropisms make literary references
("allegory" for "alligator," "antistrophe" for "catastrophe," "derangement of
epitaphs" for "arrangement of epithets"). She comments frequently on language, including women's language: though she would "by no means wish
a daughter of mine to be a progeny of learning," and "would never let her
meddle with Greek, or Hebrew, or Algebra, or Simony, or Fluxions, or
Paradoxes," yet a girl should learn a few things. "Above all, Sir Anthony, she
should be mistress of orthodoxy, that she might not mis-spell, and mis-
pronounce words so shamefully as girls usually do; and likewise that she
might reprehend the true meaning of what she is saying.—This, Sir
Anthony, is what I would have a woman know;—and I don't think there is
a superstitious article in it."[1] Part of the fun of Mrs. Malaprop derives from
the degree to which we can, in fact, understand her perfectly: *progeny* is a

good enough approximation of *prodigy* for a competent listener. The son of an important elocutionist, Sheridan subverts his own father's emphasis on precise and expressive pronunciation; native speakers know which words go with which and can simultaneously process both the expected word and the comic substitution.

But, less kindly, much of the fun must also be attributed to traditional misogyny. As an old and ugly husband-hunter, Mrs. Malaprop is a stock figure of comedy and exemplifies the potential that comedy has for cruelty. Too old for marriage, she is superfluous in a society that allows women only one role, yet her desperation cannot be comprehended (except with fear) by men who have no trouble finding wives and who in any case have other means of support. Mrs. Malaprop can stand for us as an emblem of the gap between the situated understandings of the sexes. More to the point here, she represents that gap in terms of language use. The literary predecessors of Mrs. Malaprop do include male characters, such as Dogberry in Shakespeare's *Much Ado*. But contemporaries understood that Mrs. Malaprop was ridiculous largely because of her sex.

In the preface she wrote to an edition of *The Rivals,* the actress and author Elizabeth Inchbald highlights the attack on women:

> Against the illiterate Mrs. Malaprop, common occurrence, and common sense, protest. That any Englishwoman for these five hundred years past, in the habit of keeping good company, or any company, could have made use of the words—*extirpate* for *exculpate, exhort* for *escort,* and *malevolence* for *benevolence,* seems too far removed from probability, to make a reasonable auditor smile.
>
> When future generations shall naturally suppose, that an author of Mr. Sheridan's reputation drew men and women exactly as he found them; this sketch of a woman of family and fortune, at the end of the eighteenth century, will assure the said generations—that the advance of female knowledge in Great Britain, was far more tardy than in any other European nation.[2]

Inchbald reminds us of the gap between emblematic representations of women and the real, live human beings operating in the real world. For her, not only is Mrs. Malaprop insulting, she is unrealistic. It is significant that Inchbald places her in the context of a perceived "advance" in women's learning, invoking a very eighteenth-century notion of progress. Like Mary Wollstonecraft, whom she knew, Inchbald views women as "rational creatures," who have a share in that most divine and most human attribute— reason—and who by the end of the eighteenth century had some opportunities to cultivate that faculty. Mrs. Malaprop, as written, is a voice from a dark and distant past.

But the notion that women were rational creatures—however small an extension that is of Enlightenment ideals—did not go uncontested. The eighteenth-century discourses on women's language tend to insist, rather, on women's physicality, linking women's faulty speech to biological difference. Early in the century, in an unusually hateful *Spectator* essay, Joseph Addison describes, first, the four types of "Female Orators," then literalizes his criticisms in a section on women's tongues. The dominant criticism is of the quantity and emptiness of women's conversation: "there are many among them who can Talk whole Hours together upon nothing."[3] Of the kind of female orators who deal in invectives, Addison asks, "With what a fluency of Invention, and Copiousness of Expression, will they enlarge upon every little slip in the Behaviour of another? With how many different Circumstances, and with what variety of Phrases, will they tell over the same Story?" (2:459). Similarly, a female orator classed as a gossip "launches out into Descriptions of Christenings, runs Divisions upon an Head-dress, knows every Dish of Meat that is served up in her Neighbourhood, and entertains her Company a whole Afternoon together with the Wit of her little Boy, before he is able to speak" (2:459).

But what, says Addison, is the cause of such empty verbiage?

> I have sometimes fancied that they have not a Retentive Power, or the Faculty of suppressing their Thoughts, as Men have, but that they are necessitated to speak every thing they think. . . . [A] Friend of mine, who is an excellent Anatomist, has promised me by the first Opportunity to dissect a Woman's Tongue, and to examine whether there may not be in it certain Juices which render it so wonderfully voluble and flippant, or whether the Fibres of it may not be made up of a finer or more pliant Thread. . . . Nor must I omit the Reason which *Hudibras* has given, why those who can talk on Trifles, speak with the greatest Fluency; namely, that the Tongue is like a Race-Horse, which runs the faster the lesser Weight it carries. (2:460)

Addison's satirical tone, like Sheridan's, is so exaggerated that it deflects criticism; he would certainly accuse a woman who felt insulted by it of having no sense of humor. But physically based accounts of gender difference in language remained alive through the century and also appeared in serious scientific works, like the *Philosophy of Natural History* (1790/1799) by the Scottish naturalist William Smellie. In a chapter titled "Of the Language of Beasts," Smellie describes the function of birdsong, which is performed mainly by males in order to stake out territory and to attract females. In most species, he asserts, the males "are more *loquacious* than the *females*. But, in the human species, it is likewise an unquestionable fact, that the *females* are much more talkative than the *males*." Smellie's task is to "investigate the intentions of Nature in creating such a marked distinction" (2:440; italics in original).

Like many other language theorists, Smellie highlights gender difference and minimizes other kinds of difference, in his case even the differences between animals and humans. And like others, Smellie posits what modern feminist linguists call a "female deficit theory," one that assumes not only the salience of gender difference but the inferiority of women's speech in terms of a male norm. Furthermore, the assumed deficit of female loquacity, which for Smellie is "unquestionable," is one that has cultural meaning precisely because it is false. Modern empirical studies consistently indicate that women speak less, not more than men; they explain the conflict between our stereotype of talkative women and the empirical measurement by inferring that the quantity of women's speech is judged against a norm of silence.[4] Yet the stereotype, and the strength of belief in it, work to inhibit women's speaking by equating speech and volubility.

Equally significant is Smellie's attempt to discover a natural cause for this difference, where others of his era blamed women's relative lack of educational opportunity. But given his commitment to a physical explanation, it is not surprising that Smellie derives women's quantity of speech from the needs of child-rearing, women's natural role. Women are supplied by Nature with a "wonderfully complicated system of vessels" for nursing, and with the impulse to please the baby's eyes and ears. The mother delights the baby by presenting attractive objects and repeating their names. "Thus, by habit, the *natural volubility* of female tongues is greatly improved" (2:441). Women are so quick to please their babies, and so attentive to their fretfulness, that "a person who had never attended to these scenes . . . would be apt to conclude, that both were proper inmates for a bedlam" (2:442). But no, says Smellie, this talkativeness has a natural utility. Men's occupations, "which demand either bodily or mental exertions" (2:443), exaggerate men's natural taciturnity.

> But the employments of women are of a more domestic kind. Household affairs, and particularly the nursing and training of children, are fully sufficient to engross their attention, and to call forth all their ingenuity and active powers. The *loquacity* of women is too often considered, by poets, historians, and by unthinking men, as a reproach upon the sex. Men of this description know not what they say. When they blame women for *speaking much,* they blame Nature for one of her wisest institutions. Women *speak much.* They ought to *speak much.* Nature compels them to *speak much;* and, when they do so, they are complying religiously with one of her most sacred and useful laws. It may be said, that *some men* talk as *much* as women. Granted. But beings of this kind, I deny to be *men.* Nature seems to have originally meant them to be *women;* but, by some cross-accident, as happens in the production of *monsters,* the external *male form* has been superinduced upon a *female stock.* (2:443)

Smellie differs from those theorists who consider language to be exactly that which divides men from beasts. Beasts, he argues, do have language. The difference for him lies in the gendering of language: humans are unlike all other species, whose males are gifted with greater language ability than the females. Woman's language is trivial, but it serves a natural purpose. For Smellie, women's language use neither expresses nor communicates rational thought. Rather, it serves an interactive function independent of denotative meaning. By describing language in this way, Smellie can continue the analogy with the language of beasts while diminishing the importance of women's rationality. Interestingly, male speech fares little better in Smellie's extreme form of gendered language. For Smellie, true men, rational men, speak little; talkative men are not males at all, but monsters.

Smellie's expression is extreme, but his treatise illustrates several features common in eighteenth-century discussions of language. First of all, he privileges gender difference over any other kind of difference between classes of speakers and posits the category "woman" as a homogeneous one, without even making the crudest divisions of class, age, or region. Moreover, he assumes that women's speech is characterized by its deficiency. For Smellie as for others, the greatest deficiency is women's volubility, for which Smellie proposes a "natural" explanation. Others (like Mary Wollstonecraft) would reject the notion that women are "naturally" inferior, but there were few challenges to the notions that gender is always salient and that, while classes of men may be distinguished by their speech, women can be lumped together as a single category.

The task of this first chapter is to demonstrate the power of these assumptions in eighteenth-century discourses on language. It is not my goal to offer a complete overview of eighteenth-century language theory, nor simply to collect examples of the invective against women's speech so evident in Mrs. Malaprop, Addison's female orators, and Smellie's mad mothers. And as Inchbald reminds us, we would be foolish to equate the Mrs. Malaprops with actual women speakers. But developing a sense of the discursive norm is necessary if we are to appreciate the task facing individual women who constructed identities in speech. This chapter has four sections. I consider, first, the salience of gender in language and linguistic constructions of identity. Second, I discuss the specific features of the stereotype of the deficient woman speaker. Third, I describe the best theorized work on speech in the eighteenth century, that of the elocutionists, and show how it disadvantaged women. And finally, I examine the poles of civility and sincerity within conversation and how they figure the woman speaker. My reader has already guessed, no doubt, that the discourses introduced here are rim ones, almost unrelieved in their hostility toward women. But in order to celebrate the agency and ability of women in constructing complex linguistic identities, we must understand the full weight of the forces that worked toward limiting women's speech.

The Salience of Gender

One of the foundational metaphors of women's history is that of "separate spheres," the idea that gender roles became noticeably more rigid and differentiated through the eighteenth and early nineteenth centuries, especially among the bourgeoisie. Whereas earlier middle-class women had worked beside their husbands in small businesses and shops, it became increasingly important to bourgeois status that women *not* work. The narrative implicit in the metaphor emphasizes the separation of public and private space as work moved outside the home and culminates in the Victorian model of "the angel in the house" who preserves the home as a safe and moral refuge, and who at the end of the day welcomes a husband exhausted from the trials of the rougher world of work. The narrative of separate spheres connects gender to economic history and to the development of a large middle class. Indeed, Leonore Davidoff and Catherine Hall have argued that the development of separate spheres was essential to middle-class consciousness, so that "gender and class always operate together."[5]

Like any large historical narrative, the one implied by the metaphor of separate spheres is vulnerable to critique. On the one hand, historians originally developed the metaphor on the basis of prescriptive texts, especially conduct books, rather than on the basis of lived experience. When we do examine individuals' experience, the patterns of their lives are far too complicated to fit into such a rigid, binary division. On the other hand, the narrative depends on positing an Industrial Revolution that transformed English life after 1780, where some scholars would emphasize continuity through the early modern period, both in economic and in social structures. Amanda Vickery, for example, argues that we do not have the evidence to support our narrative of radical economic change in the late eighteenth century. She remains skeptical of a separate "middle-class" ideology, seeing instead a unified local elite of merchants, professionals, and lesser gentry, who had connections that reached both "up" toward the aristocracy and "down" to the world of tradesmen and artisans. And as for women's roles, "texts extolling domestic virtue and a clear separation of the realms of men and women circulated long before 1789. . . . Visions of female nature had for centuries oscillated between impossibly pure and irredeemably depraved."[6]

Whether or not change was "real," though, commentators at the end of the eighteenth century consistently articulated their strong belief that their age was undergoing a moral and social reformation, and that women's roles were central to both. These commentators participate in a key feature of separate spheres ideology: the belief that women are the tenders of morality. After nearly a century of effort to reform manners, commentators at the end of the long eighteenth century saw their age as significantly more "genteel" than earlier periods had been. The reformation of manners can be seen, for example, in the revision of literary works whose originals by this time seemed shocking; Thomas Bowdler's *Family Shakespeare* (1807) omits everything "which may not with propriety be read aloud in a family."[7] The effect of the alteration in manners was also noted by Samuel Taylor Coleridge, with considerable ambivalence. For Coleridge, attuning literary works to a domestic, feminine moral code meant that works were gutted:

> Another cause of false criticism is the greater purity of morality in the present age, compared even with the last. Our notions upon this subject are sometimes carried to excess, particularly among those who in print affect to enforce the value of a high standard. Far be it from me to depreciate that value; but let me ask, who now will venture to read a number of the Spectator, or of the Tatler, to his wife and daughters, without first examining it to make sure that it contains no word which might, in our day, offend the delicacy of female ears, and shock feminine susceptibility? Even our theatres, the representations at which usually reflect the morals of the period, have taken a sort of domestic turn, and while the performances at them may be said, in some sense, to improve the heart, there is no doubt that they vitiate the taste. The effect is bad, however good the cause.[8]

Coleridge is typical in associating the new delicacy with wives and daughters—that is, with domestic relations. Thus, even well before the Victorian period, the home was increasingly located as the center of morality, putting greater pressure on women to focus on their identities as mothers and, in consequence, to give up other possible social roles. For example, by the 1790s even aristocratic women were discouraged from sending their infants out to wet nurses.

The reformation of manners, and the increasing emphasis on women's moral purity, developed in large part as an ideology intended to distinguish the bourgeoisie from what it considered a decadent aristocracy. Yet the opposition of bourgeois and aristocratic values decreases as time goes on. In her study of prescriptive literature on manners and morals, Marjorie Morgan argues that "relations between the aristocracy and middle class in the early industrial period progressed from being confrontational to being conciliatory and integrative. . . . By the mid nineteenth century, these two value systems had converged, as etiquette books and professional ideals reveal."[9] While norms were in flux throughout the period, for the sake of simplicity I will call the more moralistic domestic ideology "middle-class" or "bourgeois." It is this ideology that ties women's "nature" to supposed norms of "woman's language" and to calls for modesty, even silence, where the traditional aristocratic mode allowed room for some women to speak with authority and wit.

The sense that class ideologies were converging could also lead to fears about upward mobility. Many literary texts and popular caricatures depict the false gentility of tradesmen's daughters who picked up a few accomplishments at a boarding school and now considered themselves "above" their parents. In Austen's *Persuasion,* upward mobility is portrayed as the modern mode: the Musgrove "father and mother were in the old English style, and the young people in the new." The parents are "not much educated, and not at all elegant," whereas the elegance of the younger generation is demonstrated wholly by the accomplished daughters.[10] Thus, while we must remain aware that both the separateness of separate spheres and the chronology of their development are undergoing revision by modern historians, the metaphor of separate spheres captures a crucial aspect of the late eighteenth century's sense of itself. In an age of anxiety about class mobility, women became markers of change, and the definition of their status elicited much debate.

Over the course of the long eighteenth century, a number of discourses articulated an increasingly strict binary of gender difference. The legal system, notably, worked to strip women of any identity but that of wife. At the same time, according to Thomas Laqueur, the medical establishment rebelled against ancient traditions that saw sexual difference as a matter of degree, not of kind: "By around 1800, writers of all sorts were determined to base what they insisted were fundamental differences between the male and female sexes, and thus between man and woman, on discoverable biological distinctions. . . . Not only are the sexes different, but they are different in every conceivable aspect of body and soul, in every physical and moral aspect."[11] And aesthetics, as Laura L. Runge has argued, followed the same pattern: for earlier critics like Dryden, "the best literature combines both male and female attributes. . . . The language of gender in the earlier criticism tends to emphasize a one-sex model"; later on, "the masculine sublime gains its apparent authority and stability only through the definition and suppression of the feminized beautiful."[12]

Important to this book is the way in which eighteenth-century language theory, as well, pays increasing attention to a gendered binary. In 1712, Jonathan Swift associated women with speech that abounds in vowels and liquids, while men tend to rely on rough consonants.[13] Yet because *both* vowels and consonants are required for speech, both male and female orientations are required; a gendered theoretical category is not firmly attached to male and female people. By the end of the century, however, language theorists and casual commentators routinely envisioned a separate sociolinguistic category for women's speech. To differentiate the stereotype from empirical linguistic practices, I will refer to the former as "woman's language."

The gender bifurcation within eighteenth-century language theories must be understood in the context of an overall move toward the standardization of English, in which prescriptive grammarians became more attentive to "correctness" than had been the case earlier. The impulse toward a standard English can be framed as a side effect of a new sense of nationhood or of a new self-confidence among the bourgeoisie.[14] The standardization of English can also be seen as a gendered phenomenon. "Good" English was gendered male. According to Elizabeth S. Sklar, "representing English as a 'manly' language was a key strategy" in the effort to "promote English as a language worthy of national pride."[15] For many years, English and other Germanic languages had been considered too consonantal, too rough. But sometime during the eighteenth century, this "rough" quality was reinterpreted as manly and positive; the vowel-laden Romance languages became the proper study for accomplished women, but lost their stature in the linguistic hierarchy. Sklar interprets this reevaluation of English in the context of theories of the growth and decline of languages, as a move to imagine the national language—and thus the nation—as nearly at its peak. This meant that it must also be male.

The gendering of English may perhaps best be seen in attempts to impose grammatical gender on it. We see this, for example, in James Harris's *Hermes; or, a Philosophical Inquiry Concerning Universal Grammar* (1751), which influenced important English grammars like those of Robert Lowth and Lindley Murray. While sections of *Hermes* develop original ideas, even anticipating the modern concept of the "speech act," Harris relies on Aristotelian and Scholastic tradition in the logical categories he utilizes. Most relevant in this context is his section on grammatical gender, where Harris seeks to find an underlying masculinity or femininity to nouns that are given grammatical gender in other languages.

Harris first establishes a complete set of logical possibilities: "Every Substance is either *Male* or *Female;* or *both Male and Female;* or *neither one nor the other.* So that with respect to *Sexes* and their *Negation, all Substances conceiveable* [*sic*] are comprehended under this *fourfold* consideration" (41). However, he says, since hermaphrodites are rare, or possibly nonexistent, language drops that category and recognizes only masculine, feminine, and neuter (42). English, he continues, is unlike other languages in using only the neuter for substances; and other languages assign gender inconsistently: "MIND is surely neither male, nor female; yet is NOUS, in *Greek,* masculine, and MENS, in *Latin,* feminine" (43). But is grammatical gender purely arbitrary? Harris agrees that in some cases, it is. However,

> In others we may imagine a more subtle kind of reasoning, a reasoning which discerns even *in things without Sex* a distant analogy to that great NATURAL DIS-TINCTION, *which* (according to *Milton*) *animates the World.*
>
> In this view we may conceive such SUBSTANTIVES to have been considered, as MASCULINE, which were "conspicuous for the Attributes of imparting or communicating; or which were by nature active, strong, and efficacious, and that indiscriminately whether to good or to bad; or which had claim to Eminence, either laudable or otherwise."
>
> THE FEMININE on the contrary were "such, as were conspicuous for the Attributes either of receiving, of containing, or of producing and bringing forth; or which had more of the passive in their nature, than of the active; or which were peculiarly beautiful and amiable; or which had respect to such Excesses, as were rather Feminine, than Masculine." (44–45)

Harris then shows that by this logic, Virgil and Milton ranked the sun as masculine, the moon as feminine; cities and countries are feminine because they are containers and receivers, and so on. The ocean is puzzling for Harris: as a receiver, container, and producer, "it might justly have been made (like the Earth) *Feminine;* yet its *deep Voice* and *boisterous Nature* have, in spight of these reasons, prevailed to make it *Male*" (50).

Harris, to repeat, leans on a long tradition for this explanation, notably on the Scholastics. But it is the gesture that is meaningful here—the insistence that a division of all things into a neat binary, that of sexual difference, is central to logical explanation. And indeed, the binary of grammatical gender grew increasingly strict through the century. The most widely used grammar in the second half of the century was Robert Lowth, *A Short Introduction to English Grammar* (1762). In his section on substantives, Lowth devotes less than two pages to grammatical gender, noting the advantages of the relative lack of gender in English. Lindley Murray, however, whose *English Grammar* (1795) superceded Lowth's as the most widely used at the end of the century, privileges gender as a category. His chapter on substantives includes sections on number and on case. The first section, though, is the one on gender, in which he adapts Harris's explanation of assigning gender to inanimate objects. Murray also gives lists of examples (which grew much longer in later editions) in which gender is distinguished in English by using different words (*drake* and *duck*), by adding a suffix (*poet* and *poetess*), or by adding a prefix (*man-servant* and *maid-servant*). At the end of this section, Murray laments that English doesn't have enough markers for gender, for the ambiguity embarrasses the (male?) speaker:

> Of the variable terminations, we have only a sufficient number to make us feel our want; for when we say of a woman, she is a philosopher, an astronomer, a builder, a weaver, we perceive an impropriety in the termination, which we cannot avoid; but we can say that she is an architect, a botanist, a student, because these terminations have not annexed to them the notion of sex. (25)

Lurking behind the impropriety of speech, the reader feels, is the sense that there is impropriety in a woman *being* a philosopher, an astronomer, or a builder; the examples Murray gives for nonoffensive words not only don't end in the masculine suffix "-er" but are more appropriate occupations for women. There is some conflation here of social role and grammar. Indeed, Murray's attentiveness to gender reveals much more about the social construction of gender than about "logical" grammar. The insistence of Harris, Murray, and other grammarians on the salience of gender, and its centrality to logic, can be seen as an indication of the increasing rigidity of gender roles over the course of the eighteenth century.

However, it is not the case that all grammarians highlighted grammatical gender. In *The Theory of Language,* James Beattie argued that Harris's assignments of gender were "liable to many objections" (2:12) and that "As things which have not animal life cannot with propriety be said to have sex, . . . it would seem most natural, that the names of all inanimate things and abstract ideas should be of the *neuter* gender" (2:15). Harris's examples were ridiculed by John Horne Tooke in his *Divisions of Purley* (1786) because they were Latinate; in German and Anglo-Saxon, *sun* is feminine and *moon* masculine (26–27). Tooke points to the arbitrariness of grammatical gender while championing the vernacular over the elitist Latin. Joseph Priestley criticized grammatical gender in a more general way: "With respect to sex, the *English* Language seems to have followed nature, [while] other languages, by aiming at two [*sic*] great refinement, have departed from it, without gaining any advantage, which can be called an equivalent, for the absurdity and additional intricacy attending to the practice. Why is *lapis* masculine, when *rupes* is feminine, and *saxum* neuter?"[16] Tooke and Priestley, both politically radical, were also minority voices in protesting the imposition of grammatical gender.

In addition to assigning gender to substantives, eighteenth-century grammarians grew much stricter about the so-called generic masculine: the use of *he* to mean "any person." This usage is consistent with the legal concept of coverture, which defines a husband and wife as one person, that person being the husband, a notion that was strongly articulated in the eighteenth century. But as Ann Bodine points out, while defenses of the generic masculine claimed to rest on logic, the generic *he* is no more logical than the commonly heard generic *they* (e.g., "each student should bring their own pencil"), which was accepted as grammatical until the late eighteenth century. *He* agrees with a singular referent in number, but not necessarily in gender; *they* disagrees in number but includes both genders. Both *he* and *they* are equally inaccurate; we have simply chosen to favor accuracy in number over that of gender.[17]

Even more significant for my purposes than the assignment of grammatical gender to substantives or the generic masculine pronoun is the bifurcation of gender roles in conversation. In the late eighteenth century, writers articulated rigid separations between the linguistic practices of women and men, and linked usage to their (constructed) social roles. As in other discourses, the construction of gendered linguistic identity cannot be separated from identities of class and religion. "Woman's" language often implicitly means "middle-class women's" language, and it is quite distinct from representations of lower-class language. Presumably, too, aristocratic Englishwomen continued to have possibilities in conversation that were increasingly denied to bourgeois women, especially among those with conservative or evangelical ideologies. Among the latter groups, there was an increasing consciousness that men and women have and ought to have separate roles in conversation to match their separate social roles.

A good example of the trend toward gendered conversational roles can be found in the work of Hannah More, who as a young woman was associated with the "Bluestocking" salons and the London theater world, but who later was prominent among conservative evangelical educators. More wrote three separate essays on conversation, whose variations reveal the tension between traditional rules of courtly politeness, in which the (ungendered) speaker aims to please the other, and the increasing delegation of the task of pleasing to women. The best-known of the three, her poem "The Bas Bleu; or, Conversation" (1786) is remarkable for its *lack* of concern with gender. "The Bas Bleu," written in heroic style to honor the salon hostess Elizabeth Vesey, celebrates the collaborative, useful conversation at Bluestocking affairs. Like earlier conversation manuals, it praises cooperation and criticizes selfishness or the display of learning for its own sake. The cooperativeness and informality of English conversation are contrasted most strongly with the formalities and (especially) with the dueling wit of French salons, "Where point, and turn, and equivoque/Distorted every word they spoke!/All so intolerably bright,/Plain Common Sense was put to flight."[18] In this piece, More highlights national differences while deemphasizing gender divisions. Vesey is praised in masculine terms: she is skilled in geometry as she breaks the cold formal circle into small groups; and she holds the secrets of chemistry that can get her various guests to coalesce into "the very things which Nature meant" (16). More's almost Augustan sociability leads her to argue that learning acquires its value and meaning only when shared in conversation. Her bourgeois values are revealed in an economic metaphor: scholars study, travelers see, to share and to tell: "But 'tis thy commerce Conversation,/Must give it use by circulation;/That noblest commerce of mankind,/Whose precious merchandise is MIND!" (17). And the end of the poem is explicitly gender-neutral, addressed to both "the letter'd and the fair" (17). No speech, More says, can earn us love; we only gain that by giving attention—by silently listening.

"The Bas Bleu" celebrates the conversation of privileged and highly educated women. But in a work intended for boarding-school girls, a chapter titled "On Conversation" highlights traditional fears about women's voices. It begins and ends with sections on women's display. At the beginning of the essay, More rejects the conduct-book notion that women should display their accomplishments while hiding their knowledge and piety. And at the end, display is punished in a parable of a (female?) nightingale whose singing attracted a predatory (male?) hawk. More reiterates the standard criticisms that women are too often censorious, blurt out opinions without thinking, and so on, like many, assuming "women" to be a single class of speakers. More also gives much attention to an issue studied by modern feminist linguists: who proposes topics? whose topics are pursued? Women, More says, should not introduce subjects; they may, however, use their eloquent silence either to invite the male speaker to continue or to discourage him. More emphasizes the power of silence in controlling the conversation: "How easily and effectually may a well-bred woman promote the most useful and elegant conversation, almost without speaking a word! for the modes of speech are scarcely more variable than the modes of silence."[19]

As More became more conservative, the advice she had given to middle-class girls was directed also to the upper class, the explicit target audience of her Strictures on the Modern System of Female Education (1799). Conversation is no longer a marketplace for the circulation of ideas, but is rather "a field for the exercise and improvement of our virtues; as a means for promoting the glory of our Creator, and the good and happiness of our fellow creatures."[20] A traditional task, that the conversationalist bring forward the talents of others, is now attributed to both good breeding and Christianity. The misuse of the Maker's name is particularly criticized, and More urges women to declare their faith, without parade, whenever serious conversation requires. More also strengthens the injunction to silence. Whereas in the earlier *Essays,* women's silence was a way of choosing and pursuing topics, now it is a good in itself: "An inviolable and marked attention may show that a woman is pleased with a subject, and an illuminated countenance may prove that she understands it almost as unequivocally as language itself could do; and this, with a modest question, which indicates at once rational curiosity and becoming diffidence, is in many cases as large a share of the conversation as it is decorous for feminine delicacy to take" (1:373). This text expresses the convergence of bourgeois and aristocratic norms that we think of as typically nineteenth-century. For Hannah More, the proper conversational role for women of rank was approaching that for the middle class; women were becoming classed as a unified sociolinguistic category, increasingly differentiated from men.

The bifurcation of gender roles in conversation meant that gender was performed ever more linguistically. Male language and female language became recognizable modes of speech. The line between the two becomes especially evident when it is transgressed, for example, in the figure of the amazon. In Frances Burney's *Evelina* (1778), the character of Mrs. Selwyn is stigmatized as "masculine": she is willing to partake in jokes with men, is overly direct, and (not coincidentally) is the character who does the most to resolve the heroine's difficulties. Significant in this context is her unwomanly speech. While Mrs. Selwyn mockingly claims that "I only talk, like a silly woman, for the sake of talking" (275), she often uses speech to defend young Evelina, almost as aggressively as a male protector would. She says to one predatory Lord, for instance, "My Lord . . . you don't consider, that the better Miss Anville looks, the more striking is the contrast with your Lordship; therefore, for your own sake, I would advise you not to hold her" (313). Mrs. Selwyn's insults and veiled threats go beyond the norms even of the female wit and strike her audience as mannish.

Even more amazon-like is the character Harriet Freke (*sic!*) in Maria Edgeworth's *Belinda* (1801). Mrs. Freke is a cross-dresser, and while in costume she violates gender norms by being overly direct, as when she "spoke with such unbounded freedom" (44), "stared me full in the face" (45), or later on visited the heroine after she "swore to set the distressed damsel free," though the latter rejects "Mrs. Freke's knight-errantry" (225–26). Along with male attire, Mrs. Freke adopts an exaggerated male language, characterized by rejecting the loquacity and emptiness of woman's language. Mrs. Freke speaks in compressed sentences. Her greeting is typical: "How do, dear creature! . . . How do? Glad to see you, 'faith! Been long here? Tremendously hot to day!" (225). In addition, Mrs. Freke rejects the moral books Belinda has been reading ("Only ruin your understanding, trust me. Books are full of trash—nonsense" [227]) and all manner of polite dissimulation: "To cut the matter short at once, . . . why, when a woman likes a man, does not she go and tell him so honestly?" (230). Because woman's language was stigmatized as empty, Mrs. Freke's curt directness becomes part of her transgressive performance of gender.

Mrs. Freke's "male" language plays out a gendered binary. But inherent in the imagery of separate spheres is the notion that men play many roles, whereas women play only one. In his *Enquiry into the Duties of the Female Sex* (1797), Thomas Gisborne explains that women are more alike than men are: "Even the superiority of rank which elevates the peeress above her untitled neighbour . . . is far from creating a difference equal to that which subsists between the duties of an hereditary legislator and those of a private gentleman" (3). This notion is deeply embedded in the linguistic construction of gender: men may speak as orators, or professionals, or fathers; women speak only as women. Woman's language was imagined to be a unified sociolinguistic category; significantly, there was no parallel conception of "man's language" as a single sociolinguistic category. A passage from Laurence Sterne's *Tristram Shandy* makes this explicit. When Tristram's father argues with his mother about who should attend Tristram's birth, we are told,

> What could my father do? He was almost at his wit's end;——talked it over with her in all moods;—placed his arguments in all lights;—argued the matter with her like a christian,—like a heathen,—like a husband,—like a father,—like a patriot,—like a man:—My mother answered every thing only like a woman; which was a little hard upon her;—for as she could not assume and fight it out behind such a variety of characters,—'twas no fair match;—'twas seven to one.—What could my mother do?[21]

Sterne captures the sense that to be a woman was to have one's role in society fixed—socially and linguistically. To be a woman was to speak woman's language.

Woman's Language and Its Deficiencies

Addison's essay, published very early in the century, articulated the stereotype of woman's language that remained alive through the period:

women spoke too much and said too little. The quantity and emptiness of woman's language were probably its most obvious features. But it is worth sketching out other characteristic deficiencies as well. Particularly useful in literary representations (because so easily imitated) was the specialized vocabulary that marked woman's language, consisting of overused intensifiers like *vast* and *monstrous*. This vocabulary also served to characterize women as a single class of speakers, and contemporaries noted the leveling effect by which tradesmen's daughters could imitate fashionable argot. More troubling, because less easily dismissed, were the linguistic practices that supposedly revealed women's flawed characters. Most of the deficiencies that eighteenth-century commentators saw in woman's language can be traced back to ancient writers like Juvenal, yet they have special resonance in a period of increased class mobility and growing linguistic standardization.

The anxiety over women's speech produced stereotypes that reached to two extremes. On the one hand, woman's language was uncivilized, "natural" in the lowest sense, disruptive, ungrammatical, and unedifying; this is the extreme position that William Smellie attempted to convert to a positive and that I would like to pursue now. On the other hand, women were also associated with the overly civilized world of Gallic courtliness, with insincerity and formal politeness; this association will be discussed below. In both cases, women were defined as "other" against a masculine ideal of rational good sense.

As we saw in Smellie and in Addison, woman's language was associated with the undisciplined body. Women could not control their tongues, neither to rein in the flow of words nor to govern a rational idea. As Michèle Cohen says, regarding the maxim that women could not keep secrets, "the unrestrained tongue was inescapably female."[22] Traditionally, women have been associated with the spoken language (the mother tongue), while the written language has been a male realm. Carol Elaine Percy has argued that eighteenth-century critics experienced a "category crisis" when significant numbers of women began publishing works of literature, especially novels. A great many of these were published anonymously, and (consistent with my comments on the salience of gender) it became a matter of some concern for reviewers to "sex the texts," that is, to seek evidence about the sex of the author. Percy argues that one key term was "easiness," which reviewers often felt signaled a woman author. "From the ease of the language," a 1766 reviewer wrote, "we hesitate not to pronounce, that a Lady wrote it."[23] "Easy" prose was unaffected and conversational, but also often incorrect, undisciplined, unintellectual, and trifling. As Percy summarizes, "the connotations of 'easy, sprightly' language as artless, incorrect, and spoken, implicitly uncivilized the woman who had ventured into print" (329). Similarly, the many calls for women's silence (which are of course of ancient origin) must be understood as participating in the construction of women as "naturally" loquacious, given to verbiage that swung between poles of emptiness and invective.

Let us turn for a moment to Samuel Johnson, undoubtedly one of the period's linguistic authorities; his *Dictionary of the English Language* (1755) is one of the great accomplishments of the time. In his original *Plan* for the dictionary (1747), Johnson had proposed a work that would serve to "fix" the English language, in the way that the French Academy had established stable norms of linguistic purity. Authors like Swift had occasionally suggested a similar project for English. As he worked on the *Dictionary*, though, Johnson modified his goal; not only was it impossible, but its authoritarianism was an insult to English liberty. Instead of dictating what pure English should be, Johnson chose an empirical method: the *Dictionary* was compiled by marking passages from great authors and classifying their significant usages. The implication is that the best English is literary English, that is, written English as exemplified by a small number of great (male) authors. In fact, Johnson includes very little on women's or "woman's" language in the *Dictionary*; only three words—flirtation, frightful, and horrid—are described as women's "cant."

However, others sought to highlight woman's language. A few months before Johnson's *Dictionary* was published, it was noticed by two numbers in the periodical *The World,* by Philip Dormer Stanhope (Chesterfield). Stanhope had been the dedicatee of the *Plan,* but had not had any contact with Johnson in some years. Johnson reacted angrily to the essays, feeling Stanhope was claiming credit as a good patron when in fact Johnson had worked independently. The entire episode marks a turning point in Johnson's career and in a wider shift from patronage to market-driven bookmaking.[24] What has been less noticed is that, remarkably, Stanhope devotes more than half of his attention to woman's language; unremarkably, he focuses on women's deviation from correctness, in making up new words (*flirtation, fuzz*), in giving new slang meanings to old words (*vast, vastly*), and in "auricular orthography," or spelling by ear. Since the *Dictionary* had not yet been published, Stanhope could not have realized the extent to which it demonstrates that "good" English leans on the authority of literary masters. His own attitude about oral and written English is ambiguous. The target of his condescension is women's supposed inventiveness, the very opposite of the "fixed" English Johnson proposed in the *Plan:* woman's language is so flighty that it leans on no authority at all. Stanhope poses a fictional dilemma for Johnson:

> I am well aware of the difficulties he would have to encounter, if he attempted to reconcile the polite, with the grammatical part of our language. Should he, by an act of power, banish and attaint many of the favourite words and expressions with which the ladies have so profusely enriched our language, he would excite the indignation of the most formidable, because the most lovely part of his readers: his dictionary would be condemned as a system of tyranny, and he himself, like the last Tarquin, run the risque of being deposed. So popular and so powerful is the female cause! On the other hand, should he, by an act of grace, admit, legitimate and incorporate into our language those words and expressions, which, hastily begot, owe their birth to the incontinency of female eloquence; what severe censures might he not justly apprehend from the learned part of his readers, who do not understand complaisances of that nature? (299–300)

Stanhope molds his attack on women so as to be relevant to the *Dictionary*: the old complaint about women's loquacity now focuses on vocabulary and orthography. When women are in the midst of "the torrents of their eloquence, . . . if words are wanting (which indeed happens but seldom) indignation instantly makes new ones; and I have often known four or five syllables that never met one another before, hastily and fortuitously jumbled into some word of mighty import" (2:300). Stanhope then explains the words minted by women (*flirtation, fuzz*) and words given new meanings (*vastly* has been so degraded that we now hear "vastly little").[25] He demonstrates women's orthography through anecdotes about letters of assignation, and ends with the prediction that the *Dictionary* will find its place in ladies' dressing rooms or the feminized powder-rooms of the young nobility. A very generous reader could suggest that Stanhope, through this mockery, still celebrates the inventiveness of spoken English, simply using women as an exaggerated example. That reading creates an essay that is deeply critical of the *Dictionary*'s goals and methodology. As a casual piece, though, the essay probably didn't have such a serious purpose. What is striking in that case is not the actual criticisms of woman's language (they are very standard), but the scale of the criticism—more than half of the total. Johnson's *Dictionary* was an enormous undertaking, and woman's language is a very small part of it. Stanhope's essay doesn't so much react to the *Dictionary* as exemplify the cultural importance of constructing women as a class of speakers.

Two other essays from *The World* (not by Stanhope) continue this trend. The first essay appeared in the very next number (102) and picked up on Stanhope's mocking suggestion that Johnson publish a dictionary of neologisms. But this author, Richard Owen Cambridge, claims that women wouldn't want their words in the dictionary: "it would be degrading their invention to suppose they would desire a perpetuity of any thing whose loss they can so easily supply" (2:306). The essay then recommends an annual dictionary of fashionable language, as an appendix to the almanac.

The last essay (175) raises a concern that is a necessary consequence of treating women speakers as a single category: it expresses horror at the leveling effect of woman's language. In a (fictional) letter to the editor, the author first notes that women have recently become more independent in their dress (which he praises as an example of liberty) but more uniform in their speech. He then quotes his friend, who intensifies the complaint:

> [T]he conversation of the female world . . . is at present all out of the same piece: all distinctions are taken away, and the several ranks and orders among them laid into one. There is one line of sentiment, air, manner, tone and phrase, running through the whole, and no discerning for a few seconds, a young woman with six or eight hundred pounds to her fortune, from a duchess; especially if she happens to have been allowed to keep company with her betters. (4:121)

Not only do all women rely on a vocabulary of "vastly, horridly, abominably, immensely, or excessively" (4:122), too many of them adopt an authoritative tone of voice: "full and sonorous, round and peremptory, with a very decisive emphasis, as if there could lie no appeal from their sentence; taking a larger scope for utterance, by opening their mouths to a disproportionate width" (4:122). After this letter, the fictional editor concludes that distinctions must be preserved:

> Thus a duchess may be twice as loud and overbearing as a countess; a countess as a simple baroness, and so downward; but such a pompousness of elocution, phrase, and manner (as my correspondent's acquaintance seems to point at) such *great swelling words,* must, one would think, set as ill upon one of a moderate face, rank, or fortune, as a great swelling hoop is found to do upon another not five foot high. (4:125–26)

The point of this essay is intensified by its narrative structure. It consists of sections by three narrators (the letter-writer, the letter-writer's friend, and the editor), all of whom agree that middle-class women should not imitate their betters. The consistency among the three narrators, we must assume, implies they speak for all men. The three narrators of this essay reveal not only hostility toward women's speech but a shared fear that the uniformity of women's speech hides class distinctions.

While these authors emphasize the uniformity of women's speech, others devised categories or types into which women could be divided according to their linguistic behavior. Addison's *Spectator* essay is typical in this regard. His four types of "Female Orator" are all loquacious, but they have different moral failings: first, those "who are employed in stirring up the Passions"; second, "those who deal in Invectives"; third, "Gossips"; and fourth, "the Coquet" (459). Addison does list other types that include both men and women; these four, he says, are the ones under consideration because they define specifically female characteristics.

The central two, involving detraction and gossip, seem especially closely linked to verbal behavior, and they attracted much attention. For example, in his *Essay on Old Maids,* the popular author William Hayley included the following, like Addison literalizing the female tongue:

> The envious Old Maid is a complete proficient in the black art of detraction; and, if she possesses both opulence and wit, all the evils that the ignorance of the dark ages imputed to witchcraft, are inferior to those which her malicious spirit has the power of producing. Her tongue is armed with a corrosive venom, and, by its insidious application, she delights in dissolving the ties of ancient friendship, in annihilating the festive bands of Hymen at the moment of their formation, and in poisoning all the fountains of social pleasure.[26]

Sadly, the association of bitter invective and old maids is too frequent in the period. The link between women and gossip, surprisingly, was only newly strong in the eighteenth century. According to Patricia Meyer Spacks, Johnson included a third definition for the term, "for the first time connecting gossip unambiguously and officially with women: 'One who runs about tattling like women at a lying-in.'"[27] Again, woman's language is associated with bodily functions and lack of control.

Gossip, littleness, and vindictiveness become attached to the constructed norm of women's linguistic behavior. Significant, then, are the advice books addressed to women, urging them to repair their linguistic deficiencies. Occasionally, these take the form of satire. Maria Edgeworth wrote two such texts, "An Essay on the Noble Science of Self-Justification" (1795), and a fictionalized version of the essay, *The Modern Griselda* (1805). Edgeworth tells us how to torture "that common enemy, a husband" by perfecting "the art of defending the wrong":

> I take it for granted that you have already acquired sufficient command of voice; you need not study its compass; going beyond its pitch has a peculiarly happy effect upon some occasions. But are you voluble enough to drown all sense in a torrent of words? Can you be loud enough to overpower the voice of all who shall attempt to interrupt or contradict you? Are you mistress of the petulant, the peevish, and the sullen tones? Have you practiced the sharpness

which provokes reply, and the continual monotony which effectually precludes it, by setting your adversary to sleep?[28]

The "Essay," which might have been gender neutral, is certainly not; *The Modern Griselda,* about a woman who harangues her husband until she drives him away, highlights the gap between the torturing wife and Chaucer's perfectly obedient one. It is specifically *women's* verbal combativeness, not combativeness in general, that needs correction.

A different kind of linguistic correction has survived in a conduct book by Helena Wells (later Whitford), *Letters on Subjects of Importance to the Happiness of Young Females, Addressed by a Governess to her Pupils* (1799). The book consists of twelve long letters on common conduct-book topics like the duty owed to parents and the avoidance of the affectations of modern life. Then it includes an appendix of "examples of improprieties of Language frequently occurring in familiar conversation; vicious pronunciation corrected."[29]

The examples are interesting in part because they indicate the kinds of errors to which the author felt schoolgirls were prone. These are of several types, each "error" followed by a "correct" example. Some of them simply note prescriptive grammar: "I wish you and I *was* schoolfellows" becomes "I wish you and I *were* schoolfellows" (158–59); "*Was* you in town last week? *me and my* sister *was*" is corrected, "*Were* you in town last week? *my sister and I* were" (165) Another group tries to rid girls of lower-class or regional pronunciation: "*Wat* a pretty *Ouse* that is.—*What* a pretty *house* that is" (168). Or, the examples may combine the two goals: "The *orses was* very troublesome.—The *horses were* very troublesome" (168).

In preparing girls for upward mobility, Helena Wells teaches them how to behave politely in speech. She encourages a rather literary style, characterized by a more complex syntax and a more formal vocabulary. Here are three examples:

I *wrote* to my brother some time ago, and I am *very much hurt* that he has not answered my letter.
Some weeks have elapsed since I *have written* to my brother, and I am *rather* hurt that he has not acknowledged the receipt of my letter. (162)

Mamar says that if it is a fine evening to-morrow, we shall go to *Fox Hall.*
Mama has been so good as to promise, that should the weather be favourable to-morrow evening, she will permit us to accompany her to *Vauxhall.* (163)

I *was* sorry I *vext* you; but you know you began to *quarrel* first.
I *am* sorry that you imagine I intended to *vex* you. I think you were out of temper without cause. However, if I did offend you, I sincerely beg your pardon. (173)

In each case, the corrected version is couched in layers of indirectness that make it more polite. This is true even when (as in the last example) the "correct" form actually admits less than the incorrect one; here, the speaker is sorry about the listener's reaction, not her own deed.

There are, to be sure, many representations of eighteenth-century women who mastered polite speech, avoiding the flaws of woman's language and remaining within decorous norms. Literary representations include examples of witty women, modest women, and everything in between. But these representations offer individual women as contrasts to the "natural" norm of the loquacious woman with the uncontrolled tongue. The value of speaking "properly" increases as it contrasts with the bad grammar, clichéd vocabulary, loquacity and meanness of the stereotypical woman's language. One discourse, that of sensibility, did attribute to women a "natural" eloquence. Significantly, though, this is an eloquence of feelings and of the body, of silent expression, rather than of the communication of rational thought. "Natural" eloquence was theorized in the public sphere by the elocutionists, to whom we turn now.

Theorizing Speech in the Public Sphere

As noted in the Introduction, many scholars view the eighteenth century as marking the firm establishment of print culture. Perhaps, then, it is not surprising that the same period saw the development of the elocution movement, which resisted the growth of print culture, emphasizing the virtues of the spoken word along the lines of ancient tradition. As a practical matter, the elocutionists shared with men like Johnson the impulse to standardize English; elocutionists like Thomas Sheridan made their livings in part by teaching men with Irish or Scottish accents to speak "properly." In earlier periods, regional accents were not stigmatized, and even aristocrats spoke like their neighbors. By this period, though, the aristocracy and gentry had adopted a more uniform accent that marked prestige, and other accents were increasingly vilified. The movement to standardize led to the publication of several guides to pronunciation, whose motivation one author described very simply: "it is disgusting to hear continually the same words differently pronounced in the mouths of different speakers."[30]

In broader terms, the elocution movement represents the best articulated defense of speech in the period. One senses the anxiety behind the resistance to print culture in Thomas Sheridan's first important publication, *British Education; or, the Source of the Disorders of Great Britain* (1756), in which he promises to prove that the present immorality derives from the defective system of education, and "that a Revival of the ART of SPEAKING, and the STUDY of OUR OWN LANGUAGE, might contribute, in a great measure, to the Cure of those EVILS" (title page). Sheridan's millennial approach caused Johnson and others to distrust his enthusiasm; his exaggerated claims for elocution were mocked in Sterne's *Tristram Shandy*. Yet he and the other elocutionists consistently argued that proper speech, especially public speech (oratory), would revive the glory of ancient Greece and Rome.[31]

In all of his works, Sheridan stresses the "deadness" of written language as compared with oral. In the introduction to his major work, *A Course of Lectures on Elocution* (1762), Sheridan argues that written language may convey ideas, but it cannot affect the passions or the fancy (that is, imagination):

> Some of our greatest men have been trying to do that with the pen, which can only be performed by the tongue; to produce effects by the dead letter, which can never be produced but by the living voice, with its accompaniments. . . . [W]e have in use two kinds of language; the spoken and the written. The one the gift of God; the other the invention of man. Which of these two is most likely to be adapted to its end, that of giving the human mind its proper shape, and enabling it to display all its faculties in perfection? (x–xi)

However, despite their rhetoric, the elocutionists did not teach what we would think of as oratory. Rather, their attention was on the relation between speaking and writing and, especially, on the performance of texts written by others. Sheridan was particularly concerned with the performance of the church service, which many contemporary observers decried as so bad that it could not serve religion. In his *Lectures on the Art of Reading* (1775), Sheridan moves through the service almost line by line, criticizing the usual readings and showing how better to express the text's meaning. Other elocutionists, like John Walker, established rules for oral reading based on syntax. Because of its focus on the relation between speaking and writing, the elocution movement will be particularly important for this study; the elocutionists' specific instructions on reading will be considered below. For now, I would like simply to discuss three general points that relate to how the elocutionists conceived (or didn't conceive) the woman speaker: their emphases on affect, on the physical properties of the voice, and on public discourse.

The elocutionists championed a "natural" language of tones and gestures not unlike the inarticulate cries that others had theorized as the origins of language. Sheridan spoke of two languages: the language of ideas (that is, words) and that of emotions (including tones, looks, and gestures). The language of ideas was complex and often led to miscommunication. The language of emotions, on the other hand, was simple and universal; it had merely been corrupted by bad teaching and bad reading. The elocutionists relied heavily on schemes that codified the language of the passions. Though these follow from ancient tradition, the most immediate influence in England was Charles Le Brun, *A Method to Learn to Design the Passions* (1734, French original 1698), a guide for artists. Each of the passions is described and illustrated as a universal: "Fright, when excessive, raises the Eye-brows exceedingly in the middle . . . ; the Eyes must look wide open . . . ; the Muscles of the Nose and Nostrils also swelled" (31); "Jealousy is expressed by the Forehead wrinkled, the Eye-brow quite depressed and knit; the Eye flashing fire. . . . One part of the face will appear inflamed and the other inclined to yellow" (38); and so on. Because Le Brun was developing a language of pictorial representation, he did not mention the voice. Others, however, did, most notably James Burgh, in his *Art of Speaking* (1761). The specificity of Burgh's instructions can sound comical to us: "*Malice,* or spite, *sets* the *jaws,* or *gnashes* with the *teeth;* sends blasting *flashes* from the *eyes;* draws the *mouth* toward the *ears; clenches* both *fists,* and *bends* the *elbows* in a *straining* manner. The *tone* of voice and *expression* are much the same with that of *anger;* but the *pitch* not *so loud*" (24). What matters is the assertion that the language of the passions is universal.

The elocutionists felt strongly that it wasn't words that persuaded, so much as the sincere expression of emotion, to which the hearer responds sympathetically. In an "Essay on Oratory," Francis Gentleman argued that eloquence works by moving the audience's passions; rational argument is an afterthought:

> [Eloquence] should enforce the clearest proof of any useful truth, with such interesting motives as may affect the hearers, and work their passions to virtuous purposes; to raise indignation against ingratitude; horror against cruelty; detestation against vice; abhorrence against slavery; compassion for misery; love for virtue; reverence for religion; obedience to superiors; and benevolence to all. Thus employed, eloquence appears in its full force and beauty: mere harangues seldom fail to catch the ear, but rarely touch the heart, and as seldom inform the head.[32]

As Jay Fliegelman has demonstrated, the paradox of the elocutionists' emphasis on affective persuasion is that it presents a "natural" language theatrically. In order to persuade, the orator must appear sincere in his emotions: "The elocutionary revolution made the credibility of arguments contingent on the emotional credibility of the speaker. . . . The quest for a natural language led paradoxically to a greater theatricalization of public speaking, to a new social dramaturgy, and to a performative understanding of selfhood."[33] Indeed, several of the elocutionists (including Sheridan and

Gentleman) were actors, and their instructions are very much geared toward the performance of texts written by others. In utilizing a performative concept of selfhood, the elocutionists seemingly allow the possibility that gender roles, too, are performed. To a certain extent, as I will argue in later chapters, the elocutionists' insistence that the reader takes on the character of the author as "he" performs a text can offer a means by which women can perform a variety of roles. But the possibilities of the performative self are limited by the female body.

Far from arguing that women were "naturally" emotional and thus especially eloquent, the elocutionists' focus on the physical properties of the voice set up dichotomies in which female voices were judged inferior. Because one of the elocutionists' concerns was the way written language did not provide enough clues to pronunciation, the description of the voice along musical lines was a common feature of elocution texts. Several authors developed schemes for notating the sounds of oral language. Abraham Tucker proposed a phonetic alphabet that would better reflect pronunciation and facilitate the learning of new languages. In one of his schoolbooks, John Walker published side-by-side versions of speeches, one with just text, the other with markings indicating emphasis, pauses, "passions," and (his particular hobbyhorse) inflections. Most radical, though, was the *Prosodia Rationalis* of Joshua Steele. Using a version of musical notation, Steele could indicate melody and rhythm as well as pauses and emphasis.[34]

One consequence of using musical analogies is that high voices are ranked as inferior to low ones. In his "Essay on Oratory," Francis Gentleman notes that there are three voices appropriate to oratory, all of which may be found or created, more or less perfectly, in every voice: they are countertenor, tenor, and bass (37); for him, "every voice" means every male voice. Focusing on the voice and breath as an instrument, John Herries criticized a feminizing tendency in genteel education, in which boys are taught to mince their words: "What is the consequence? His voice as he grows up retains the same unmanly quality. He dare not, he will not, he cannot exert it. He speaks upon the most important, most alarming subjects, with the delicate tone of a waiting-gentlewoman."[35] Herries recommends, instead, that boys perform manly breathing exercises, "to draw in, and expel the breath with the utmost VEHEMENCE and bodily exertion" (98). Furthermore, Herries argues that a low voice is the most powerful. Too often, the public speaker

> elevates his voice to a HIGHER pitch, instead of speaking in a LOUDER or stronger tone. We have already observed that the voice becomes smaller, and consequently weaker, in proportion as the larynx ascends and the glottis con-

tracts. What custom then can be more injurious to the purposes of speaking than to degenerate into a squeaking, inarticulate tone, at the very time when the voice should be exerted with vigour and fulness? (157–58)

Finally, of course, elocution excludes women because it occurs in the public sphere; the elocutionists focused on speech in the public realms of the senate, the pulpit, and the bar. We will see below (Chapter 4) that the rules of elocution were reproduced in schoolbooks and in that way reached a domestic audience. Even there, however, the instruction was framed in terms of persuasion in the public sphere. John Herries is not unusual in slipping from speech, which characterizes all humans, to men-only oratory:

> Of all the faculties which belong to the human nature, there is none more admirable or excellent, than the power of SPEECH.
> By the voice in a peculiar manner we are distinguished from other animals. By the voice we convey our sentiments and feelings to one another. . . . What but the skilful command of this faculty, can enable one man, not only to attract the attention of a numerous audience, but to convince every judgment, to please every taste, to delight every ear, and to animate every heart! (1–2)

And while we cannot absolutely separate the realms of public and private, there is no question that the penalties for women who attempted public speech were very high. A painting by the social satirist John Collet, entitled "The Female Orators," portrays the typically misogynist view: women who speak are viragos. These two women are the only women in a man's world, and they have everyone's attention. Their dispute presumably arises from a pitifully trivial business conflict (the women's class status is part of the "joke"), and their noisiness disturbs the judge, the sole representative of bourgeois order, who attempts to escape. Another man points to a poster on the wall: "Epicoene, or the Silent Woman" (the title of a Ben Jonson play). Admonitions for women to be silent are nothing new; rather, I would underscore the significance of this painting's title, which echoes Addison's. An earlier work might have been called, simply, "The Fishwives"; "The Female *Orators*" highlights the renewed attention to public speech in the second half of the eighteenth century and a heightened anxiety about women's participation in the public sphere.[36]

Theorizing Conversation: Gendering Civility and Sincerity

In the eighteenth century, the term *conversation* still retained the dual meaning of talk and of all human interaction, and it is impossible to sepa-

2. "The Female Orators" (1768). Fishwives disturb the peace. Engraved from a painting by John Collet. (© Trustees of the British Museum)

rate speech norms from the norms of politeness that construct social identity. It is not surprising, then, that writings on conversation form a pattern of competing discourses, differing over questions like what it is to be human, what it is to be female, or which social class best exemplifies virtue. Very often, the differences are framed in terms of the balance between civility and sincerity, in which we can see a historical shift after the middle of the century. Earlier prescriptive texts generally emphasize a courtly and relatively gender-neutral model of complaisance, or pleasing, and easy elegance. Later in the period, texts tend either to foist pleasing onto women or to recommend a bourgeois model of plain speaking or "manly" sincerity. This shift is consistent with increasingly rigid gender divisions and with the convergence of aristocratic and bourgeois values discussed above. As ever, we must be clear that general trends in the prescriptive literature may say little about actual practice, recognizing at the same time the power of discursive norms.

The earlier, Augustan paradigm of pleasing leans on a long tradition in polite conversation. Defining rules for the semipublic spaces of the polite world, it recapitulates norms that go back to Cicero and that were codified through many sixteenth- and seventeenth-century conversation manuals. (In fact, very similar norms appear in the classic modern studies of conversation by H. P. Grice.) The emphasis is on "pleasing," cooperation and turn-taking. As Samuel Richardson expressed it, "Conversation, where it is rightly managed, must be so conducted, as to let each member of the company have a share in the *pleasure* and *applause* it affords."[37] Various specific rules follow from the cooperative model, such as that no one should dominate or that one shouldn't use foreign words or specialized vocabulary that might exclude a listener. The cooperative norm, however, must be seen in the context of a hierarchical society. The norm assumes that cooperation remains appropriate to the social roles of the participants; turn-taking does not mean reciprocity when the conversationalists are not equals. While celebrating sociability, the model of complaisance is constructed for a stable courtly society.[38]

This model is well represented by Henry Fielding's "An Essay on Conversation," which recapitulates Augustan commonplaces. The essay demonstrates the tension between the injunction to please and an acceptance of social hierarchy. Most important for my purposes, Fielding describes "pleasing" in an essay directed only to men; pleasing is not yet gendered female. And pleasing has no taint of hypocrisy here. Fielding's advice rests on a view of human nature as social; pleasing is doing what is most human, that is, most benevolent. As he says later in the essay, "every Man is best pleased with the Consciousness of pleasing."[39] Fielding devotes the first section of the essay to pleasing through our actions, with small narratives of a visit to a country house and of a public assembly. The rules he offers of avoiding giving offense and paying proper respect are linked to a qualified version of the Golden Rule: "*do unto Men what you would they,* IF THEY WERE IN YOUR SITUATION AND CIRCUMSTANCES, AND YOU IN THEIRS, *should do unto you*" (124). Pleasing, that is, must always be appropriate to "the Degree of the Person" (124).

The second half of the essay, on "Good-Breeding . . . with respect to our Words" (142), also participates in the goal of pleasing within the framework of maintaining hierarchy. The most general rule is that of inclusive cooperation: "the Pleasure of Conversation must arise from the Discourse being on Subjects levelled to the Capacity of the whole Company; from being on such in which every Person is equally interested; from every one's being admitted to his Share in the Discourse; and lastly, from carefully avoiding all Noise, Violence, and Impetuosity" (146). Pleasing also involves not making others uncomfortable, and Fielding lists specific offenses to be avoided: first of all, argument; then slander; general reflections on countries, religions, and professions; blasphemy; indecency; anything that brings discomfort; inappropriateness to situation; and raillery (146–49). Over all, the point is that men, being fundamentally benevolent, please themselves by pleasing others.

This model of civility as pleasing politeness has sometimes been described as a "feminized" ideal. Lawrence E. Klein emphasizes the extent to which women were represented as agents of civilization in the seventeenth-century French discourse of salon culture, which then "made an important contribution to the construction of the public sphere in eighteenth-century England."[40] Women's conversation alone was insipid, but men's threatened to become argumentative; both sexes were required for sociable conversation (105). Klein sees Addison and Steele, in particular, as forwarding a notion of polite discourse that must qualify any strict dichotomy between public (male) and private (female) spheres. The world of polite conversation falls somewhere between public and private; it occurs neither in the public world of oratory nor within the intimacy of the family.

But by the middle of the eighteenth century, texts that still engage the norms of salon culture tend to view women as dispensable. Fielding's examples tend to take place after the "ladies" have left the room. That is also true of the courtly model proposed in James Burgh's *The Dignity of Human Nature* (1754). Like Fielding, Burgh considers conversation in the context of overall behavior; in his case, in the section "Of Prudence." Prudence includes not speaking ill of others, not venting "singular opinions," and not boasting (8). Burgh advises the reader "to accustom one's self to speak as little as possible in the first person. The figure Egotism is one of the most ungraceful that can enter into any man's conversation or writings" (15). Burgh even acknowledges that "the elegancy of behaviour, and that universally-engaging accomplishment of complaisance, are no where to be learned but in the conversation of that delicate part of our species" (17). He continues:

> But as on the other hand, it must be confessed, that their being deprived of the advantages we have for enlarging our knowledge, renders their conversation less improving, it must be allowed, that to spend the bulk of one's leisure in their company is not to be justified; nor indeed do they expect it, but, on the contrary, heartily despise the effeminate tribe of danglers. A prudent man will therefore only seek the conversation of the ladies occasionally. (17)

At least in this later period, then, the Augustan notion of the complementarity of the sexes, in which each works to improve the other, may more fruitfully be seen as archetypal than as a meaningful inclusion of female people. That is, it deals with qualities of the mind that were conceived of as gendered. In other ways, too, civility invokes particular views about human nature. Leland E. Warren argues that advice given in the conversation manuals depends, on the one hand, on a faith in our fundamental benevolence, and on the other, on a fear that separation from the social risks madness. Sociability is celebrated in part because the alternative is so bleak. Yet there is something paradoxical about instructional manuals that celebrate spontaneous benevolence. Indeed, Warren contrasts these with others that openly urge a more calculated approach. These latter rely on a more Hobbesian view of human nature and see conversation as a way of controlling others; dissimulation is part of the game.[41]

At issue is whether or not the desire to please is selfishly motivated. For Fielding and others committed to natural benevolence, pleasing in itself satisfies our desires. But there is always the risk that pleasing is merely a performance, designed to achieve one's less noble ends. Later in the century, when the discourse on sensibility emphasized spontaneity and sincerity, Augustan conversational rules began to ring false. Not surprisingly, the formal conversation manual, which both codified the rules of the game and offered stock phrases for memorization, became rare.[42] A historic shift is evident in the public reaction to the publication of Stanhope's (Chesterfield's) *Letters to his Son* in 1774. The *Letters* epitomize a courtly mode in which one's behavior is consciously shaped to achieve one's goal. And they were read, perhaps unfairly, as scandalously cynical, indeed immoral—particularly by bourgeois authors like Johnson and Cowper.[43] Sincerity and authenticity became more important than pleasing.

As Michèle Cohen has argued, the later eighteenth-century ambivalence about civility was framed in national, class, and gendered terms: formal politeness accrued negative connotations when it was identified as French, aristocratic, and female, and Stanhope epitomizes aristocratic Francophilia. By contrast, in his comment on "effeminate danglers," James Burgh expresses an anxiety about the risk to masculinity posed by conversation with women, which Cohen sees as captured in the stereotype of the fop.[44] And comments about the superficiality of French manners abound in the period. But the shift also has to do with a danger inherent in pleasing: that one might try to please the wrong people. While some authors, like Isaac Watts, felt confident that in pleasing man we please God, others felt that "the desire to please universally generates weakness . . . because it implies subservience to the opinions of others," who may or may not be godly themselves.[45]

Later in the century, the task of pleasing is generally assigned to women. And because young women were likely to be indiscriminate in choosing whom to please, the many conduct books written in the late eighteenth century took great pains in defining pleasing in moralistic terms. These texts often jumble Augustan notions of sociability with later, more conservative (evangelical) tendencies toward separate spheres for women. In advising women on moral behavior, many of the most widely read conduct books urged what can only be read as dissimulation—with the proviso that dissimulation should be in the service of pleasing; pleasing, in turn, would best serve women's interests of getting a husband and keeping him. And if pleasing traditionally involved the reduction of ego while drawing others out, the most conservative conduct books reduce ego to zero, and speech to silence. For John Gregory, women please best by being good listeners: "The great art of pleasing in conversation consists in making the company pleased with themselves. You will more readily hear than talk yourselves into [men's] good graces."[46] Gregory discusses women's speech in the context of modesty, which "will naturally dispose you to be rather silent in company" (119). However, "People of sense and discernment will never mistake such silence for dulness. One may take a share in conversation without uttering a syllable. The expression in the countenance shews it" (119). Wit should never be displayed, and women are urged to "be even cautious in display-ing your good sense. It will be thought you assume a superiority over the rest of the company. But if you happen to have any learning, keep it a pro-found secret, especially from the men" (122). As Mary Wollstonecraft pointed out, Gregory's advice always has an instrumental goal, that of catch-ing a husband.[47] We see this in his distinction between "companions" and "women." Lively speech "on some occasions . . . might render you more agreeable as companions; but it would make you less amiable as women" (125–26). Gregory recommends verbal modesty for its strategic value.

The year after the first edition of Gregory's book appeared, John Trusler lifted sections of it into his *Principles of Politeness* (1775). He expands and clarifies Gregory's advice, in intensifying the rules for conversation. Modest conversation, he says, is even harder than modest action. And his rules for modesty approach the ideal of silence: "A woman by no means should talk loud" (4); "A woman had better say too little in company than too much" (4). Like Gregory, Trusler couches his advice in terms of its strategic value. When a woman does occasionally express an opinion, she should be diffident and deferent:

This would win the hearts of all present, whereas the reverse would disgust them. There are many proper opportunities for a young woman to speak with advantage and credit to herself; and if she does it without conceit or affectation, she will be far more agreeable than such as sit motionless and insensate as statues. Even in silence, your looks should shew an attention to what is saying [*sic*]; for a respectful and proper attention never fails to gratify and please. (5)

Perhaps the most widely read conduct book of the period was James Fordyce's *Sermons to Young Women* (1766). In his chapter on conversation, Fordyce is less attentive to verbal performance than other authors were. Instead, he advises cultivating a generally sober, even melancholy air. He rails against gaiety, vivacity, silliness, and especially wit. It is not good humor, but sadness that touches men's hearts: "Never, my fair auditory, never do your eyes shine with a more delightful effulgence, than when suffused with all the trembling softness of grief" (83). Fordyce mentions several traditional failings in women's speech and conversation, but it is talkativeness that arouses his outrage: "But what words can express the impertinence of a female tongue, let loose into boundless loquacity? Nothing can be more stunning, except where a number of Fine Ladies open at once— Protect us, ye powers of gentleness and decorum, protect us from the disgust of such a scene" (89).

Gregory, Trusler, and Fordyce articulate the most conservative conduct-book norm, in which women should strategically utilize speech (sometimes) and silence (more often) to attain their goals. We should note that even when they recommend silence, they put it in the context of women's agency. In this, they are not that distant from the norms articulated by Stanhope: the speaker constructs the character that is most likely to succeed. The desire to please, which was inherently human in Fielding, is now both specifically female and not at all spontaneous. Not surprisingly, other authors criticized not only the end (husband-hunting) but the recommended dissimulation.

This critique is most vivid in the *Vindication of the Rights of Woman* (1792) of Mary Wollstonecraft, in which she addresses the English conduct books along with Rousseau's *Émile*. By devoting most of her attention to Rousseau, Wollstonecraft frames her attack in part in nationalistic terms: the French have elevated pleasing to a degree that is disgusting to the English. However, her main objection is to the idea that women's sole purpose is to please men; for Wollstonecraft that notion is appalling and irreligious. Wollstonecraft dismisses Fordyce for his sensibility and Gregory for his praise of dissimulation. This leads her to Stanhope (though he had not addressed women and was thus not obviously relevant to her argument) and "his unmanly, immoral system."[48] Instead, she recommends an honest English sturdiness, in which the self is constant: "for where are rules of accommodation to stop? The narrow path of truth and virtue inclines neither to the right nor left—it is a straightforward business" (5:168).

What Wollstonecraft proposes links plain speaking with civic virtue. If pleasing, the hallmark of civility, was read by the bourgeoisie as dissimulation, this second paradigm privileges manly sincerity. We may associate this mode with the Ciceronian "plain style" that was self-consciously adopted by scientists and by Puritans in the seventeenth century. In written prose, the plain style favors content over form; rhetorical flourishes are minimized in favor of a style closer to everyday language. More important for my purposes is the implication of a mode of interaction: straightforward, sturdy, and manly. This must be contrasted with aristocratic and polite forms that were increasingly stigmatized as French and effeminate. Michèle Cohen describes this process as dichotomizing nationality, language, and gender in parallel pairs. To be English, to speak English, was to be male.[49] Thus, if the stereotype of woman's language represented women as uncontrolled or even bestial, the rejection of formal politeness figured them as effete and insincere against an ideal of manly sincerity.

In the late eighteenth century, the model of straightforward, honest speech and behavior was especially commended by rational Dissenters like Wollstonecraft's mentor, Richard Price. Price's theology depends on liberty of conscience: as moral beings, we must be free to determine moral principles and to act upon them; we must also test all received opinions and beliefs by rational criticism.[50] Obviously, this has radical political implications in an age of an established and hierarchical Church, and Price is perhaps best known to modern readers as the orator whose speech praising liberty provided the occasion for Edmund Burke's antirevolutionary *Reflections on the Revolution in France*. But for my purposes, what matters is that Price's emphasis on individual conscience requires that we each seek truth openly and impartially; this then implies an openness in our dealings with each other that violates polite norms. Speakers like Price favor sincerity over civility.

The link between radical politics, freedom of conscience, and personal sincerity is most explicit in the work of William Godwin (not coincidentally, Wollstonecraft's future husband). Godwin's *Enquiry Concerning Political Justice* (1793) secularizes the moral philosophy of the Dissenters; Godwin had left the ministry a few years before he wrote this, his major work. In *Political Justice,* Godwin offers a strictly utilitarian system: it is our duty always to do whatever will promote the greatest good for the greatest number, and that duty trumps any possible rights, even the right to life. But, consistent with the rationalist emphasis on individual conscience, Godwin does allow one right, the right of private judgment, which enables us to decide for ourselves where the route to the greatest good lies. And private judgment is soundest when we deal with each other openly and sincerely. Godwin describes three degrees of sincerity: first, a man might consider himself sincere "if he never utter any thing that cannot be explained into a consistency with truth." Second, he might say "nothing which he knows or believes will be understood by the hearer in a sense that is untrue." But "the third and highest degree of sincerity, consists in the most perfect frankness, discards every species of concealment or reserve, and, as Cicero expresses it, 'utters nothing that is false, and withholds nothing that is true'" (1:338–39). Godwin illustrates how sincerity might work in everyday life in a section on the euphemisms used to exclude unwanted visitors. By asking servants to lie for us, we corrupt them. And then, isn't it better that the visitor know why he is excluded? If we are simply busy, he will understand. If we do not like him, he should be told why, so that he can have the opportunity to improve himself (1:357–60).

Godwin's *Political Justice* is the most extreme statement of valuing sincerity over civility, but it must be noted that no eighteenth-century author wanted to claim that the two are incompatible. Even Godwin recognized that perfect sincerity is possible only in an ideal world. In an essay in *The Enquirer* on "The Reciprocal Claims of Politeness and Sincerity," Godwin admonishes us to balance truth-telling with kindness.[51] At issue, always, is the proper relationship between the individual and society, with some authors more committed to an "authentic" and relatively independent self, and others thinking more about the roles we play in society. But for many authors, independence was "manly," whereas women were taught to focus on their social role. Thus sincerity becomes gendered male, and civility female.

Godwin, like Price, writes within a civic tradition that consistently links luxury, femininity, and weakness. True virtue is to be found in the manly virtues of the middle class. The gendered nature of this rhetoric is well illustrated in Mary Wollstonecraft's *Vindication of the Rights of Men* (1790) and *A Vindication of the Rights of Woman* (1792). The first piece was a direct response to Burke's *Reflections on the Revolution in France* and attacks Burke in part for his ornamented, "pretty" style; Burke, of course, had earlier articulated an aesthetic in which beauty was associated with the weakness of women and was less noble than the (masculine) sublime. Wollstonecraft begins by asserting her own directness:

> Sir,
> It is not necessary, with courtly insincerity, to apologise to you for thus intruding on your precious time, nor to profess that I think it an honour to discuss

an important subject with a man whose literary abilities have raised him to notice in the state. I have not yet learned to twist my periods, nor, in the equivocal idiom of politeness, to disguise my sentiments, and imply what I should be afraid to utter: if, therefore, in the course of this epistle, I chance to express contempt, and even indignation, with some emphasis, I beseech you to believe that it is not a flight of fancy; for truth, in morals, has ever appeared to me the essence of the sublime; and, in taste, simplicity the only criterion of the beautiful.[52]

Wollstonecraft continues here and in the second *Vindication* to associate her rhetoric and her morals with sturdy manliness, and to attack Burke and others who defend hierarchical societies as effeminate. Wollstonecraft works hard to redefine manliness as a human, rather than a male quality: the "manly virtues" for her are "those talents and virtues, the exercise of which ennobles the human character, and which raise females in the scale of animal being, when they are comprehensively termed mankind" (5:74). Her goal is to convince women to abandon the trivial pursuits and false sentiments that society seems to value, and "to persuade them to become more masculine and respectable" (5:76). Wollstonecraft thus applies the term "masculine" or "manly" to plain and straightforward speech and behavior, which members of both sexes should favor over courtly hypocrisy.

This effort constitutes part of Wollstonecraft's overall effort to emphasize human virtues (those common to both sexes) over the schemes by which women and men had separate or "sexual" virtues. While consistent with liberal Enlightenment philosophical principles in favoring similarity over difference, Wollstonecraft's arguments went against the tide of increasing gender bifurcation at the end of the eighteenth century. Unfortunately, Wollstonecraft's proposal of a gender-neutral norm of manly sincerity could not be acceptable in her society, and indeed contained the seed of the most vitriolic attacks upon her. Even before her death and the scandals erupting from Godwin's publication of the facts of her personal life, Wollstonecraft was frequently vilified for being "masculine." Her attempt to separate "manly" and "male" was a failure.

By the end of the eighteenth century, civility came to be associated with aristocratic and French artificiality or with female dissimulation; the discourse on bourgeois speech championed manly sincerity. Where, then, is there linguistic space for middle-class women? I would like to end with two conduct books that do encourage women to participate in conversation as rational creatures. In *Emily: A Moral Tale,* Henry Kett defines rules that are gender-neutral: "The rules of good manners seem to require that conversation, in mixed companies of grown persons of both sexes should be divided nearly in equal proportions between all present. It is the most agreeable, when it resembles a *round game,* where each person has his turn to play. It is most instructive when, as in a cricket match, the most skilful strikes the ball most frequently" (1:271). (And it is notable that this is *not* followed by any hints that men are the most skillful.) Kett recognizes that loquacity is not characteristic only of women, and his critique of exaggeration and praise for good storytelling explicitly include both sexes. Kett devotes an entire chapter to scandal, but again, he asserts that "what is generally called *Scandal,* is as common to men as it is to women" (2:1).

An equally reasonable position is articulated by the conservative Jane West, in *Letters to a Young Lady* (1806). Instead of one constant mode of speech, West envisions a kind of discourse competence in which the speaker masters a range of styles. In the beginning of her essay, West allows several roles for women, though here each woman plays one part:

> Conversation was never so happily allegorized as by a resemblance to a collection of musical instruments; and I believe we never return from a pleasant intellectual concert, without acknowledging that our gratification proceeded from its *variety* as well as its *sweetness.* We felt obliged to the leading kettle-drum (provided she did not play too long or too loud), as well as to the harmonizing flute; and the sprightly kit would have given us less amusement, had it not been contrasted with the sober strains of the virginal. (3:10–11)

West explicitly writes for "the middle orders" (3:12), and she notes the sameness of aristocratic conversation and its French insubstantiality: "among high circles, conversation is more like a *déjeuné* than an old English repast" (3:14–15). But she disdains the notion that sincerity and civility are incompatible: only "among the rougher forms of society [is it] not infrequent to hear civility and sincerity contrasted, as if they were in their natures irreconcilable" (3:24–25). With due adaptation for specific circumstances, "A few general rules seem to constitute the fundamentals of agreeable manners" (3:26): we should not offend or mislead; we should avoid egotism and affectation, contradiction, slander, and flattery. While reiterating the commonplaces of many earlier conversation texts, West tries to negotiate a middle ground between the norms of upper-class civility and bourgeois sincerity. Her essay is notable because, although written for women, it returns to a gender-neutral ideal. It is sometimes explicitly inclusive, and nowhere does it advocate silence.

Regrettably, Kett and West were minority voices among the conduct-book authors. Most others worked to enforce the stricter standards of decency and increasingly rigid norms for women's behavior that so many commentators have noted. We cannot separate this increasing emphasis on propriety from the coming to dominance of norms that had been characteristic of an Evangelical or Dissenting middle class. But this is not to say that class-based rules for conversation disappeared. There was still room for salon conversation and even wit among aristocratic women. The power relations inherent in speech norms are perhaps even more clearly seen in an advice book for servants, Jonas Hanway's *Advice from Father Trueman to his Daughter Mary upon her Going into Service* (1789). Hanway presents speech as nearly always dangerous: Mary should avoid speaking altogether. If her mistress should ask her opinion, she should either plead ignorance or, at most, offer facts, never an opinion. In any case, "remember to express thyself in as few, not in as many words as possible . . . , as happiness in service depends so much on the government of the tongue" (132–33). For a servant, who is dependent on pleasing a mistress, there is no ambiguity: silence is safer than speech.

But middle-class women spoke in contested space and, for that and other reasons, will be the subjects of this book. These women were told that their speech was idle, insipid, malicious, too high, and too long. On the one hand, they were to win husbands by their silence; on the other, the ideal wife "enlivened his social pleasures by the sprightliness and pleasantry of her conversation."[53] Commentators described women's speech as either uncontrolled and disruptive or effete and un-English; in either case, women were urged to speak less.

Still, we must avoid the temptation to accept prescriptive norms as descriptive of any individual's behavior. Even the conduct books exhibit a range of opinions. The discursive power of the conduct books and other writings on language was undoubtedly strong, but we will see that when we look at any individual woman's speech, they were only one influence among many. Individual women could position themselves as dutiful daughters or modest wives; they could also stake claims to other roles.

I began this chapter with literary representations of women's speech, which are useful in delineating stereotypes and in highlighting the constructedness of gender roles. My examples of negative stereotypes derived, not coincidentally, from texts written by men. But in closing, I would like to consider one example of the subtlety with which the stereotypes of women and language could be used. Jane Austen, as we might expect, made masterful use of woman's language, and often in fun. Woman's language may signal a character's inferiority. We must be on our guard against someone like *Northanger Abbey*'s Isabella Thorpe, who speaks in exclamations and exaggerations: "Oh! heavens! You don't say so! Let me look at her this moment. What a delightful girl! I never saw any thing half so beautiful! But where is her all-conquering brother?" (*NA* 57). Isabella often stuns this novel's heroine, Catherine Morland, by controlling the conversation and blinding Catherine with her exaggerations. The reader sees instantly that Isabella is a hypocrite.

If Isabella represents the worst stereotype of woman's language, Austen more often offers complex representations of gendered speech. Gendered sociolects are especially pertinent to the action of *Emma*. Emma herself is extraordinarily skilled in managing conversation according to polite rules. She makes everyone feel welcome and included; she also knows when to steer the conversation away from potential conflicts, and when reticence is the most tactful option. We are frequently told that Emma changes the topic, "feeling [the old one] to be an unsafe subject" (101); that Mr. Knightley's vexation "made Emma immediately talk of something else" (150); that in an uncomfortable moment she was "always putting forward to prevent Harriet's being obliged to say a word" (156); that Emma did not protest combining two parties because "it could not be done without a reproof to [Mr. Weston], which would be giving pain to his wife" (353); and so on.

Emma's politeness is never criticized, because it is motivated by true benevolence and appropriate to her position and her sex. For the male characters, politeness is treated with more ambivalence; the conflict between civility and sincerity is an important component of the tension between Frank Churchill and Mr. Knightley. Austen utilizes the vocabulary of nationhood in contrasting these characters' linguistic practice. When John and George Knightley greet each other with a simple, "How are you," they speak "in the true English style" (99). Even more telling, when Mr. Knightley criticizes Frank Churchill's "professions and falsehoods," he attacks Frank's Gallic civility: "No, Emma, your amiable young man can be amiable only in French, not in English. He may be very 'aimable,' have very good manners, and be very agreeable; but he can have no English delicacy towards the feelings of other people: nothing really amiable about him" (149). Unlike Mr. Knightley, Emma appreciates Frank's "well-bred ease of manner," his "readiness to talk" (190), and the fact that "he knew how to make himself agreeable," the "proof of his knowing how to please" (191). But if Emma does not engage Mr. Knightley's national vocabulary, she does recognize the traditional connection of politeness and class: part of Frank's appeal for her is that he is decidedly aristocratic.

By contrast, Mr. Knightley's plain speech is rather bourgeois, most associated with men a notch below him like Robert Martin (whose speech we never hear directly). For Mr. Knightley, this kind of speech is simply manly, and he explicitly rejects Frank Churchill's language as less than masculine. Yet Austen highlights Emma's sensitivity to the ways in which conversational interactions reflect class, and Mr. Knightley's obliviousness, when the two of them discuss Frank's difficulty in leaving his demanding aunt to pay an overdue visit to his father. While she argues it is unfair to judge Frank's conduct without knowing the social context, Mr. Knightley says plainly,

> "There is one thing, Emma, which a man can always do, if he chuses, and that is, his duty; not by manoeuvring and finessing, but by vigour and resolution. . . . A man who felt rightly would say at once, simply and resolutely, to Mrs. Churchill—'Every sacrifice of mere pleasure you will always find me ready to make to your convenience; but I must go and see my father immediately. . . . I shall, therefore, set off to-morrow. . . .'"
> "Such language for a young man entirely dependent, to use! Nobody but you, Mr. Knightley, would imagine it possible. . . . Standing up in the middle of the room, I suppose, and speaking as loud as he could!" (146–47)

Emma sees clearly that Mr. Knightley's devotion to sincerity is a luxury. While Mr. Knightley asserts that his behavior is simply manly, it is his financial independence that enables him to practice plain sincerity.

Emma may tease Mr. Knightley for his bourgeois sturdiness, but Frank's Gallic civility is not necessarily preferable. Frank's insincere courtliness toward Emma, while he is secretly engaged to someone else, deserves the censure it receives at the end of the novel. And Mr. Elton's civilities, while at least sincerely meant to court, are vague enough that Emma and Harriet are confused as to their object. Civility has its dangers. Yet on the other hand, civility may protect feelings where sincerity risks hurting them. At the end of the novel, after Emma and Mr. Knightley are engaged, Emma performs one of her kindest actions in keeping a secret: she never tells Mr. Knightley that Harriet was in love with him. Here, Emma's discretion is nobler than Mr. Knightley's sincerity, although it causes her some discomfort:

> "Mystery; Finesse—how they pervert the understanding! My Emma, does not every thing serve to prove more and more the beauty of truth and sincerity in all our dealings with each other?"
> Emma agreed to it, and with a blush of sensibility on Harriet's account, which she could not give any sincere explanation of. (446)

In *Emma,* neither plain sincerity nor polite civility is an absolute good: either may be used for good or for ill. Austen invokes her period's characterizations of these two modes of language, especially as they differ in their construction of masculinity, but both modes may be the target of her admiration or of her wit. The conflicts over pleasing politeness and plain sincerity were well covered by various commentators. Austen is perhaps unique, though, in challenging the stereotype of woman's language with which I began.

It is Mr. Knightley, not surprisingly, who uses the term, when he contrasts Harriet Smith's volubility with his own no-nonsense version of Mr. Martin's proposal: "Your friend Harriet will make a much longer history when you see her.—She will give you all the minute particulars, which only woman's language can make interesting.—In our communications we deal only in the great" (472). The novel includes several examples of the stereotype, from the naive Harriet Smith, to the loquacious Miss Bates, to the spiteful Mrs. Elton. But curiously, we first come upon woman's language in the person of Emma's father, Mr. Woodhouse. As a rather sweet hypochondriac, whose domestic orders are nearly always subverted, Mr. Woodhouse epitomizes a kind of "feminine" powerlessness. And his speech exemplifies the littleness of woman's language, with his repetitious exclamations and his focus on bodily functions. Even his vocabulary is "feminine." Here is a conversation with Mr. Knightley:

> "It is very kind of you, Mr. Knightley, to come out at this late hour to call upon us. I am afraid you must have had a *shocking* walk."
> "Not at all, sir. . . ."
> "But you must have found it very damp and dirty. I wish you may not catch cold."
> "Dirty, sir! Look at my shoes. Not a speck on them."
> "Well! that is quite surprizing, for we have had a *vast deal* of rain here."[54]

Finally, Austen warns us not to be too judgmental. One of the most serious breaches of decorum in any of her novels occurs in *Emma,* when the heroine has lost patience with the dithering, gossiping, loquacious Miss Bates. When a game is suggested in which each person must say one very clever thing, two moderately clever, or three dull things, Miss Bates is sure she can manage the last. But "Emma could not resist. 'Ah! Ma'am, but there may be a difficulty. Pardon me—but you will be limited as to number—only three at once' " (370). For a fine conversationalist like Emma, this is a shocking breach of politeness. What is worse, and what Mr. Knightley points out, is that Miss Bates is a poor old maid, while Emma is wealthy and young.

> Were she a woman of fortune, I would leave every harmless absurdity to take its chance, I would not quarrel with you for any liberties of manner. Were she your equal in situation—but Emma, consider how far this is from being the

case. She is poor; she has sunk from the comforts she was born to; and if she live to old age, must probably sink more. Her situation should secure your compassion. (375)

The foolish speech of women may be a legitimate target for criticism, Austen tells us, but the woman who speaks foolishly must be seen as a whole person, a situated being. Like Mrs. Malaprop, Miss Bates is a "useless" creature in her society, poor because unmarried. Her language is silly, but her pitiable condition should protect her from our ridicule. The stereotype of woman's language treated women as a single, unified class of speakers; Austen reminds us of the differences among women. It is the specificity of individual women's patterns of speech that we turn to now.

CHAPTER 2

Polite and Plain Language; or,
Amelia Opie "Quakerized"

She has assumed the garb, and even the shibboleth of the sect, not
losing in the change her warmth of heart and cheerfulness of spirit.
—Robert Southey, *Colloquies on the
Progress and Prospects of Society*

Amelia Alderson, the only child of a prominent Norwich physician, lived most of her life in the spheres of rational Dissent. Her father worshiped with the Unitarians, hosted visits by revolutionary thinkers like William Godwin and Thomas Holcroft, and attended meetings of the radical Norwich Corresponding Society. In 1794, on her first visit to London, Amelia Alderson witnessed the famous treason trials of Thomas Hardy, John Thelwall, and John Horne Tooke, commenting knowledgeably on the legal issues and on the oratory in letters home. In 1798, she married the painter John Opie, the son of a carpenter, and helped resuscitate his career as a society portraitist; after his death in 1807, she returned to Norwich to live with her father, but visited London regularly. In addition to performing a role at the center of Dissenting and radical society, Opie wrote books that, while not now canonical, had a steady readership and decent reviews. But at the age of fifty-five, Amelia Opie turned away from her glitterati existence and joined the Religious Society of Friends (Quakers). She had long been close to her Norwich neighbors, the Gurney family, who counted two members who would transform Quakerism: Joseph John Gurney and Elizabeth (Gurney) Fry. Amelia Opie's conversion must be seen, then, within a network of personal attachment. But joining the Quakers meant adopting a social identity quite different from that of the salon hostess and conversationalist. Among other strictures, it meant giving up writing novels, which the Quakers considered frivolous and untruthful; Opie even abandoned a work-in-progress, to the disappointment of her publisher. The alteration that is most relevant here, however, is that joining Friends entailed adopting a new language—joining a new linguistic community.

This shift in language was remarked upon by Opie's worldly friends, and not always kindly. Opie's friend Mary Russell Mitford commented thus:

> She is all over Quakerized, as you of course know—to the great improvement, as I hear (for I have not seen her), of her appearance. It is certainly a pretty dress. She *thee's* and *thou's* people; calls Mr. Haydon "friend Benjamin;" and directs to the Rev. William Harness after the same fashion, "William Harness, Hampstead." With all this, she is just as kind and good-humoured as ever; and Mr. Haydon told me that, in about a quarter of an hour's chat, she forgot her *thee's* and *thou's,* and became altogether as merry as she used to be.[1]

Amelia Opie's speech demonstrates the kind of discourse competence discussed in the Introduction. By unselfconsciously switching from one linguistic code to another, she constructs multiple identities, choosing to affiliate herself with the conversational partner of the moment. In so doing, however, she violates the stringent rule of Quaker speech prescribing an unchanging mode of language in all circumstances: the Quakers deliberately spoke to the king as they would to their neighbor. Opie thus exemplifies one facet of the complexity of language use. The representations of her speech after her conversion point to the ways in which she negotiated identities that were each supposed to have one fixed mode of speech. Opie refused to speak *either* "as a woman" *or* "as a Friend"; her practice demonstrates the great distance between the descriptions of fixed sociolects and the flexible ways in which actual women speak. Opie's speech, and the ways Quaker speech in general was represented in the period, can thus offer us a case study of historical linguistic practice.

I begin with Quaker women for several reasons: first, because Quakers are so conscious of themselves as a separate speech community. When people joined the society, they often wrote of the shift to "plain" language as the key moment in their conversion. (The use of *thou* was the clearest marker of the shift, though as we shall see, not the only one.) Even the name of the sect was carefully delineated; the use of the term *Quaker* can express distance from the group. The Quakers themselves never used that term, referring rather to "Friends" or "members of our society." At most, they would use the phrase "the people called Quakers" in titles of polemical tracts, as a concession to a non-Quaker audience. The Quakers thus offer an unusually well defined speech community, one that was both explicated in detail and self-consciously oppositional to mainstream patterns. If we are to find linguistic purity anywhere, we would expect to find it here.

Second, I begin with the Quakers because their use of silence was so well theorized. The Quakers conceived of their meeting for worship as a mystical experience in which they waited in silence until moved by God to speak; their spoken messages were felt to be directly inspired. Speech, in meeting, was understood not to be of human origin, and silence was an active listening for the Divine spirit. In everyday life, of course, silence and speech accrued something closer to their ordinary meanings, but there was always a sense that the Divine might be present at any moment, so that silence always had a sacred element. Obviously, this is quite different from the polite norms of mainstream society and must complicate our picture of linguistic practice in the period.

Third, and especially, I begin here because Quaker speech raises a number of issues about gender and language. Quaker speech as described in the eighteenth century was the very opposite of "woman's language" as discussed in Chapter 1. Far from exemplifying the loquacity assumed to be natural to women, Quaker women, like Quaker men, conceived of silence as offering access to the Divine. With the stringent enforcement of plain language, Quaker women did not utilize the exaggerated vocabulary of "monstrous" and "vastly" that was described as typical of women. More important, when Quaker women expressed their affiliation in speech, the Quaker features are much more obvious than those identifying them as women. Yet unlike other women who deemphasized gender in their speech, Quaker women were never presented as masculinized. We are faced with a set of contradictions. As discussed in Chapter 1, plain speech was gendered male ("manly sincerity"), yet this group of women who used it was never vilified. Similarly, the locutions of politeness and indirectness, used to smooth social interaction, were consistently rejected by the Quakers, yet the speech of Quaker women was not generally interpreted as face-threatening. These contradictions are at the heart of this chapter.

I begin with a brief consideration of the woman conversationalist, Opie's linguistic persona before her conversion. I turn then to the special features of Quaker language that were furthest from mainstream norms: women's preaching, the use of silence, and the rejection of polite locutions. Then, I look at representations of Quaker women's speech and behavior in non-Quaker texts. Finally, I examine how one speaker, Amelia Opie, negotiated the complexities of expressing affiliation in language. Since she converted so late in life, Opie's gender identity and habits of speech had already been fixed; her writings and the representations of her speech demonstrate the difficulties inherent in performing a new speech identity.

Witty Women and Polite Conversation

In Chapter 1, I explored the negative stereotype of woman's language, which emphasized the quantity and emptiness of women's speech. While obviously not descriptive of the range of women's linguistic practices, the stereotype had discursive importance because it attempted to define what was essential to women's speech. That is, while Addison, for example, recognized a number of ways of speaking badly, only some of these are (to his mind) peculiar to women. In turning now to the good conversationalist, I move to a type that is not so clearly gendered: both men and women might be included. But I hope to show, even if sketchily, that the female conversationalist performed a role that was often in conflict with late-eighteenth-century gender expectations. To the extent that someone like Amelia Opie was known as a witty woman, that is, her claim to being a modest one was threatened.

Wit was a contested term in the eighteenth century. Wit had been favored by writers of the Restoration, but was later considered hostile or cynical. Stuart M. Tave has argued that biting wit was replaced by "amiable humor," which substituted good nature for the hostility barely concealed in raillery. Looking back at the Commonwealth and Restoration from the early eighteenth century, he says, Englishmen saw two equally unacceptable models: "As they saw it, first had come the Puritan, enthusiastic, morose, and austere, then the rake, cynical, gay, and debauched: two extremes in agreement on the natural depravity of human nature, and either intensely holy or intensely profane. What good-natured men wanted was a more equable way of life, in which the archetype was neither the saint nor the wit but the benevolent and good-humored gentleman."[2] Tave describes a shift to a latitudinarian and benevolent concept of "cheerfulness and innocent mirth," epitomized in the appreciation of "amiable humorists" like the gentle "my uncle Toby" in Sterne's *Tristram Shandy* (viii).

Even such gentle humor, however, can disrupt the comfort and cooperative nature of pleasant conversation. Modern linguists describe jokes as violations of H. P. Grice's "cooperative principles" governing conversation, especially the "maxim of quality," which precludes saying something you believe to be false. Jokes are "non-bona-fide" communications—statements that deny their own truth value. This quality of "deniability," in turn, means that speakers may express socially unacceptable beliefs in jest (in racist jokes, for example, or Addison's jokes about female tongues), because they leave the hearer uncertain of the speaker's commitment to the expressed belief. And because jokes nearly always invoke judgments about others, they convey social norms in ways that may include the listeners, in a gesture of solidarity, or exclude them.[3]

What matters here is that neither Tave's amiable humorist nor the modern mode of framing humor would have allowed linguistic space for witty women. The amiable humorist was a gentle eccentric whose foibles we could love; he was necessarily male. And wit nearly always involves a judgmental attitude that is at odds with the modesty prescribed for bourgeois women of this period. Hester Lynch Thrale (later Piozzi) provides a good example of how carefully the woman conversationalist must be described. A close friend of Samuel Johnson's, she recorded many evenings of his conversation; later on, her own conversation was recorded by others. Edward Mangin, who published *Piozziana; or, Recollections of the Late Mrs. Piozzi* in 1833, described her power thus:

> She told a story incomparably well; omitting every thing frivolous or irrelevant, accumulating all the important circumstances, and after a short pause (her aspect announcing that there was yet more to come), finished with something new, pointed, and brilliant.
>
> To render all this more fascinating, she would throw into her narrative a gentle imitation—not *mimicry,* of the parties concerned, at which they might themselves have been present without feeling offended.[4]

Mangin must stress the gentleness of Thrale's speech, its inoffensiveness, because pointedness, brilliance, and especially mimicry are essentially unfeminine. They are hard, sharp, and inherently offensive. Indeed, storytelling in itself is a form of display that "holds the floor" longer than is perhaps appropriate for bourgeois women.

The increasing emphasis on modesty as women's privileged virtue inevitably meant that women conversationalists spoke in contested space. The conservative conduct-book author James Fordyce rejected wit for women both because it was judgmental and because it was a way of grabbing attention for oneself:

> The faculty termed Wit, is commonly looked upon with a suspicious eye, as a two-edged sword, from which not even the sacredness of friendship can secure. It is especially, I think, dreaded in women. . . . But when I speak on this subject, need I tell you, that men of the best sense have been usually averse to the thought of marrying a witty female? . . . We are never safe in the company of a critic; and almost every wit is a critic by profession. . . . Who is not shocked by the flippant impertinence of a self-conceited woman, that wants to dazzle by the supposed superiority of her powers?[5]

On the other hand, more moderate writers like Henry Kett and Hester Chapone allowed raillery as long as it was "delicate." For Kett, a woman may tell stories and even laugh at folly, as long as "she never endeavours to do so at the expense of benevolence or decorum" and never forgets "the tenderness that may be due to another's feelings." Chapone goes even further:

> I would not condemn you to perpetual seriousness—on the contrary, I delight in a joyous temper, at all ages, and particularly at yours. Delicate and good-natured raillery amongst equal friends, if pointed only against such trifling errors as the owner can heartily join to laugh at, or such qualities as they do not pique themselves upon, is both agreeable and useful; but then it must be offered in perfect kindness and sincere good humour; if tinctured with the least degree of malice, its sting becomes venomous and detestable. . . .
>
> You will wonder, perhaps, when I tell you that there are some characters in the world, which I would freely allow you to laugh at—tho' not in their presence. Extravagant vanity, and affectation, are the natural subjects of ridicule, which is their proper punishment. . . . You are welcome to laugh, when you leave the company, provided you lay up a lesson for yourself at the same time.[6]

The kind of raillery that Chapone allows is well represented by Jane Austen, in *Pride and Prejudice*. Elizabeth Bennet has been trained by her father to treat the follies of others as occasions for mirth, and she defends the ridicule of "follies and nonsense, whims and inconsistencies," and notably of "vanity and pride" in a conversation with the overly serious, vain, and proud Mr. Darcy (*P&P* 57). But we are always aware that Elizabeth's playfulness borders on impropriety, and while her father's raillery can be cruel, her own must always be sweetened by smiles and sensitivity to the feelings of others. Whatever moral effect humor can have, then, its use must be tempered by reference to the humorist's gender.

In other Austen works, as well, we see how wit is qualified by gender. In *Northanger Abbey*, Henry Tilney resembles his father in always controlling the conversation, though he does so with wit rather than by command. When he first meets the heroine, Catherine Morland, he "talked with fluency and spirit—and there was an archness and pleasantry in his manner which interested, though it was hardly understood by her" (*NA* 25). Catherine does understand his ridicule of the platitudes strangers must utter about Bath, but she is stymied by his witty comparison of dancing and marriage (76) and is often utterly oblivious to Henry's meaning when he is anything but completely straightforward. Catherine is, to be sure, an exceptionally naive heroine. Still, Henry is permitted to mystify her, indeed to control her, and to remain a desirable marriage partner only because he is male.[7]

Wit functions differently in Austen's female characters, most especially in *Mansfield Park*'s Mary Crawford. Miss Crawford is introduced as a woman of fortune, who doubts that the sister she comes to stay with is fashionable enough to suit her (*MP* 41). Her propriety is always questioned by the more serious Edward and Fanny, even when they appreciate her good qualities, and it is usually her witty speech that signals impropriety. As Edward says, "She does not *think* evil, but she speaks it—speaks it in playfulness—and though I know it to be playfulness, it grieves me to the soul" (269). Edward is initially shocked at Mary's tendency to speak so freely of the uncle who has raised her, particularly at her witty acceptance of his immoral behavior: "Certainly, my home at my uncle's brought me acquainted with a circle of admirals. Of *Rears,* and *Vices,* I saw enough. Now, do not be suspecting me of a pun, I entreat" (60). Edward works hard to claim that Mary "is perfectly feminine" (64) in spite of her sharp tongue, but the more delicate Fanny is always ambivalent about Miss Crawford. Toward the end of the book, Fanny is justified, for Miss Crawford's wit is closely tied to her decadent morals: first, in admitting (in jest) that she wishes the elder son, Tom, would die, leaving Edward as heir to the estate and title, and second, in viewing Edward's sister's adultery as a mere folly that can be hushed up. She responds to Edward's horror with a joke and then with "a smile ill-suited to the conversation that had passed, a saucy playful smile, seeming to invite, in order to subdue me" (459). Mary Crawford's wit and her acceptance of "immoral" behavior work with her birth to mark her as a member of a "decadent" upper gentry, who aspire to reach even higher. She constructs a linguistic identity that marks those aspirations, one far from the modest demeanor prescribed for bourgeois women.

In Amelia Opie's letters, as well, we can see the construction of an identity whose performance of gender alters slightly as it moves toward the aristocracy. Opie lost her mother at a young age, and the woman who in part took her place is described by a male observer as a good bourgeoise: Susannah Taylor was "a most intelligent and excellent woman, mild and unassuming, quiet and meek, sitting amidst her large family, occupied with her needle and domestic occupations, but always assisting, by her great knowledge, the advancement of kind and dignified sentiment and conduct. Manly wisdom and feminine gentleness were in her united with such attractive manners, that she was universally loved and respected."[8] Many of Opie's published letters were written to Taylor, and one senses the check on Opie's high spirits. Opie can ironically look forward to meeting her friend again, when they will "rejoice in the absence of husband and father" (Brightwell 41), and she can report on social successes and on her real anxiety and dismay during the 1794 Treason Trials. But these early letters always keep within decorous bounds. For example, Opie makes gentle fun of a "fine, jolly, florid young countrywoman, a great deal fatter than I am," who claims

her friends will be shocked at her loss of weight: "I could hardly keep in my
laughter at this. Her Deptford friends must be droll persons, and great amateurs in fat indeed, to be dissatisfied with her magnitude, and regret what
she had lost" (119). But the raillery is kept behind this woman's back.

It is after her husband's death in 1807, and especially in the series of letters written during the 1814 season, that Opie represents speech in ways that
violate bourgeois norms for women. It is not so much that Opie herself
speaks immodestly. Rather, she depicts a salon culture in which wit and
repartee are appreciated, in which women as well as men tell stories (though
rarely without some critique, at least, expressed), and in which many of the
participants are titled. In 1813, she attended a gathering hosted by Germaine
de Staël. "Lady Crewe, Lord Dudley, William Spencer, the Mackintoshes,
the Romillys, were among the brilliant group, who, witty themselves, were
the cause of wit in others; and, while they grouped around her, called forth
the ever-ready repartees, and almost unrivalled eloquence, of our hostess"
(Brightwell 144). On another occasion, in 1814, "the wonder of the crowd,
and the persons who sucked us all in turn into their vortex, were Professor
Spurzheim and Lady M. Shepherd. Her ladyship fairly threw down the
gauntlet, and was as luminous, as deep, as clever in her observations and
questions . . . as any professor could have been. . . . The professor looked
alarmed, and put on his pins; and Lady Mary began her dialogue at ten, and
it was not over at a little past twelve" (151). As Opie's evocative language
shows, there is something discomforting about women who speak forcefully
even in this aristocratic salon culture, though clearly aristocratic women
have linguistic freedom that bourgeoises did not. And Opie seems to be sit-
uating herself as a hopeful entrant to the aristocracy: she writes on 25 May
1814, "My *levée* on Sunday was rather splendid, consisting of twenty-seven
persons, who (men excepted) chiefly came in carriages" (149).

It was very shortly after this, the height of her social success, that
Amelia Opie began to move toward the Religious Society of Friends and a
new social and linguistic identity. Let us leave her for a bit and turn to the
very different norms of speech among the Quaker community.

The Quakers on Language

The eighteenth century is considered a rather dull period in the history
of the Society of Friends, even among Quaker historians. It is overshadowed
on the one hand by the turmoil and heroism of the seventeenth-century
origins, when Quakers were actively persecuted for their beliefs, and on the
other by the schisms and social activism of the nineteenth century, when

Friends turned their attention to prison reform, the abolition of slavery, and women's suffrage. Eighteenth-century Quakerism can be characterized by its Quietism: its sense, theologically, that the self must be annihilated in order to be filled with the Divine spirit, and its literal quiet waiting. While silence had been theorized by the founders of Quakerism, their meetings saw very little of it; hours-long impromptu sermonizing was the norm. By contrast, eighteenth-century meetings might go for years without any vocal ministry. At the same time, the Society turned inward. In contrast to both earlier and later periods, Friends of the eighteenth century were admonished not to get involved in worldly politics. Friends took no official interest in the turmoil surrounding the French Revolution, and their political agenda was confined to ensuring their own religious freedom regarding marriage law, tithes, and so on. The period seemingly offers little of interest to historians.

The privileging of voice over silence among feminist scholars, as discussed in the Introduction, has directed them, too, to the surrounding periods of Quakerism. In her book on seventeenth-century Quakers, Phyllis Mack vividly captures the excitement of what it meant for women to join a sect whose tactics we might now call street theater:

> Standing alone or accompanied by other Friends, they chastised neighbors, judges, clergymen, and monarchs, face to face, in churches, graveyards, private houses, and before the doors of Parliament. As worshipers they had melted, wept, and quaked in an atmosphere of ecstatic, sympathetic bonding. In public they shouted, insulted, and provoked, seeking to trigger in their audiences a process of self-scrutiny and inward repentance, proving the authenticity of their message by their own upright bearing as they were punched, bludgeoned, and whipped by enraged ministers and magistrates.[9]

But historians working on the eighteenth century tend to adopt an apologetic tone toward women who valued self-discipline and whose speech was not so flamboyant. Sheila Wright states, for example, "By the late eighteenth century Quaker women's ministry had little of its original verve and vigour. The ranter and prophecy element of the seventeenth-century ministry had given way to a more seemly and 'quiet' style of preaching. The Quaker ladies, for ladies they were, undertaking work in the ministry in our period would no doubt have preferred to forget some of the earlier antics of their founding sisters."[10] Although it is understandable that modern feminist scholars tend to look for heroic foremothers, I would prefer to begin with a less judgmental approach toward women of this period. Whether or not the historian prefers "ranters" to "ladies," the historical project enjoins us to allow these women to define their own terms.

One of the most notable features of Quaker women's speech was the tradition of women's preaching. As early as 1666, Margaret Fell had defended the practice, on a scriptural basis, in a pamphlet entitled *Womens Speaking Justified*. Her task involved, on the one hand, providing scriptural examples of women's prophesy and, on the other, interpreting the Pauline injunction against women's speaking in church in a way that limited its ban to idle talk. But preaching, Fell argues, is a matter of articulating the Spirit with which we are inspired, and no human force should constrain this Spirit. She concludes, "And so let this serve to stop that opposing Spirit that would limit the Power and Spirit of the Lord Jesus, whose Spirit is poured upon all flesh, both Sons and Daughters, now in his Resurrection" (11).

Needless to say, the tradition of women's preaching continued to receive attention through the eighteenth century. The most famous comment is, undoubtedly, Samuel Johnson's, made to James Boswell after Boswell had visited a Quaker meeting: "Sir, a woman's preaching is like a dog's walking on his hinder legs. It is not done well; but you are surprized to find it done at all."[11] The issue arose again with the growth of Methodism in the eighteenth century, which also incorporated women's prophesy. John Wesley, however, distinguished the practice of his followers from that of the Quakers by insisting that women's preaching should be the exception, not the rule.[12]

Quakerism was not unaffected by the increasing influence of conservative evangelicalism toward the end of the eighteenth century. The traveling ministry of Joseph John Gurney, Amelia Opie's friend, led to a major schism in American Quakerism between more mystical and more evangelical branches (that is, between those who continued the traditional Quaker emphasis on the direct experience of the Divine and those who leaned more heavily on historical [scriptural] revelation). With the increasing emphasis on Scripture as the source of truth, the defenses of women's preaching become somewhat testier—more insistent that it is not "really" the women who preach, but rather the immediate inspiration of the living Spirit. Joseph John Gurney included a chapter on women's ministry in his *Observations on the Distinguishing Views and Practices of the Society of Friends*. He repeats the traditional Quaker justification of it, that all true ministry is prophetic, and that God's power to inspire cannot be limited. But he sounds halfhearted, to say the least: "Since we conceive, on the one hand, that all true ministry is uttered under the immediate influence of the Spirit of Christ—and since, on the other hand, we confess that the wind bloweth where it listeth—we cannot, reasonably, do otherwise than make way for the exercise of the gift by those persons, of every description, whom the Spirit may direct into the service" (181). Gurney treats the Pauline passages with great respect, merely offering the possibility of alternate interpretations. And he emphasizes that women preachers are not demanding a new place in the social hierarchy: "Women who speak, in assemblies for worship, under such an influence, assume thereby no *personal authority* over others. They do not speak in their own name" (188). Gurney's very qualified approval of women preachers is typical of other Quaker texts of the period, such as John Bevans's *A Defence of the Christian Doctrines of the Society of Friends* (1803) or Henry Tuke's *The Principles of Religion, as professed by the Society of Christians, usually called Quakers* (1805).

Yet in spite of the evangelical influences, the Quaker tradition of women's ministry flourished, and in a new way. The period 1775–1825 was a peak period for traveling ministry: Friends who felt a concern to travel received a certificate from their home meetings and visited meetings throughout England, Ireland, Europe, and America. Many individuals traveled thousands of miles, usually in same-sex pairs; half of the traveling ministers were women.[13] These public Friends framed their ministry as a duty that came before all other duties, even the responsibilities of motherhood. Mary Dudley describes the struggle between the call to public ministry and her duty to her children:

> Having a disposition naturally prone to affectionate attachment, I now began, in the addition of children, to feel my heart in danger of so centering in these gifts, as to fall short of occupying in the manner designed, with the [prophetic] gift received; and though at seasons I was brought in the secret of my heart to make an entire surrender to the work I saw that I was called to, yet, when any little opening presented, how did I shrink from the demanded sacrifice, and crave to be excused in this thing.[14]

Yet in 1788, she journeyed to the Continent, leaving seven children to her husband's care, the youngest only ten weeks old.

One sign of the esteem in which these public Friends were held is the fact that their memoirs were often published; many were included in the canon-forming nineteenth-century anthology, *Friends Library*. The autobiographies tend to be formulaic, describing childhood, a struggle with worldliness followed by convincement, the developing sense (resisted at first) of the obligation to speak publicly, then an account of the minister's travels.[15] The formulaic nature of these memoirs can be attributed in part to the fact that all were edited, often by Quaker authorities, who molded them into the conventional genre. That censoring process and the reiterative memoirs that result reflect the antiindividualistic bias within Quakerism. The Quietism of this period, to repeat, emphasized a "clearing" of self as a way of opening to the Divine. While this rejection of self can seem masochistic to modern feminists who prefer assertiveness, it is what allowed eighteenth-century women to speak, travel, and serve.

Unfortunately, since Quaker ministry is spontaneous and purely oral, it is normally lost to history. A very rare exception is a sermon given in New York province, as the title page says, "by the celebrated Rachel Wilson, (One of the People called *Quakers.*) To a numerous Audience of different Persuasions, Taken in short Hand, from the Mouth of the Speaker, by one of the Audience" (Newport, 1769); the transcriber says in a preface that he did not ask Rachel Wilson's permission either to take notes or to publish the sermon, which was delivered extemporaneously. Rachel Wilson was a traveling minister, based in Westmoreland in the north of England, who had ten children (the youngest only seven) when she felt called to travel to America. Her discourse as printed is twenty-four pages long and would have taken at least half an hour to deliver. Except that she addresses a portion of the sermon directly to youth, perhaps a concession to her position as mother, there is nothing in it that points to her gender. On the contrary, Rachel Wilson emphasizes the powers available to and the duties incumbent upon all. She begins with a typical Quietist gesture toward releasing the self:

> The soul that has its thoughts fix'd upon God . . . is certainly happy beyond any finite comprehension. The divine image, when grafted in the soul, utterly excludes all vain and ostentatious thoughts of our own sufficiency; a confidence in which would be inconsistent with the character of a Christian, as well as repugnant to the express command of God, given to the prophet, *to debase the creature, and exalt the Creator.* (3)

In urging her audience to attend to God, Rachel Wilson stresses the simplicity of her message: "There are too many, now a days, who forget the plain parts of scripture (of which there are enough for every man to profit withal) and from a want of understanding the more obscure ones, are too apt to think irreverently of the Deity. . . . But, my friends, the word of God is plain to every man who has the light of reason" (13). Indeed, while Rachel Wilson frames her discourse as a commentary on a text from Isaiah, she emphasizes the God-given reason that is available to every human being. It is our use of reason that will be judged: "since morality is founded upon that reason which is a common gift to mankind, every man must answer for the use of his reason" (16). We should not overreact to Rachel Wilson's use of the generic masculine here, since that was the standard of her time. Rather, in typical Quaker fashion, she locates the faculty by which we discover God in all people. Her focus on the simplicity of Scripture and the commonality of reason creates an opening for women's full humanity. Her discourse illustrates a third trend in eighteenth-century Quakerism, in addition to mysticism and evangelicalism: a tendency toward Deism.

Preaching is a very specialized, and ill-documented, use of language, and it will not be of central concern here. What is relevant about the traveling ministers is that they—and their audience—privilege their identity as "minister" over their identity as "woman." For Gurney and the evangelical Quakers of a slightly later period, that becomes troublesome; gender identity becomes more salient. Individual speakers thus had to negotiate conflicting demands regarding how they expressed affiliation in their speech.

By beginning with this brief excursus on women's preaching, I have to some degree misrepresented what happens during meeting for worship. Speech often corrals our attention. But the linguistic feature that most typifies Quaker worship is the use of silence. I have already noted that eighteenth-century Quietism set the bar very high as to when to break silence with prophesy; many hours of worship were completely silent. In his chapter titled "On Silent Worship," Joseph John Gurney outlines a three-step program for worship, each of which requires silence. First and most essential is "a deep humiliation and subjection of soul before the divine Majesty" (202), which Gurney then illustrates with scriptural references to silence. Second is a "waiting upon God" (205), best exemplified in the "silence of expectation" (207). Third, we must be silent in order to hear God's message: since "the periods appointed for the public worship of God are times when the immediate teaching of Christ may reasonably be expected; the propriety of *silence,* on such occasions, is at once established" (209). Many witnesses attest that during this period of Quakerism, there was less certainty that "waiting upon God" would result in spoken ministry. Silence became the rule, speech the exception.

Since Quakers do not believe in segmenting life into sacred and secular realms, the devotional use of silence extended into "ordinary" life. Quakers were noted for their sparing use of words and for their sense that the Divine could visit them at any time. In his sympathetic *Portraiture of Quakerism,* the (non-Quaker) abolitionist Thomas Clarkson describes the peculiarities of Quaker conversation. Clarkson explains that "Their conversation is usually cramped or fettered," because of their caution in the use of idle words and commitment to the truth (146). The subjects of their conversation are also limited, excluding as they do politics, scandal, fashion, and the arts. But Clarkson especially remarks on the way silence can fall on the group:

> In the company of the Quakers a circumstance sometimes occurs, of so peculiar a nature, that it cannot well be omitted in this place. It sometimes happens that you observe a pause in the conversation. This pause continues.

Surprised at the universal silence now prevailing, you look round, and find all
the members in the room apparently thoughtful. The history of the circumstance is this: In the course of the conversation, the mind of some one of the
persons present has been either so overcome with the weight or importance of
it, or so overcome by inward suggestions on other subjects, as to have given
himself up to meditation, or to passive obedience to impressions upon his
mind. This person is soon discovered by the rest, on account of his particular
silence and gravity. From this moment the Quakers in company cease to converse. They become habitually silent, and continue so, both old and young, to
give the apparently meditating person an opportunity of pursuing uninter-
ruptedly the train of his own thoughts. Perhaps, in the course of his meditations, the subject, that impressed his mind, gradually dies away, and expires in
silence. In this case you find him resuming his natural position, and returning
to conversation with the company as before. It sometimes happens, however,
that, in the midst of his meditations, he feels an impulse to communicate to
those present the subject of his thoughts, and breaks forth, seriously explaining, exhorting, and advising, as the nature of it permits and suggests. When he
has finished his observations, the company remain silent for a short time; after
which they converse again as before.

   Such a pause, whenever it occurs in the company of the Quakers, may be
considered as a devotional act. (149–50)

That is, consistent with their belief that the Divine spirit could appear spon-
taneously and unpredictably, Quakers kept worship as a possibility during
ordinary conversation. Clarkson does note, however, that the practice he
describes is most likely to occur in the presence of traveling ministers.

   To exemplify the way an "ordinary" person conceptualized silence in
her life, we can look to A Diary of the Religious Experience of Mary Waring
(1809). Unlike the majority of published diarists, Mary Waring was not a
traveling Friend, nor does her journal relate her childhood or conversion.
Rather, it records the routine events of her life from 1791, when she was
thirty-one, until her death in 1805. Like the other autobiographies, though,
the work was edited (the preface notes that "family occurrences" were
deleted) and made more uniformly religious in character. What remains are
brief entries, describing rounds of visits, illnesses, personal spiritual struggles, and—most notably—records of meetings for worship. Waring's comments are surprisingly judgmental. Each meeting is given an overall characterization, almost a "thumbs up" (or down): "a low stripping season" (18),
"a humbling time" (45), "a searching time" (50), "a favoured time" (21 and
often), "a time of labour" (27 and often). The judgments depict a mind and
soul constantly seeking and evaluating; there is no "feminine" tentativeness
here. Moreover, Waring's comments offer an unusual record of the activity
that Quakers sensed in the silence. She often perceives the silence as a time

of conflict, sometimes imagined as between God and Satan, at others imagined as a conflict within herself. She says on 18 Twelfth Month, 1791, "In the fore part of the meeting the enemy was near spreading his snares, and seeking to draw my poor mind off its watch; but my eye and cry being to the Lord, who beheld the conflict, he was pleased, in gracious condescension, to appear for my help, and the renewal of my strength" (43). On the other hand, the conflict is internal on 4 Second Month, 1803: "By giving way to a roving disposition on first sitting down at meeting, my way became so hedged up, that I could not discern a path; but, after struggling a while, I was enabled to press through the crowd of difficulties, and approach Him who is the health of my countenance, and my God" (229–30). Often the silence is a time for consideration of her own unworthiness. At other times, consolation comes to her in the silence, generally described as a visitation from the living Spirit: "Was favoured with an extraordinary degree of divine favour, in my silent waiting this morning. Methought it somewhat resembled the morning stars singing together for joy" (195). Lest we think that the silence is always active, though, Waring reminds us that drowsiness can overcome: "Though a silent meeting, yet to my mind a very favoured one, far beyond my deserts: yet towards the conclusion, attacked with sleepiness; which I had reason to fear had prevailed with some, much to their hurt" (25). Finally, while Waring says little about conversation, and includes no reported dialogue, we do get hints of the stress on silence and seriousness in everyday life, which can make Quakers appear dour. She says of one day, "Took a walk. Was too light and airy in my conversation, for which I quickly felt gently corrected, which humbled me" (78).

Like Rachel Wilson's, Mary Waring's speech and silence emphasize her solidarity with Quakers over her identity as a woman. In the wider world, silence (like speech) is frequently interpreted in ways that reflect gender. Women's silence, as we saw in the Introduction, is interpreted even by feminists as passivity. A silence of resistance is more usually linked to men. Women can be "meek"; men are "taciturn." But the Quakers imagined silence as a site of both contestation and consolation; as a time to examine the self or as an open space into which the Divine might enter. What they did not imagine was that silence is gender-specific.

In ordinary conversation, as in spoken ministry, Quaker language utilized both a specialized vocabulary and a mode of interaction rather different from that of the wider culture. This specialized language served to identify the speaker as a member of the group. Converts often commented on the effort required to adopt the new mode of speech, and even birthright members occasionally slipped. Mary Waring's entire diary entry for 27 Seventh Month, 1791, reads: "Favoured in my retirement to-day; yet was guilty of a weakness in the evening, in saying *Sunday* [instead of *Firstday*] to a person not a Friend, for which I felt condemnation, and desire to abide humbly under it" (32). Quaker discipline was strict enough that Waring may have condemned herself or may literally have been scolded by a Friend who was present. Certainly the lines marking Quakers as a speech community were very sharply drawn.

As we saw in Mary Russell Mitford's description of Amelia Opie's speech, it was the *thee*'s and *thou*'s and the refusal to use honorifics that most clearly marked Quaker language use. In addition, Quakers used numbers for the names of the days of the week and of the months of the year, which they considered pagan. Since they didn't practice water baptism, they didn't call first names "Christian" names. Because all days are equally good, they didn't say "Good morrow" or "Good evening." Because they believed their lives were directed by God, they wouldn't say something had happened "luckily," "fortunately," or "by chance."[16] But it was the use of *thou* and the refusal to use honorifics that attracted the most comment.

George Fox, founder of the Society, had fostered both on the grounds that to do otherwise amounted to flattery. In the seventeenth century (Fox's time), the *thou/you* distinction still had the force of *tu/vous* in French: *you* was used both for the second-person plural and as a mark of respect, often by someone of lower status who would be addressed in turn as *thou*. Fox promoted a kind of egalitarianism before God that led him to reject the "polite" *you*. A second argument for the use of *thou* was grammatical: saying *you* to a single person was untruthful. However, by the late eighteenth century *you* had developed its modern usage, as both plural and singular, whereas *thou* became limited, for the most part, to sacred usages. At the same time, Quaker usage was changing: the nominative *thou* was more and more replaced by the accusative *thee,* as in "thee knowest." Thus, the arguments both from grammatical correctness and from avoidance of flattery were less convincing. It becomes much more clear that the main reason to retain the traditional usage was that of group identity, both to keep the boundaries between the sect and the outside world and to maintain solidarity with those in the past whose commitment to plain language had incurred great suffering. One author emphasized this to Quakers who were drifting away from the old ways. After describing the extreme suffering of several earlier Friends, he continues:

How can you act so inconsistently with the profession you are making as to salute persons by the title of Mr. or Mrs., bow, and take off your hats to them,

and designate the days of the week and the month by the vulgar names which
the heathens gave them in honour of their idols, thus violating and trampling
under foot those precious testimonies, the faithful support of which cost many
of our predecessors in religious profession the loss of all in this world that is
most dear[?][17]

The refusal to use the conventional forms of address had two purposes:
to insist that all were equal before an ever-present God and to avoid exposing the other to potentially harmful flattery. In his widely read *Observations,*
Joseph John Gurney reiterated both of these purposes. But, again in keeping with his general tendency to move closer to the mainstream, he softens
the potentially brutal honesty of Quaker speech: "I have been very far from
any intention to disparage so useful and amiable a quality as *courtesy.* On the
contrary, experience has thoroughly convinced me of the great practical
importance of that quality, as a means of smoothing down the little asperi-
ties of society, and of rendering the communications between man and man
profitable, easy, and agreeable" (283).

Gurney is right to hedge, for Quaker plainness of speech is indeed the
opposite of conventional politeness: the Quaker sociolect rejects the face-
saving conventions of mainstream society. In their classic book *Politeness:
Some Universals in Language Usage,* Penelope Brown and Stephen C.
Levinson theorize politeness in terms of "face." Normal social intercourse
involves many acts that may be understood as aggressive or threatening to
the face of the hearer. To counter that, politeness demands that each potentially face-threatening act be expressed in language that reflects recognition
of the hearer's power over the speaker (we must be especially protective of
the face of someone of higher status than us), the social distance between
the two (bonds of personal affection may diminish the need to protect face),
and the degree of the imposition. The speaker then chooses among four
overall strategies: "Bald on record" includes direct statements that reflect
concerns other than saving face ("Watch out!"). Positive politeness expresses
approval or solidarity ("What a great party!"). Negative politeness preserves
the hearer's face by allowing autonomy and softening imposition ("Would
you mind softening the music?" rather than "Turn that stereo down!"). And
"off-record" statements make requests only implicitly. Within each of these
higher strategies, Brown and Levinson list specific linguistic strategies by
which the speaker's goals are implemented.

A remarkable number of these are exactly the kind of thing the Quakers
didn't do. For example, positive politeness includes several strategies rejected
by the Quakers. One is, simply, "Exaggerate (interest, approval, sympathy
with H[earer]," with the example, "What a fantástic gárden you have!"

(104). Another is to avoid disagreement, including through the use of white lies (115). A third is, "Joke" (124). Brown and Levinson discuss the use of honorifics as a part of negative politeness, under the strategy "Give deference" (178–82). By refusing to say "Your Honour" to a judge, they would say, the Quakers threatened his face. In addition to these linguistic strategies, Brown and Levinson recognize behavioral rituals that work to save face, like bowing or removing one's hat. Again, these are exactly the rituals that the Quakers refused to perform.[18]

Brown and Levinson present their strategies as structural and universal, but note that they are "the subject of much cultural elaboration" (13). They continue: "Furthermore, cultures may differ in the degree to which wants other than face wants (such as the want for efficiency, or for the expression of power) are allowed to supercede face wants. If there is a norm of sincerity, for example, sincere disapproval is less of [a face-threatening act] than it would be in societies not having such a legitimization of non-face wants" (249). We cannot say that the Quakers were not polite, then, only that they valued sincerity, directness, and the rejection of hierarchy over saving face. Within the group, these features serve to establish solidarity, which is itself a kind of positive politeness. For example, Thomas Clarkson describes how Quakers behaved toward visitors to their homes. Instead of pressing food or drink upon them,

> The Quakers appear to be particularly gratified, when those, who visit them, ask for what they want. Instead of considering this as rudeness or intrusion, they esteem it a favor done them. The circumstance of asking on such an occasion is to them a proof that their visitors feel themselves at home. Indeed, they almost always desire a stranger, who has been introduced to them, 'to be free.' This is their usual expression. (145)

But solidarity within the group only reinforced the group's distance from wider society. The difficulties with Quaker norms of politeness came when Quakers interacted with others.

The solidarity fostered by Quaker speech had obvious advantages in a subculture that was both very communitarian and committed to an oppositional relation to the wider society. Clarkson remarked,

> They would say, again, that this, as well as the other alterations in their language, has had a moral influence on the Society, and has been productive of moral good. . . . This language has made the world overseers of the conduct of the Society. A Quaker is known by it as much as by his dress. It operates, by discovering him, as a check upon his actions. It keeps him, also, like the dress, distinct from others. And the Quakers believe that they can never keep up their Christian discipline, except they keep clear of the spirit of the world. (137)

But Clarkson also devotes considerable attention to the disadvantages caused by the linguistic strategies used by Quakers. For example, he says, Quakers were considered devoid of affection and animation, which we can understand as not following Brown and Levinson's strategies of positive politeness (such as praise and exaggeration). Quakers were considered evasive: "Their great desire to speak the truth, and not to exceed it, occasions often a sort of doubtfulness of speech" (446). Quakers were reluctant to make promises (another feature of positive politeness); Clarkson explains that "Quakers, knowing the uncertainty of all human things, . . . seldom . . . promise anything positively, that they may not come short of the truth" (446). Finally, and most shocking to Clarkson: "The last charge against the members of this community will be seen in a vulgar expression, which should have no place in this book if it had not been a saying in almost everybody's mouth. The expression is, 'Though they will not swear, they will lie'" (447). Clarkson rejects this entirely, admitting only that Quakers' hesitancy may have "produced an appearance, which the world has interpreted into evil" (448).

Clarkson uses the masculine pronoun, of course, and it is not clear whether he always means to include women. We have noted before that Quaker women's language use emphasizes their Quaker rather than their gender identity. This was true also of other polite behaviors. Clarkson comments on after-dinner behavior: "This custom of the females withdrawing after dinner was probably first insisted upon, from an idea, that their presence would be a restraint upon the circulation of the bottle, as well as upon the conversation of the men. The members however, of this Society seldom submit to this practice. Men and women generally sit together and converse as before dinner" (159–60). That is, gender difference was somewhat mitigated, at least in this ritual that is often a figure for different patterns of conversation.

More important, insofar as politeness is figured as "feminine," Quaker women occupy an ambiguous position. Quaker speech is not "polite." Ever since Robin Lakoff claimed that women habitually "weaken" their speech through overpolite indirectness, hedges, and so on, there has been a stream of work by feminist linguists on women and politeness. Deborah Tannen emphasized the positive politeness that women articulate, by expressing interest in the other, paying compliments, and so on. More recently, Janet Holmes has used the criteria developed by Brown and Levinson to argue that women are in fact more polite than men.[19] Not everyone agrees that the claim that women use more polite forms is empirically true, and some would claim that the issue isn't so much gender as power hierarchies (Brown and Levinson would agree that a lower-status person must use more polite strategies to avoid threatening a higher-status person's face). For my purposes, it is the representational force of the notion that matters. Women are perceived to be more polite, or, to put it the other way around, a woman uttering a direct statement risks being perceived as rude or masculine. Then, Quaker women were adopting a position that was not feminine.

Quaker women, by all accounts, rejected the modes of speech that were designated "female" in the larger society. Furthermore, the habits of speech expected of members of the Society of Friends were considered definitely masculine. This seems to controvert the schema of Chapter 1, in which men were allowed various speech identities, but women were clumped together as a single class. However, eighteenth-century Quaker women, even considering the prominence of public Friends, were not threatening in the same way as earlier Quakers. Brown and Levinson theorize that "the problem for any social group is to control its internal aggression while retaining the potential for aggression both in internal social control and, especially, in external competitive relations with other groups" (1); politeness can be seen as a way of signaling nonaggression. Their first premise seems to this Quaker culturally biased; however, it does offer a way to understand the seeming conflict around Quaker women's impoliteness. The Quakers, historically adamantly pacifist, signaled their nonaggression through their testimonies. Perhaps, then, it was less important for them to perform the rituals of nonaggression encoded in politeness.

Mainstream Representations of Quaker Women

In Chapter 1, I argued that eighteenth-century language theorists privileged gender as a sociolinguistic category: where the speech of men might be imagined along a spectrum representing differences of class, region, age, or individual temperament, "woman's language" was a stable category that did not differentiate among groups of women. Clearly, Quaker women represented a challenge to this system. They did not use the stereotypical exaggerations of woman's language; they did not gossip or speak at length; their speech was closest to the model of manly sincerity, but they were never considered masculinized. Within the Society of Friends, communitarian discipline worked to make the representations of women's speech that have come down to us surprisingly uniform. But let us turn for the moment to the ways in which "outsiders" represented the speech of Quaker women. These representations offer us insight into how authors imagined women not bound by mainstream norms of femininity.

I have already noted that Quaker women of this period were less threatening to outsiders than were Quakers of earlier times, and that this was in spite of the fact that Quaker women did not follow the norms outsiders expected. Attitudes toward Quaker women, as expressed in literature at least, changed markedly over the course of the century. In the early 1700s, while no longer persecuted as evil or mad, Quaker women were still mocked for their enthusiasm. In the *Spectator,* for example, a letter described inverted priorities: "Sir, I am one of those unhappy Men that are plagued with a Gospel-Gossip, so common among Dissenters (especially Friends). Lectures in the Morning, Church-Meetings at Noon, and Preparation-Sermons at Night, take up so much of her Time, 'tis very rare she knows what we have for Dinner, unless when the Preacher is to be at it."[20] Literary works such as Defoe's *Captain Singleton,* Centlivre's *A Bold Stroke for a Wife,* and Fielding's *Tom Jones* included Quakers (men and women) who were by no means wholly admirable. Even the Quaker landlady in Defoe's *Roxana,* who is a great friend to the heroine, is tainted for the reader because all of her qualities are filtered through the corrupt first-person narrator. For Roxana, it is no doubt a positive feature that the (unnamed) Quaker is "a cunning, as well as an honest Woman" (356), or that she deceives Roxana's persecutors even where she declines to lie—the reader, however, may be skeptical. But by the time of Robert Bage's *Man as He Is* (1792), to be Quaker was unambiguous in adding dignity to a woman's characterization. Bage's character, Miss Carlill, holds her own in theological arguments with clergymen. Described as having eyes that conveyed "a certain archness" (1:91), traveling about Europe with a worldly friend, and marrying a non-Quaker, Miss Carlill would not have been appreciated by the Society of Friends; the honorific "Miss" in itself is off-putting. But several reviews of this novel identify her as a Quaker—and enough said. Anna Laetitia Barbauld wrote in 1810, "the best sustained character is that of Miss Carlill, a quaker, in which the author has exceedingly well hit off the acuteness and presence of mind, and coolness in argument, by which the society she is supposed to belong to are so much distinguished."[21] By the end of the eighteenth century, the representational status of Quaker women had changed significantly.

This shift is reflected in the changes made in *The Fair Quaker of Deal,* a comedy by Charles Shadwell, which went through many performances and printings after its debut in 1710. The play involves the romance of Dorcas Zeal (a wealthy Quaker) and the non-Quaker Captain Worthy, and the complications that result when another man, Captain Mizen, wants Dorcas for her money, while Dorcas's non-Quaker sister Arabella loves Captain Worthy. Both subplots involve characters assuming the guise of Quakers. When Worthy learns that Mizen plans to kidnap Dorcas and marry her against her will, he manages to provide a substitute victim, a whore, who pretends to be Dorcas and "catches" Mizen. Meanwhile, Arabella sends a forged letter to Dorcas claiming that Worthy already has a family; she then takes the disguise of a Quaker man who wants to marry Dorcas and whose (false) honesty is to contrast with Worthy's (slandered) perfidy. We thus have three supposed Quaker voices: Dorcas's, the whore Jenny Private's, and Arabella's as the suitor, plus Mizen's attempts to match his false Dorcas's speech.

Dorcas is a sensible character whose commitment to sincerity leads to the comic complication: on the one hand, it doesn't occur to her to question Arabella's lying letter; on the other, believing that Worthy has lied to her is devastating. Her speech is generally straightforward. One always senses the tensions between her subculture and the wider world, though. For example, when she visits her friend Belinda, she begins: "Friend Belinda, I am come resolved to chat away the Evening with thee." Belinda responds in a language that partly imitates Dorcas's but that challenges her separateness: "My pretty Saint, thou'rt welcome, I need not ask you how Worthy does, I see it in your Eyes; the demure Aspect is vanish'd, and you begin to look like one of us." To which Dorcas retorts, "Why, I am Flesh and Blood as well as thou art; and did not my Spirit get the better of my Clay, I should be vain as thou art."[22]

Shadwell has more fun when non-Quaker characters attempt "Quakerese." When Jenny Private disguises herself as Dorcas in order to thwart Mizen's plot and get him to marry her, she mangles the sociolect. Meanwhile, Mizen tries to court "Dorcas" by attempting to imitate her speech. Here is a sample, showing that while Jenny can't maintain the use of *thou,* she does know how to eroticize Quaker spirituality:

> *Jen.* Will you change your vain Religion then? Will you stand fast to the Faith? In Perseverance, will you come over to the Congregation of the Upright? Will you put off these Gaudy Cloaths, those Vanity of Vanities?
> *Miz.* Yea verily, I will put off my Gaudiness, I will strip my self to the Nakedness of the Spirit.
> *Jen.* Why then thou hast overcomed me, and verily I will be thine in a few Months.
> *Miz.* Oh, thou Lovely Lamb, set not so terrible a time; the Spirit moveth me to make thee Flesh of my Flesh, and Bone of my Bone, before the Sun shineth again. (44)

Finally, when Dorcas's sister Arabella disguises herself as a suitor as part of a plot to gain Worthy for herself, she adopts an elaborated biblical language. Language like this gains her access to Dorcas: "Verily, I could wish thou could'st dispense with giving her some small Disturbance, my Business is very urgent; for behold my Errand is from her Brother, and concerneth her much, and we must be in private" (71). Yet Dorcas is suspicious. Arabella introduces herself as "the chosen Man, selected by thy Friend and thy good Brother to greet thee with a holy Kiss, and tell thee I love thee, fair one." To which Dorcas responds, "Love me at first sight!—Have a care thou talk not in the Language of the World, and play the Deceiver" (73).

While Dorcas is reasonably believable as a Quaker speaker, the plot of *The Fair Quaker of Deal* is not a credible representation of Quaker practices. Most notably, consistent with their communitarian outlook, Quakers planning a marriage must announce their intention to the Meeting, which is responsible for ensuring that the partners are free from prior commitments; a Quaker wouldn't need to hear this through an anonymous letter. But Dorcas is portrayed as an isolated individual; even her sister is not a member of the Society. Shadwell was not really interested in Quakerism; his representation of it must have some other purpose.

Partly, of course, using Quakerism heightens the comic effect. The Quaker emphasis on truthfulness highlights the comedy of disguise. The Quaker costume and distinctive language make it simpler for Jenny Private to "play" Dorcas, since her social identity is so distinctive. Even Dorcas herself uses her honesty to tease her friend Belinda. When Belinda pretends she is not in love, Dorcas replies, "Why, Friend Belinda, art thou not asham'd to dissemble so? I must tell thee my Conscience will not let me do it; if thou dost not shew a great deal of Kindness to Rovewell forthwith, I will discover what pass'd in thy Closet between us just now" (57). On a different level, though, Dorcas's Quakerism is just an eccentricity that must be shed to complete the comic resolution. At the end of the play, Dorcas leaves the stage while the others perform a country dance; Quakers did not dance. When she returns, however, she announces that she is converting—she says to Worthy, "to make our Marriage Yoak more Chearful still, from this bless'd Hour I'll joyn thy holy Worship" (90). This conversion is unmotivated and unprepared; it changes Dorcas's faith into an amusing foible that was useful for comedy but has no place in married life. On a more political level, it expresses a hope of avoiding religious schism, still a real threat in 1710.

In 1773, the play was revised (now titled simply *The Fair Quaker*) by Edward Thompson, whose first motivation in an era of reformed manners was to make those characters more refined, whose "seasoning may be too high for the palates of the present age" (iii). The revisions affect primarily the language of the naval characters. For example, where Shadwell's Worthy ends his first speech to his cockswain with an offer ("There's something for the Boat's Crew, go and refresh yourselves" [1]), Thompson's qualifies his gift: "Cockswain, there is something for the boat's-crew to drink; but mind that you all go off sober" (1). Thompson consistently makes the characters' language more polite and more literary, in keeping with late-eighteenth-century norms of gentility. But throughout the play, there is almost no change in Dorcas's language, and her language seems more antiquated against the modernized text. Yet one element of the plot is altered: in the 1773 version, Dorcas does not convert. By 1773, Quakerism was no longer an eccentricity, and the threat of religious schism was no longer so fearful. Quaker women were now seen as modest and unthreatening, whose behavior outsiders could read in terms of conduct-book norms. The end of another comedy, John O'Keefe's *The Young Quaker*, offers the most conservative version of this kind of representation. The heroine says:

> I will tell thee, my Reuben, and this good company,
> No more nam'd Primrose, I'm my Reuben's wife
> And Dinah Sadboy I am call'd for life,
> There will I rest tho' altered in my name
> My faith and manners shall remain the same:
> Still shall my cheek show *Nature's* white and red,
> No cap shall rise like steeple from my head.—
> Ye, who in marriage, wealth and grandeur seek,
> Think what a blessing is a wife that's meek.
> A help-mate true of heart, and full of love;
> Such unto Reuben, Dinah means to prove.
> My mind shall still be pure, my thoughts serene,
> My habit simple, and my person clean:
> No pomps, and vanities *will I* pursue
> But love my home, and love my *husband* too. (62)

But the presumed modesty and domesticity inherent in these representations of Quaker women—the very fact that they were not threatening—also enabled them to speak more powerfully. This kind of representation of Quaker women is exemplified in the religious novels of Harriet Corp, *An Antidote to the Miseries of Human Life* (1807) and *A Sequel to the Antidote to the Miseries of Human Life* (1809), which respond to James Beresford's 1806 work (no surprise) *The Miseries of Human Life*. This latter is a comic piece, a sequence of dialogues in which characters list the horrors of everyday life. For example, the miseries of reading consist in "Unfolding a very complicated map in a borrowed book of value, and, notwithstanding all your care, enlarging the small rent you originally made in it, every time you open it" (171); "in attempting, at a strange house, to take down a large book from a high, crowded shelf, bringing half the library upon your nose" (172);

"receiving, 'from the author,' a book equally heavy in the literal, and the figurative sense; accompanied with intreaties that you would candidly set down in writing your detailed opinions of it in all its parts" (172), and so on. The point is, of course, to laugh readers out of their tendency to whine, a point made explicit at the end by a sermonizing brother of one of the characters, an addition felt to be both dull and unnecessary by at least one reviewer.

In Corp's original *Antidote,* we meet characters who did miss the point. The slightest ripple is a misery to them, and they believe that Beresford has invited them to express their feelings as long as they do so with wit. One of these is Miss Finakin, a society lady of a certain age, who speaks in exaggerated woman's language: "Heavens! that we should be so horridly early! Dear George, desire the coach-man to hasten, or I shall absolutely fall asleep in this hideous place, and all the powers on earth will not be able to awaken me!" (3). (" 'A new misery! A new misery!' replied [her nephew]; 'upon my honour, set that down.'") But Harriet Corp does not leave the sermonizing for the end of her book. The novel takes place in an overcrowded coach, and most of the text is a telling of her life story by the Quaker Mrs. Placid (as with Bage's Miss Carlill, the honorific "Mrs." already marks this as not an accurate representation), who has faced real adversity with faith and serenity. At the end, having related hardships including the deaths of her husband and her son, fire, poverty, an illness that deprives her daughter of her understanding, and so on, she meets and forgives a man who had robbed her.

Since Harriet Corp was not Quaker (Quakers, to repeat, did not write imaginative literature), we must ask what she felt was to be gained by representing her heroine as a Friend. Mrs. Placid's religion is first introduced when the coachman, who has oversold seats, "made no doubt but that his other two passengers would be brought round, for they were *yeas* and *nays.* 'What's that?' said [the narrator], not taking his meaning. 'O, quack, quack, I suppose,' replied the 'squire" (4; "yeas and nays" refers to the Quakers' refusal to swear oaths and its source in Matthew 5:33–37). That is, Mrs. Placid is introduced as a figure of ridicule whose identity is figured in her speech. And indeed, her first speech, in which she scolds the coachman for not saving the seat she had paid for, sounds remarkably "modern" and assertive: "turning to the coach-man, [she said], 'thou hast acted very indiscreetly in this matter; thou knowest our places were taken two days since,' . . . 'Well, then, you must both go to-morrow,' said the ungracious driver, 'but mind you have paid the fare'—'Which in that case thou wilt return,' meekly observed the fair Friend" (6). Mrs. Placid is of course the moral center of this little book and convinces all the sensible characters to take more heed of their spiritual lives. But what is unusual is that her identity as a Quaker enables her to be both meek and assertive. A non-Quaker author chose this character not for her specific faith but for this combination of gentleness and power.

In the *Sequel,* it becomes clearer that the author is making use of a Quaker character for evangelical purposes. For example, one scene represents a supposed Quaker meeting that begins with silence, but has a preacher giving a written sermon on a biblical text as well as the singing of hymns (93–94). And by the end of the book, Mrs. Placid has converted the Squire of the *Antidote* to a religion of an evangelical stripe. As with the Shadwell comedy, the question is not "is this an accurate representation of Quakerism?" (it certainly is not), but rather, what was to be gained by labeling a woman character a Quaker? I quote the author's praise for her character:

> Female influence is universally acknowledged, in its effects upon society as well as individuals. The influence which the Widow Placid gained over the mind of Squire Bustle has been described; and it only remains briefly to consider by what means it was effected. It was not by means of the adventitious advantages of youth, beauty, or accomplishments; but her unaffected piety, and sweetness of manners. The latter quality has been greatly recommended, but too often with no other view than that of *pleasing:* from the example of Mrs. Placid, we hope the female reader will be encouraged to cultivate it for *use* as well as *ornament.* Without this amiable trait in her character, even her piety might have passed unknown or unregarded. It disposed her indeed to speak for the honour of religion; but the *manner* with which she spoke rendered her words acceptable. She advised without dogmatism; she reproved without acrimony; she aimed at pleasing the ear by the correctness of her language; and, above all, when she conversed on the sublime truths of Christianity, she betrayed no *party* prejudices which could excite displeasure in those she was desirous to instruct. Here, then, is a character not only worthy of imitation, but which every intelligent female is capable of imitating. (166–67)

To the modern reader, Mrs. Placid is annoyingly judgmental, a tiresome busybody. But what matters here is that through her figuring as a Quaker, she is enabled to use a speech strategy that combines effectiveness and femininity. Later on in the nineteenth century, Quaker women will be imagined as heroic actors like Rachel Halliday, the central figure of a utopian community in Stowe's *Uncle Tom's Cabin.* In the late (long) eighteenth century, what is remarkable is the representation of Quaker women's speech. Mary Knowles, Miss Carlill, and Mrs. Placid speak plainly and persuasively. Their speech could not be further from woman's language, yet they are never considered unfeminine.

Amelia Opie's Polite Truth

In *Adeline Mowbray* (1804), the novel that is now the most widely read of all Amelia Opie's works, the heroine rejects social convention in favor of abstract principle: because her lover has written a philosophical argument against the institution of marriage, she refuses to marry him and suffers the consequences of being considered a kept woman. The novel is (obviously) in part a roman à clef about Mary Wollstonecraft and William Godwin, and it argues strenuously that women cannot live outside of social norms whether they agree with them or not. In the book, social norms are represented by a range of characters, from predatory aristocrats to mean-spirited gossips to genuinely kind acquaintances. Of these, the most powerful is a Quaker, Mrs. Pemberton, who enters at key moments to assist or advise Adeline. In her most conservative speeches, Mrs. Pemberton uses a vocabulary that evokes the antirevolutionary rhetoric of Edmund Burke and others of the period: "Poor thing, . . . I understand thee now—Thou art one of the enlightened, as they call themselves—Thou art one of those wise in their own conceit, who, disregarding the customs of ages, and the dictates of experience, set up their own opinions against the hallowed institutions of men and the will of the Most High."[23] But despite her admonitions, Mrs. Pemberton is Adeline's most effective ally. Indeed, at the end of the novel she serves almost as a dea ex machina, reuniting Adeline with her long-estranged mother, ousting a thieving cousin, and making Adeline's death as morally and physically comfortable as possible.

Mrs. Pemberton thus shares the moral weight and the willingness to speak truth that characterize representations of Quaker women in this period. But while she dresses and speaks as a strict Quaker (apart from the occasional honorific), Mrs. Pemberton has a unique history. She was "born and educated in fashionable life; and she united to a very lovely face and elegant form, every feminine grace and accomplishment" (1:218). When she married a gay Quaker, he was disowned by the Society for a time, until he returned to the "strict habits of his sect" and brought her into the fold. Thus she "became in time a convert to the same profession of faith, and exhibited in her manners the rare union of the easy elegance of a woman of the world with the rigid decorum and unadorned dress of a strict Quaker" (1:218). *Adeline Mowbray* was published some twenty-one years before Amelia Opie joined the Religious Society of Friends, but it already points toward Opie's evident wish to moderate the strict practices of the sect with a dollop of elegance. It also points to a paradox in Opie's own speech: after her conversion, Opie utilized a unique blend of Quaker and mainstream linguistic practices. Her language was, then, in some sense individualistic, yet it was intended to honor the social customs of others.

Like Harriet Corp, Amelia Opie adopted a very mediated form of Quaker language, used for particular ends. Before her conversion, Opie was known for her verbal stylishness; even the memorial plaque in Norwich describes her as "a brilliant conversationalist."[24] Though a modern reader could not infer it from Opie's literary works, which seem to us mawkish and dreary, we must accept the contemporary evidence that Opie was a gay and extremely social woman. As such, her conversion to Quakerism surprised many; as one biographer wrote, "one would as soon have expected [Pope's] Belinda to turn Quakeress."[25] What I would like to explore for the rest of this chapter are the ways in which Opie's language, after her conversion, combined the strategies of "polite" and of Quaker language. So far, I have described Quaker language as a "pure" sociolect; my task now is to see how abstract concepts of Quaker language were put to work in one person's speech. In working through the complexities of Opie's (or anyone's) actual usage, we must consider the strategic advantages of her adoption of a mediated language.

Strangely enough, Opie began the process of conversion when she was at the very peak of her social whirl, in 1814. By that time, she had been widowed for several years and had moved back to Norwich to live with her father. However, she generally went to London for at least part of "the season" each year. The 1814 season was particularly brilliant, a celebratory break from the Napoleonic wars. In her letters home, Opie described her many evenings with aristocrats and famous men; on July 1, she went to a masked ball given for Arthur Wellesley (Wellington), wearing "high feathers; with a pink domino" (Brightwell 166). Mary Russell Mitford even claims that Opie was at this time engaged to Herbert Stuart, son of the fourth Earl of Bute.[26] Throughout her letters, Opie delights in the glamorous costumes and the witty repartee of the polite world.

At the same time, she was receiving letters from Joseph John Gurney warning her against excessive vanity. Opie had known the wealthy Gurney family when she was a child. She renewed the friendship when she moved back to Norwich, becoming especially close to Priscilla and to Joseph John, both of whom were much younger than she (by ten and nineteen years, respectively). In the 1780s and 1790s, the Gurneys had been what the Quakers called "gay" Friends. That is, they attended weekly meeting and addressed other Quakers as *thou,* but otherwise fulfilled mainstream expectations for a wealthy banking family: they had a large property (Earlham Hall), wore fashionable dress, intermarried with non-Quakers, and so on.

Elizabeth Gurney (later Fry) was the first to return to the norms of "plain" Friends; her conversion was inspired by hearing a traveling minister, William Savery, in 1798, when she was a teenager. Other members of her family followed her lead. As we have already noted, Joseph John Gurney's work after his conversion significantly altered the course of Quakerism, especially in America, by bringing an evangelical fervor that reinvigorated the Society. It also divided the Society between those retaining the traditional mysticism and those (called "Gurneyites") who moved closer to other forms of Protestantism, even hiring paid preachers. Gurney's family history may help explain both his privileged position and his comfort with mainstream forms of worship and behavior (it was he who asserted that Quaker speech is not incompatible with civility, above). Opie's conversion involved a combination of abstract belief and personal connection; many even suspected that it was motivated by her wish to marry Joseph John Gurney. What matters here is that her conversion was to a particularly mediated form of Quakerism, one only partially incompatible with the fashionable world.

In early September 1814, one of Joseph John's brothers died, and Opie came down for the funeral. She dated this as the beginning of her conversion, saying, "in 1814 I left the Unitarians" (Brightwell 173). But it was not until 1825, as Opie's father was dying and with his approval, that she formally requested membership in the Religious Society of Friends. Within this gradual process, Opie marks a turning point when she began to use *thou*. She had used it to address members of the Gurney family fairly early, but in 1824 she still had reservations about joining the Society:

> To say the truth, much as I should like to belong to a religious society, and much as I see, or think I see, the hand of my gracious Lord in leading *me*, to whom have been given so many ties to a worldly life, in the various gifts bestowed on me, (I mean *accomplishments*, as they are called,) to communion with a sect which requires the sacrifice of them almost *in toto*, thereby trying my faith to the uttermost, still I feel no necessity for haste in doing so. (Brightwell 192)

Yet later that same year, in another letter to Elizabeth Fry, she says she has decided to act, "and that a gentleman, a stranger, chancing to come and call on her that morning, she spoke the 'plain language' to him, and had continued to do so ever since; and she says, 'Nor have I had a misgiving, but feel so calm and satisfied, that I am convinced *I have done right*'" (193–94). For Opie, then, the adoption of Quaker language signaled her new identity.

Joining the Religious Society of Friends had many practical implications for Amelia Opie. Among other things, she abandoned a writing project that the publisher had already advertised, causing not only a financial loss but a broken promise.[27] It meant getting rid of paintings her husband had done, since the Society allowed only portraiture (Menzies-Wilson and Lloyd 217). It meant, of course, changing her dress and, more seriously, taking on much charitable work. But Opie never became a dour Quaker. She continued to go to London annually, visited Paris, even continued watching the courts in session. Many anecdotes demonstrate that she never lost her sense of fun. Her visiting card used the Quaker form ("Amelia Opie," without an honorific title), but had a circle of roses drawn on it. Even late in her life, it is said, someone reported her "laughing heartily and impetuously thrusting a somewhat starched-up Friend into a deep arm-chair exclaiming, 'I will hurl thee into the bottomless pit.'"[28] And in 1851, she visited the Great Exhibition. By this time, she was using a wheelchair; seeing another aged friend in a chair, she reportedly proposed a race (Brightwell 389).

Like her behavior, Opie's language retained features that the Quakers considered "creaturely" or worldly. Her journal often sounds as Quakerly as Mary Waring's: "All things here, right and well; to bed, with a grateful heart for the mercies shewn me, and the blessings that remain" (Brightwell 206) or "A sweet, favoured meeting. Silence, I trust, blest to me; the ministry lively and touching" (208). But Opie did not use the Quaker forms consistently. We began this chapter with Mitford's comment that she slipped in and out of her *thees* and *thous*. In her journal, Opie made jokes and quoted *Hamlet*. She has her tongue in her cheek in a way that is not at all Quakerly, as when she says, after describing a day spent on religious duties, "Mem. Made a resolution not to speak slightingly again of —— if I can *help it*" (Brightwell 202). Most notably, she continued for her entire life to use titles, not only "Mr." and "Mrs." but the "Lords" and "Ladies" about which Quakers had been so stubborn. What are we to make of a letter in which she quotes herself as saying, "Oh! *dear* Lord Morpeth! how glad I am to see thee!" (379)? Or of the following letter, which uses stereotypical female exaggeration? "Thanks for thy kind inquiries, and still more for thy graphic description of the Cambridge show; it made me long to have been there! thy account of the behaviour of the students carried me back to 1810, when I was at Oxford, at Lord Grenville's installation, and was excessively amused by the thundering and hissing of the students" (373).

Opie's worldly friends were puzzled by her conversion and tended to doubt her sincerity. Henry Crabb Robinson wrote the following in his diary for July 14, 1824:

> At the Assizes at Norwich. Called on Mrs. Opie, who had then become a Quakeress. She received me very kindly, but as a Quaker in dress and diction.

I found her very agreeable, and not materially changed. Her dress had something coquettish in it, and her becoming a Quakeress gave her a sort of éclat;
yet she was not conscious, I dare say, of any unworthy motive. She talked in
her usual graceful and affectionate manner. She mentioned *Lord* Gifford,—
surely a slip of the tongue.[29]

Mary Russell Mitford was even more harsh, after reading the *Memorials:*

What a miserable hash *she* made of her own existence! Nothing is clearer than
the hankering she had after her old artistic and literary world. She even con-
trived to mix gay parties with May [annual Quaker] meetings to the very last.
But the want of congruity jars in the book, and must have jarred still more in
actual life; more especially as those Fry and Gurney people—popes male and
female in their way—seem to have taken upon them to lecture the dear soul.
How she declined in taste and in intelligence after joining the Friends! (3:293)

The incongruities are indeed jarring, and invite us to wonder what value
they had for Amelia Opie. Why use "thou" *and* "Lord"? Surely the one precludes the other. Why put on Quaker dress *and* act coquettish? Surely the
point of Quaker dress is that it is sober. These two incongruities—to be
Quaker and "polite"; to be Quaker and "feminine"—epitomize Opie's
mediated position.

Yet in one important respect Opie's language was unmediated. We
remember that Quaker language privileges other qualities (especially truthfulness) over politeness. Truthfulness was a quality that was particularly
important to Amelia Opie, as indeed it was to the Dissenting circles in
which she had grown up and to her friend William Godwin. Opie wrote
several didactic works about truthfulness, including a tale, "White Lies," and
the two-volume *Illustrations of Lying, in All its Branches* (1825, the year of her
membership). The latter work categorizes lies into ten kinds, each of which
can be either active (speaking an untruth) or passive (withholding the truth).
Most common, Opie claims, are lies of vanity, but she proceeds in order
through lies of flattery, of convenience, of interest, of fear, and so on. The
first nine kinds of lies are discussed, then illustrated with a tale; the last third
of the work offers arguments against lying and cites authorities on the subject, both secular and religious. The Quakers are given a privileged position
(the final chapter), but this is not a Quaker work: for Quakers, there was no
significant difference between fiction and lies, so they would consider
Opie's text itself untruthful. It shows, however, that Opie valued truthfulness almost to the degree that the Quakers did. Polite lies, for her, are not
excusable.

The use of honorific titles, however, was rejected by the Quakers not
because they were lies, but because they were a kind of flattery. As noted

above, Quakers deviate most from polite norms in "positive politeness," features that express approval. Brown and Levinson include "white lies" as one kind of positive politeness; others include joking, promising, exaggerating, and avoiding disagreement. In her speech as it is represented, Opie seems to adopt those polite strategies that don't include untruthfulness. She does exaggerate, praise, and joke, whereas other Quakers did not. Although she seems to have deliberately maintained the use of *thou* as a marker of her own identity, Opie's politeness included allowing her conversational partner to define him or herself. Opie, that is, declined to use a more confrontational aspect of Quaker language, the refusal to recognize titles.

As noted above, since the features of polite speech overlap with those of stereotypically female language (exaggeration, praise, and so on), Quaker rejection of the former meant that Quaker women did not typically adhere to the stereotyped norms of female speech. In the representations of Quaker women, this enabled a mediated position of female strength, respect, and authority. In speaking plainly, Quaker women also avoided the expressions of modesty that were expected of women. Yet here again, Opie's speech combines elements of the Quaker and of the polite world. The preface to *Illustrations of Lying* reveals this dichotomy. Opie first emphasizes her directness, her refusal to use euphemism: "My first apology is, for having throughout my book, made use of the words lying and lies, instead of some gentler term, or some easy paraphrase, by which I might have avoided the risk of offending the delicacy of any of my readers. . . . But, when writing a book against lying, I was obliged to express my meaning in the manner most consonant to the *strict truth*."[30] After this strong assertion of truth over politeness, though, Opie offers a second apology, a stereotypically female one:

> My second apology is, for presuming to come forward, with such apparent boldness, as a didactic writer, and a teacher of truths, which I ought to believe that every one knows already, and better than I do.
> But I beg permission to deprecate the charge of presumption and self-conceit, by declaring that I pretend not to lay before my readers any new knowledge; my only aim, is to bring to their recollection, knowledge which they already possess, but do not constantly recall and act upon. (414)

Another way of reading Opie's mixed linguistic practice, then, one related to her evident desire to be polite, is that it enabled her to retain a gender identity that was more "mainstream" than Quaker. Politeness, to repeat, is often considered a marker of gender; women are required to uphold a higher standard of politeness than are men. It is an oddity that Quaker women, who are not conventionally polite, are not considered masculinized. But Opie retained markers of femininity after her conversion: the flowers on her calling card, the attractive clothing that visitors found un-Quakerly, and so on.

Late in her life, Opie began to write a memoir. Only a few pages were written (or survive), which describe first her childhood fears and then an incident in which a Quaker friend of Opie's discovered and tried to rehabilitate a woman who had been successfully passing as a (male) sailor. Opie recounts her fascination and horror at this freak and her eagerness to hear more details about her. Finally, Opie visited the woman, who was working as a tailor and still wearing men's clothing. At first, the woman's story is "touching," but very soon Opie finds her "utterly offensive," "not pleasant," with "terrible eyes" that may indicate a "deranged mind" (Brightwell 20). The woman does attend Friends' meeting in a dress, "but when she walked away, with the long strides and bold seeming of a man, it was anything rather than satisfactory, to observe her" (20). The memoir breaks off with this episode, perhaps a sign of Opie's powerful ambivalence about it. Certainly this narrative points to Opie's fascination with the possibility of rejecting gender norms, while she emphasizes her commitment to them.

It is the commitment to traditional social norms, however, that remains most obvious in Opie's writings (like *Adeline Mowbray*) and in the representations of her speech. In a letter from 1807 (well before her conversion), Opie lambastes a member of Parliament who doesn't use aristocratic titles: "I do quarrel with him for the affectation, the proud humility, or the presumption, call it which you will of talking of them by the familiar appellation of Spencer, Holland, Minto. . . . This makes me sick—& I will call another subject."[31] Opie's continuing use of titles after her conversion attests to her commitment to a society organized hierarchically, even while that commitment was rejected by both Opie's Dissenting and radical friends and by the Quakers she joined. Most important, embedded in that hierarchical society is the commitment to separate spheres. Opie's linguistic practice retained features of politeness and of woman's language that made her a very feminine Quaker indeed. Where strict Quaker usage privileges religious over gender identity, Opie's mediated language kept the two in tension.

In Chapter 1, I argued that the language theorists and conduct-book authors posited women as a single class of speakers, with habitual failings and set responsibilities. The norms of Quaker speech offer a different mode, in which gender is less salient than membership in a faith community. Yet when we move to the level of an individual's practice, linguistic purity becomes less important than strategies appropriate to specific circumstances.

Her biographers asserted that Opie "did honour to her profession of [Quaker] principles, by shewing that they were not incompatible with good manners and refined taste" (Brightwell vii). In the end, Opie's strategy left her an anomaly. People expect unchanging consistency of the Quakers, who are after all persnickety about their linguistic purity. Both Opie's worldly friends and her fellow Quakers found her language odd or unsatisfying.

Finally, although it seems not to have received comment, what is perhaps most un-Quakerly in Amelia Opie's language is her lack of attention to silence. Her works on language—"White Lies," *Illustrations of Lying,* and *Detraction Displayed*—all deal with faults in speaking and could be the work of any Dissenting moralist. What Opie never considered are the opportunities offered by silence. She never articulates the richness of silent experience the way we saw Mary Waring do. The Quaker use of silence is probably its most "peculiar" linguistic feature, and perhaps Amelia Opie continued to assign the negative meanings of the polite world to silence. In Chapter 3, we will see that the use of silence by one speaker, Sarah Siddons, was indeed less kindly received than her speech.

CHAPTER 3

Acting, Text, and Correct Display:
Sarah Siddons to Fanny Price

> She does not speak much, and that modestly enough, but in a slow,
> set, and studied sort of phrase and accent very like the most familiar
> passages of her acting, but still in a degree theatrical.
> — *Life and Letters of Gilbert Elliot*

On the 10th of October, 1782, Sarah Siddons returned to the London
stage. She had first appeared in the 1775–76 season, David Garrick's last as
manager of the Theatre Royal, Drury Lane, and had failed to make an
impression; she spent the next few years practicing her craft in the relative
exile of the north and in Bath. But on her return, at the age of twenty-seven,
she was an instant star. Footmen were sent to the theater at dawn to wait in
line at the box office, and the crush when the doors opened threatened to
become riot. The press treated her as an event, which she was, and young
fans imitated her clothing and hairstyle. As one biographer wrote, "Like
Lord Byron she awoke one morning to find herself famous, and famous she
remained for the rest of her days."[1] Until and even after her retirement in
1812, Siddons was a celebrity.

Sarah Siddons was the first English actress to be a recognizable grande
dame. It had only been just over a century that women had appeared at all
on the English stage, and her success may be seen in the context of the gradual rise in status of both actors and actresses. Far from being a vagabond or
a royal mistress, Siddons socialized on equal terms with the great figures of
the London cultural world; she was the first actress to play command performances for the royal family, and she was the frequent houseguest of aristocrats. Moreover, her success was due largely to a carefully cultivated persona of extreme dignity. Siddons was considered "sublime," or "noble," or

"majestic." Her contemporary biographers, James Boaden and Thomas Campbell, praised her "male" dignity. As Boaden said, "The commanding height and powerful action of her figure, though always feminine, seemed to tower beyond her sex."[2] Even her portraits etch her features in ways that can only be called masculine.

Yet along with the majestic, Siddons projected the virtues of bourgeois domesticity. Her critics sometimes complained that she was stingy, but that flaw was mitigated in the context of her domestic duties. Married to an actor who was much less successful than she, Siddons consistently claimed that she performed primarily to support her family. When Siddons left Bath for London, she incorporated her three children into her farewell address; she was visibly pregnant with the fourth. Why does she leave, the audience asks? "My reason I produce [enter children]—These are the moles that bear me from your side," and, speaking to the children, she explains that they must leave "in hopes that you may profit by my gain."[3] Siddons's first biographers cooperated in sustaining her claim to "good" female morality. Neither Campbell nor Boaden mentions the messy scandals involving Thomas Lawrence or Catherine Galindo's husband, and both explain away Siddons's separation from her husband. Throughout her life, Siddons was able to maintain a character that combined masculine power and feminine virtue.

This combination of majesty and femininity was typified in Siddons's interpretation of her most famous role, Lady Macbeth. Siddons departed from her predecessors in conveying not only the fiendish side of Lady Macbeth but also her domesticity. As she wrote in her "Remarks on the Character of Lady Macbeth," "According to my notion, it is of that character which I believe is generally allowed to be most captivating to the other sex,—fair, feminine, nay perhaps even fragile— . . . Such a combination only, respectable in energy and strength of mind, and captivating in feminine loveliness, could have composed a charm of such potency as to fascinate the mind" of Macbeth.[4] Siddons, that is, imagines Lady Macbeth not only as an independent subject but as someone situated in a conventional (subordinate) relationship. Not surprisingly, this was the character Siddons constructed for herself, as well.[5]

In recent years, scholars have looked to Siddons as a test case for how the public (male)/private (female) boundary might be negotiated. As a public woman, an actress and object of the (male) gaze, Siddons risked being reduced to an exemplar of passive female sexuality; the assertion of her "masculine" strength was one way to address this. At the same time, to the extent that female virtue was necessarily domestic and private, Siddons's assertion of her virtue was transgressive. Kristina Straub describes the dilemma in this way:

> As women whose profession is undeniably public, actresses resisted the assumption that feminine sexuality was the private (and passive) opposite of masculinity. Whereas the discourse of professionalism helped to legitimate actors' "feminine" excesses, it intensified the contradiction between femininity as a public spectacle and emergent definitions of the middle-class woman as domestic and private, veiled from the public eye.[6]

Siddons seems to have had two modes of resolving this dichotomy, which were to some extent irreconcilable. On the one hand, she deflected the old association of actresses and aristocratic lovers by aligning herself with aristocratic *women* rather than men. On the other hand, Siddons emphasized her involvement in a bourgeois domestic world. Indeed, she furthered her domestic image by repeatedly playing the roles of virtuous, wronged wives. As Judith Pascoe says, "Siddons's performances both on the stage and off, in character roles and in the role of respectable matron, served as an enabling model for other women looking for ways to enter the public sphere without damaging their personal reputations in the process."[7]

But if Sarah Siddons successfully combined the demands of majesty and femininity as an actress and public person, the contradictions were perhaps less successfully negotiated in her private speech. She was often felt to be so dignified as to be dull. Even the sympathetic Campbell acknowledges that "she had very little light conversation in mixed company" (259); the convivial John Byng commented, "Mrs. Siddons is a woman of such retired notions as to drive off my conversation." And when Frances Burney met Siddons at a party, she wrote: "She behaved with great propriety; very calm, modest, quiet, and unaffected. She has a very fine countenance, and her eyes look both intelligent and soft. She has, however, a steadiness in her manner and deportment by no means engaging. Mrs. Thrale, who was there, said, 'Why, this is a leaden goddess we are all worshipping!'"[8]

In her private life, Siddons had to enact qualities that are irreconcilable: the quiet dignity of the majestic persona that was the basis of her success; the modesty of the good domestic female; and the vivacity of the celebrity conversationalist. The representations of her speech that have survived indicate that what struck witnesses was Siddons's silence. But unlike the Quaker women discussed in Chapter 2, Siddons was not well served by adopting silence. Campbell describes one reaction to her silence. I quote it at some length because it highlights the conflict between the private (silent) woman and the public persona:

I had once by chance the honour of seeing Mrs. Siddons and the Duke of Wellington in the same party at Paris. They were observed, after a first mutual recognizance, to stand by each other without conversing. I overheard a group of English people angrily remark, "What a proud woman is that Mrs. Siddons: she will not condescend to speak even to Wellington!" Now I had seen the duke, two evenings before, meet the great actress, and he addressed her with peculiar courtesy and graciousness. On this latter occasion I put no bad construction on his taciturnity. His grace was most likely as deficient in small talk as the great actress. But still less did I blame Mrs. Siddons's silence; on the contrary, I regarded it as a trait of her true character. Her reserve in mixed company was independent and equal; and she behaved to the Duke of Wellington exactly as she would have done to any other person slightly acquainted with her, for she had no extra courtesy for rank. (258–59)

Arthur Wellesley (Wellington), as noted in the Introduction, was famous for his taciturnity, and taciturnity can be a positive quality for men, a sign of strength. But silence is interpreted differently in women. On the one hand, women's silence reveals a virtuous deference; on the other hand, women should do the "conversational work." For her failure to do that work, Siddons might have been called impolite or incompetent. But calling her "proud" may point, rather, toward a conflict between her public role and her private one. The English observers of this scene seem to codify a gendered linguistic norm in which silent men are strong, silent women are proud. To counter that, and to rescue Siddons from the sin of pride, Campbell must assert a nongendered norm in which the silences of Siddons and of Wellesley are exactly parallel and in which Siddons's behavior becomes an expression of liberal politics. But the very fact that Campbell must perform this rescue reveals the strength of the conflicting attitudes toward women's speech.

This chapter will address several questions invited by Siddons's success and the discourses surrounding her. In particular, Siddons's position as actress invites a consideration of the performance of text and of the ways in which acting, reading, and speech were linked in the period. I look first at acting theory and elocution and at how these discourses (while not addressing gender directly) offered strategies by which women could maintain their claim to modesty while displaying their talents.

I turn then to representations of Siddons's speech in private life: what were the consequences of carrying her majestic stage persona into ordinary conversation? I will argue that to the extent that Siddons carried her stage persona and the habits of her craft into private life, she *failed* to "perform" her gender role. Or, to be more precise, the representations of Siddons's speech emphasize her failures and the ways her roles as tragic actress and domestic woman were incompatible. My hope in this section, as in Chapter 2, is to illuminate the complexity of language use as we move our gaze from a general discourse to the linguistic practice of individual women.

Finally, I consider how the discourses surrounding Siddons also affected "ordinary" (private) women. In this section, I utilize two novels that explore the discourses of elocution, accomplishment, and speech. Frances Burney's *The Wanderer* praises accomplishments and accomplished readings as they reveal the high status of a nameless heroine. In Austen's *Mansfield Park,* on the other hand, accomplishments and the performance of text render women objects of suspicion. This novel, famously, seems to foster an anti-theatrical attitude of modest seriousness. My task here will be to show how deeply this novel is engaged in contemporary debates on the relation between acting, text, and speech. This last section will serve as a transition to Part II of *Speaking Volumes,* which will have as its focus the interrelations of discourses on reading and speech in the late (long) eighteenth century.

Acting, the Passions, and the Text

Siddons's negotiated position as a celebrity actress must be understood within the controversies over acting theory in the eighteenth century. These have been framed in various ways, often employing dichotomies between "rhetorical" and "natural" styles—dichotomies that seem rather suspect, since all acting is "rhetorical" in that the actor wishes to move an audience, and every era finds its own style "natural." In the eighteenth century, the distinction between "rhetorical" and "natural" has often been drawn with regard to vocal style: "rhetorical" actors utilized a singing or chanting tone; "natural" ones attempted a more conversational style. In gesture, similarly, "rhetorical" implied a larger-scale movement that accords with the codified schemes for expressing passion; "natural" gestures are not considered exaggerated. But these distinctions are only relative; every generation tends to accuse the previous one of being "rhetorical," whereas its own practitioners are "natural."

A second distinction among eighteenth-century acting theories concerns the degree to which actors were advised to follow inherited traditions on the one hand or strive for originality on the other. For much of the period, actors were expected to perform roles exactly as their predecessors had. Siddons describes the pressure she felt to hold a candle in a scene in *Macbeth.* Just before her first performance, Richard Brinsley Sheridan (then the theater manager) pounded on her door.

But, what was my distress and astonishment, when I found that he wanted me, even at this moment of anxiety and terror, to adopt another mode of acting the sleeping scene. He told me he had heard with the greatest surprise and concern that I meant to act it without holding the candle in my hand; and, when I urged the impracticability of washing out that "*damned spot*," with the vehemence that was certainly implied by both her own words and by those of her gentlewoman, he insisted, that if I did put the candle out of my hand, it would be thought a presumptuous innovation, as Mrs. Pritchard had always retained it in hers.[9]

"Romantic" originality was not yet privileged. On the contrary, a highly involved and experienced audience expected performers to treat classic roles as rituals that must be reenacted without any changes.

A third distinction can be drawn between a sense that gesture is a universal and indeed codifiable language and one that pays attention to unique characterization: whether all human beings experiencing fear will raise their eyebrows, or whether Lady Macbeth, for example, had a particular tendency to use certain facial expressions. Thus, acting may be seen either as the expression of a sequence of universal passions or as the embodiment of a unified and unique character. These three distinctions result from different attitudes about what human nature "is," and thus what features of human nature are most essential to represent. The distinctions are partly historical, with the first of each set representing an older mode, though as Siddons's comment on Lady Macbeth's candle shows, all of these various orientations existed simultaneously.

In addition to making distinctions about what human features are most important to represent, we can frame issues around the intended effect on an audience. William B. Worthen understands these disagreements within an overall shift toward a theater of sentiment. In 1698, Jeremy Collier had argued that theater should inculcate virtue by addressing the audience's rational faculties; emotional appeals were all too likely to corrupt. But in keeping with eighteenth-century moral philosophy, later theorists argued that virtue is best aroused by moving the audience, by stirring feelings of sympathetic identification. Affective performance was the best route to the improvement of morals and of taste.[10] Audiences moved by the suffering they witness would be most likely to act to relieve suffering.

But if by midcentury a consensus had developed that the actor's job was to move the audience, there was some disagreement about the proper role of the actor's own feelings: should the actor recreate his character's passions—that is, feel them himself? Or, was it equally effective, and perhaps more practical, to simply represent them as an illusion? To what extent was the actor's sympathetic identification with the character real or essential?

Indeed, is character even in "real life" sincere and authentic, or is theatricality central to social interaction?

The two poles are expressed in two texts, John Hill's *The Actor* (1750), and Diderot's response, *The Paradox of the Actor*.[11] Hill's position is clear: "The performer who does not himself feel the several emotions he is to express to the audience, will give but a lifeless and insipid representation of them." Or, as Aaron Hill put it: "Be what you seem."[12] Moreover, John Hill posits that the best actors are not those who merely feel strongly, but those whose own personality is pliant and can thus take on another's emotions. Earl R. Wasserman says that, in this orientation,

> the ideal actor must avoid being deeply affected by the events of his private life, lest he develop a distinctive personality and be unable therefore to assume whole-heartedly all personalities at will. . . . The perfect actor, [Thomas] Wilkes explained, "must not only strongly impress [the character he portrays] on his own mind, but make a temporary renunciation of himself and all his connections in common life . . . ; forget, if possible, his own identity."[13]

The actor loses himself in the character; his emotions then become the character's authentic own.

For Diderot, at the other extreme, the actor's own feelings are irrelevant. The point is to move the audience, which the actor does "through a conscious manipulation of the theatrical languages of speech and gesture."[14] Diderot's motivation is partly pragmatic: performances must be repeated many times, so that even if the actor's feelings are required to create the role, they cannot and need not be aroused night after night: "the actor who plays from thought, from study of human nature, from constant imitation of some ideal type, from imagination, from memory, will be one and the same at all performances, will be always at his best mark; he has considered, combined, learnt and arranged the whole thing in his head."[15] But Diderot's orientation also conforms to a very eighteenth-century notion of social performativity. In everyday life, the rational man self-consciously creates a character that will achieve the desired goal. As Worthen puts it, "The actor reflects a society in which all values have become theatrical."[16]

In his essays "On the Profession of a Player" (1770), James Boswell makes this connection explicit. On the one hand, "a good player is indeed in a certain sense the character that he represents, during the time of his performance" (14). But only in a certain sense: "my notion is, that he must have a kind of double feeling. He must assume in a strong degree the character which he represents, while he at the same time retains the consciousness of his own character" (18). Moreover, this double consciousness is exactly what facilitates normal social interaction:

The double feeling which I have mentioned is experienced by many men in the common intercourse of life. Were nothing but the real character to appear, society would not be half so safe and agreeable as we find it. Did we discover to our companions what we really think of them, frequent quarrels would ensue; and did we not express more regard for them than we really feel, the pleasure of social intercourse would be very contracted. It being necessary then in the intercourse of life to have such appearances, and dissimulation being to most people irksome and fatiguing, we insensibly, for our own ease, adopt feelings suitable to every occasion, and so, like players, are to a certain degree a different character from our own. (19)

In distinguishing conscious dissimulation from the adaptiveness of social ease, Boswell's theory is softer than that of Diderot, and in its emphasis on the pliable self it approaches John Hill's. But Hill had argued that the actor truly became the character; Boswell's "double feeling" retains a site for the authentic self.

For my purposes, the most notable feature of this debate is that neither approach is advantageous for women: neither giving up the self in sympathetic identification with the character, nor performing the calculation required for conscious deception. Samuel Johnson, famously, commented on the moral danger of sympathetic identification. Boswell described it this way:

Talking of it one day to Mr. Kemble, he said, "Are you, Sir, one of those enthusiasts who believe yourself transformed into the very character you represent?" Upon Mr. Kemble's answering that he had never felt so strong a persuasion himself; "To be sure not, Sir, (said Johnson;) the thing is impossible. And if Garrick really believed himself to be that monster, Richard the Third, he deserved to be hanged every time he performed it."[17]

As Johnson's comment shows, sympathetic imagination has risks for men. But those risks are heightened for women. For women, as for Garrick, "becoming" a character could entail "becoming" a less moral being; one only has to alter Johnson's example to "Siddons" and "Lady Macbeth." But in addition, for women, the very act of giving up oneself is hazardous. Losing oneself in a role means abandoning the self-monitoring that protects against improprieties. The pliancy of personality that Hill's theory urges is at odds with the decorum required for virtuous domestic women.

Similarly, Diderot's calculated striving for effect can certainly evoke negative judgments against men. But the judgments are much harsher against women. The qualities of mastery and control, even if tinged by cynicism, are admirable and imply masculine power. For women, however, illusionism is degraded; what comes to mind is not the politician but the coquette. This gender difference is perhaps best captured in Johnson's quip about the courtier-like cynicism of Philip Dormer Stanhope (Chesterfield), whose *Letters to his Son* urge rational dissimulation in social interaction. For Johnson, "they teach the morals of a whore."[18]

Thus, the debate over sympathetic identification and calculated illusion would have been a lose/lose proposition for an actress. But framing the issues differently did open the possibility of staking out a proper feminine role. The acting style of Siddons and her brother John Philip Kemble invited a new question, the one most salient to the concerns of this book: does the actor focus more on the passions to be portrayed or on the text? In this conversation, David Garrick represented the portrayal of the passions. As he wrote in his *Essay upon Acting* (1744), Garrick stressed means by which the actor "imitates, assumes, or puts on the various mental and bodily emotions arising from the various humours, virtues and vices, incident to human nature."[19] Garrick was particularly admired for the transitions he made between passions: passions, here, meaning the classically defined emotions of anger, fear, loathing, and so on, whose physical manifestations were universal and universally understood. In contrast to Garrick's expression of passions, Siddons and Kemble were thought to focus their attention on the text. As Elizabeth Inchbald put it, Siddons was "a character of declamation rather than of passion," while Johnson told Siddons, "Garrick, Madam, was no declaimer."[20]

Expressing the passions meant using a universal language of gesture to portray universal and universally understood emotions. The passions had been categorized by the ancients and, most influentially, by Thomas Aquinas. Aquinas divided the eleven passions into those whose objects were simple good or evil (love/hate, desire/loathing, joy/sadness) and those whose objects were more remote (hope, despair, courage, fear, and anger).[21] For the British stage (as mentioned in Chapter 1), the most immediate source for this material was the French painter Charles Le Brun, whose 1698 treatise was translated in 1734 as *A Method to Learn to Design the Passions*. Le Brun organized the basic passions and their variations according to how they were expressed by the eyebrow, which "is the only Part of the whole face, where the Passions best make themselves known" (20–21); he does, of course, also describe the expressive qualities of the nose, mouth, and neck. For example, "If there be Desire, it may be represented by the Eye-brows being close pressed and advancing over the Eyes, which will be more open than usual, the Pupil situated in the middle of the Eye and full of fire, the Nostrils drawing upwards, the Mouth also more open than in the preceding Action, and the corners drawn back" (35). Le Brun's text was influential enough that it is possible to read eighteenth-century portraits in its terms. Even Siddons was painted this way, in George Romney's "Sidonian Recollections," in which her three poses clearly illustrate Le Brun's "acute pain," "fear," and "horror."[22]

The focus on the expression of the passions, though, however universal these were asserted to be, put women at a disadvantage. Whereas men were entitled to the full range of passions, and were allowed to feel them strongly, women "properly" felt only some of the passions, and always in moderation. For example, Le Brun illustrates contempt, horror, hatred, rage, despair, and other strong passions with drawings of men. The only passions illustrated with women are pure love, desire, hope, and sadness (some of the illustrations are schematic and androgynous). Veneration merits two illustrations: if based on esteem (that is, judgment) it is male; if on faith, it is female. The acting manuals, too, set limits on how much passion it is appropriate for women to display. For example, the unnamed author of *The Thespian Oracle* (1791) introduces his anthology with the standard instructions on how to express the passions. However, "Female performers, in particular, should be careful how they go beyond the limits which nature has set them . . . , as few of them having the compass of a man's abilities, they often, by great pains, render themselves pecularly disagreeable" (xvi).

Thus, Siddons's attention to the performance of *text* carved out a space in which she could excel without breaking the bonds of decorum. This is not to say that audiences were unmoved by Sarah Siddons. They clearly were. Leigh Hunt's praise for her focuses entirely on her passion: "Mrs. Siddons . . . is always natural, because on occasions of great feeling it is the passions [that] should influence the actions: . . . feel the passion and the action will follow." But a debate framed in terms of expressing a text, which is prevalent, gives a little wiggle room for respectability. Boaden answers objections that Siddons "was for the most part a declaimer only" (that is, not sufficiently passionate), by asserting that "the lead taken by the ladies in our public amusements demanded a kind of exhibition of which the excellencies were more particularly feminine."[23] The relevant point here is that a focus on the text is much less threatening than one on passion; the stakes are smaller.

In their focus on text, Siddons and Kemble were strongly influenced by the elocutionists. As noted in Chapter 1, the elocutionists nominally address orators, conventionally of "the senate, the pulpit, and the bar." However, insofar as they deal only with the performance of texts that are already written, the elocutionists treat orators as actors. Indeed, many of the elocutionists (notably Thomas Sheridan) *were* actors, and Siddons was personally trained by Sheridan, whom she always regarded as a mentor. Sheridan and

the other elocutionists taught the analysis of text in such a way that there
was always one correct reading. Correctness could be based on the grammar
or on the content of the text, but in either case, the performance of text
entailed strictness and decorum. As one theorist wrote, "It is proper for
every actor to be well-studied in *grammar;* as this is an art which teaches the
relation of words to each other, it will instruct him in their force and meaning, and consequently enable him to speak with emphasis and correctness."[24] As a performer of text, Siddons could be "correct" without going
beyond the bounds of female decorum. Even the king commented on the
correctness of Siddons's elocution. When Siddons read at the palace, she
says, he was "the most gratifying of auditors, because the most unremit-
tingly attentive. . . . He told me he had endeavored, vainly, to detect me in
a false emphasis, and very humourously repeated many of Mr Smith's, who
was then a principal Actor."[25]

Boaden even describes text as a protective shield between the actress
and her audience. He comments that when Siddons gave her 1812 farewell
address, she was criticized for reciting a poem rather than speaking prose.

> But I think they did not consider, that there is always something indelicate in
> sending on a LADY, in her own person, to *talk* to a mixed assembly of some
> thousand people. . . . A poetical address partakes more of dramatic representa-
> tion—the care as to just recitation, and the uttering [of] the studied composi-
> tion of another mind, relieves in a great degree the performer's own, and
> ensures almost the requisite and graceful composure of the last obeisance.[26]

Thus, refocusing attention on the correctness of the recitation deflects
attention from the person of the actress or from any moral effect the text
may be having on her.

In the hands of Siddons, her mentor Thomas Sheridan, and her brother
John Philip Kemble, the study of text reached a pinnacle of "close reading"
that is unlike any other critical work of their period. Whereas eighteenth-
century book reviewers dealt in generalities of "pleasing morality" and
"descriptive scenes," the elocutionists pinpointed linguistic subtleties that
can remind us only of twentieth-century New Critics. The degree of
specificity in their analyses is remarkable; what seems *un*modern is their
insistence that close analysis leads to one correct reading.

Sheridan was the first. In 1761, Sheridan gave a well-attended series of
lectures that became one of the most important texts of the elocution movement, *A Course of Lectures on Elocution* (1762). In his definition of reading,
Sheridan (unlike others) put gesture last: "A just delivery consists in a distinct articulation of words, pronounced in proper tones, suitably varied to

the sense, and the emotions of the mind; with due observation of accent; of
emphasis, in its several gradations; of rests or pauses of the voice, in proper
places and well measured degrees of time; and the whole accompanied with
expressive looks, and significant gesture" (10). Sheridan then explores, in
turn, articulation, pronunciation, accent (within a single word), emphasis
(within a phrase or sentence), pauses and stops, pitch, tones, and gesture.
Like other elocutionists, Sheridan is especially attentive to emphasis, which
can alter the meaning of a sentence. He uses a variation of an example frequently cited:

> Thus, to use a trite instance, the following sentence may have as many different
> meanings, as there are words in it, by varying the emphasis. "Shall you ride to
> town to-morrow?" If the emphasis is on shall, as, shàll you ride to town to-
> morrow? it implies, that the person spoken to had expressed before such an
> intention, but that there is some doubt in the questioner, whether he be deter-
> mined on it or not, and the answer may be, "Certainly, or, I am not sure." If
> it be on you, as, shall yoù ride to town to-morrow? the question implies that
> some one is to go, and do you mean to go yourself, or send some one in your
> stead? and the answer may be, No, but my servant shall. If on ride, as, shall you
> ride, &c. the answer may be, No, I shall walk, or go in a coach. If on town, as,
> shall you ride to tòwn to-morrow, the answer may be, No, but I shall ride to
> the forest. If on to-morrow, as, shall you ride to town to-mòrrow, the answer
> may be, No, not to-morrow, but the next day. (58)

Other elocutionists, notably John Walker, felt that a grammatical analysis
could point toward correct emphasis; Walker developed elaborate rules for
emphasis in antithesis, enumeration, and so on. That is, Walker used emphasis to clarify syntax. But for Sheridan, emphasis must be discovered within
the specific meaning of the passage.

Sheridan exemplifies his method in his *Lectures on the Art of Reading*
(1775), a work addressed both to clergy and to schoolteachers. This time,
Sheridan organizes his material as if for beginning readers: first the reading
of syllables, then of words, and so on. In the last two lectures, he turns
definitely to the clergy, offering a line-by-line analysis of the church service,
explaining how it is usually misread and how it should be properly performed. The elocution movement, as mentioned in Chapter 1, was motivated partly by a sense that the church service was usually very badly read;
Sheridan devotes several pages to making this point. But what is striking is,
first, that the church service is conceived as an acting text, waiting to be
performed, and second, that Sheridan works at a remarkable level of detail.
Throughout the analysis, he focuses on emphasis and (to a lesser extent) on
pauses, saying little about tone, gesture, or any other feature of delivery.

Here is an excerpt of the section on the Lord's Prayer (which runs to eight pages in the original):

> In the first words of it, "Our Father which *art* in Heaven"—that false emphasis on the word, *art,* has almost universally prevailed. This strong stress upon the affirmative, *art,* looks as if there might be a doubt, whether the residence of God were in Heaven, or not. . . . "Give us this *day* our *daily* bread"—Here the emphasis on the word, *day,* is unfortunately placed, both with regard to sound and sense. The ear is hurt, by the immediate repetition of the same sound, in the word daily . . . —And the true meaning is not conveyed; for this is supposed to be a prayer to be daily used, and a petition to be daily preferred, composed for our use by him, who bade us take no thought for the morrow; wherefore it should be thus pronounced—"Give us *this* day our *daily* bread."[27]

Throughout this work and others, Sheridan posits that there is one correct reading, discernible from an analysis of the text's meaning.

In preparing his roles for the stage, John Philip Kemble followed Sheridan's practice of using emphasis to clarify a text's sense. In so doing, he elicited criticism when his reading led him to depart from tradition. For example, Kemble questioned a fellow actor who emphasized "bid" in a passage from *Macbeth:* "Who can impress the forest, bid the tree / Unfix his earth-bound root?" In an exchange of letters, Kemble argued that, in this case, no emphasis was necessary, for "bid the tree" was just an amplification of "impress the forest," and "all unnecessary emphasis must be bad emphasis."[28] Often, when Kemble went against modern usage, he did so based on what he considered historical accuracy. Kemble was noted for attempting historically accurate sets and costumes, and he claimed that his pronunciation was also historical. During the 1809 "OP" riots at Covent Garden, the crowds jeered Kemble for pronouncing "aches" as two syllables, which Kemble felt was implied by the versification. As before, he exchanged letters on the subject, citing not only meter but a historical source implying "that anciently the monosyllabic and dissyllabic pronunciation distinguished the verb and the substantive."[29] Again, what is remarkable for the late eighteenth century is the attempt to pursue a linguistic correctness based on historical evidence.

Sheridan had treated pauses, along with stresses, as a means of marking emphasis. And in addition to his deliberate but idiosyncratic pronunciations, Kemble was often criticized for his excessive use of pauses. Not surprisingly, Boaden links this to his study of text: "What I have above endeavored to point out may be termed the academic or critical style of acting: it is built on a metaphysical search into our nature, and a close attention to all the minutiae of language. It deals, therefore, in *pauses,* which were not before made;

for the unlearned actor cared little about the transitions of thought" (1:175). But while the justification may have been scholarly, the effect of these pauses struck some members of the audience as comical. The actress Ann (Barry) Crawford revealed a loyalty to the older style: " 'The Garrick school,' she cried, 'was all *rapidity* and *passion,* while the Kemble school was so full of *paw* and *pause,* that, at first, the performers, thinking their new competitors had either lost their cues, or forgotten their parts, used frequently to prompt them.' "[30] It is possible that Kemble was ridiculed in part because the focus on emphasis did not serve the same function for a male actor that it did for a female. Certainly Kemble's slow speech and precise pauses made him a figure of fun, whereas Siddons's pacing was praised as dignified.

The focus on text and on correctness situated the performer differently than had the discourse on expressing passions. The enacting of passions served a rhetoric of sensibility, in which the audience would be moved through sympathetic identification. The attention to correctness, on the other hand, establishes a more distanced mode, in which both actor and audience utilize their rational, critical faculties. This may seem something of a diminishment, a less engaging style. Yet it worked to the advantage of an actress like Sarah Siddons. Again, I do not wish to imply that Siddons did not move her audience. But elocutionary performance helped her to retain a claim to propriety; indeed, the focus on correctness emphasizes propriety and is thus eminently suitable for an actress conscious of gender expectations.

Paradoxically, then, Siddons's attentiveness to decorum allowed her to stretch the norms for her gender, to be a virtuous public woman. She even, remarkably, became something of a role model for orators, the ostensible target audience of the elocutionists. According to Campbell, "The greatest pleader of his age, Erskine, said that her performance was a school for orators,—that he had studied her cadences and intonation, and that to the harmony of her periods and pronunciation he was indebted for '*his best displays*'" (255). As discussed in Chapter 1, elocution was based on "affective persuasion"; proper acting of the text moved the audience. The connection of acting and oratory was an elocutionary commonplace; what is notable here is that the power of elocution was recognized in a virtuous public woman.

As a model for orators, Siddons was unique among women of her period. While she can be seen in the context of the overall upward mobility of actresses, as noted above, Siddons herself felt the fragility of her position. Early in her career, she had been accused of stinginess for not being willing to act in benefits for two colleagues. She was hissed on the stage "and stood the object of public scorn." Siddons spoke directly to the audience in her own defense and managed to quiet the crowd. But, she said, the cheers she received throughout that season, "however gratifying as testimonials of their changed opinion, were not sufficient to obliterate from my memory the tortures I had endured from their injustice, *and the consciousness of a humiliating vocation.*"[31] Campbell explains Siddons's dignified air as a defense against the scorn actresses often faced: "In addition to the gravity that was natural to her, she had a coldness of manner on slight acquaintance, habitually acquired by the consciousness of her vocation. She felt that her profession would have exposed her both to the insolence and familiarity of patronage, if she had not possessed a great degree of defensive dignity" (257).

While Campbell implies that Siddons's dignity was an assertion of her independence from the aristocracy, the fragility of her position reveals, in part, a conflict between aristocratic and bourgeois (domestic) attitudes toward display. Eighteenth-century attitudes about theatricality and authenticity in personal presentation are consistent with the conversational norms discussed in Chapter 1. Older courtly norms accept a level of theatricality that would be intolerable to adherents of bourgeois domestic ideology; the bourgeois mode favors sincerity. This difference becomes especially salient in regard to amateur theatricals (discussed below), which seemed more threatening to the bourgeoisie than to the aristocracy. The task for Sarah Siddons was to succeed (spectacularly) at display while maintaining a claim to bourgeois modesty and domesticity. Theorizing her acting in terms of the correct expression of text was important in enabling her to do just that.

Public Readings

One of the essential features of the elocution movement is that it blended the concerns of acting, reading, and speech. As my argument moves from the public arena of the theater to the realm of bourgeois domesticity, we must pause at an intermediate step: public readings of literary works. Today, we are most familiar with Charles Dickens's public readings of the 1850s and 1860s, in which he self-consciously recreated the atmosphere of the family circle while performing to packed halls. In the eighteenth century, as we might expect, public readings were less pointedly domestic, more theatrical. Thomas Sheridan began the practice of public readings during his lectures on elocution in the 1760s, when he performed some exemplary literary works. He turned more fully to entertainment in performances he called "Attic Evenings," which mixed instrumental music, song, and readings, sometimes including a lecture on elocution; the term "Attic" expresses Sheridan's explicit belief that he was reviving an ancient practice. In 1785, he teamed up with the actor John Henderson and presented a series of "English Readings" at Freemasons' Hall; Boaden tells us "the grand room of that building literally overflowed on these nights."[32] Of the two, however, Henderson was better received than Sheridan. Although Sheridan had explicitly championed a "natural" reading style, the reviewers thought his performance was mannered. One attendee commented,

> Old Sheridan had a pompous emphasis; his elocution was of the old school; but as he was occasionally spitting or taking snuff, it did not altogether so well please. His day had passed by, *le rideau tombe.* Henderson had a deal of comic humour, and he used to recite the tale of John Gilpin [by Cowper], in excellent style. The hall was always crowded, and whenever it was his turn to read, there was a general buzz of approbation. Being a constant attendant there, I could not but feel for poor Sheridan.[33]

These performances were popular enough to inspire at least one parody, an afterpiece by James Cobb presented at the Haymarket by George Colman and published in 1787, which articulates popular reactions to elocution and which highlights gender concerns. In *English Readings,* a public contest in reading is used as a diversion by Capt. Wilmot and his lover, Charlotte, whose father wishes her to marry one of the contestants, her cousin Bob Bootekin; Bob's performance allows the lovers enough time for a hurried wedding. By transferring a London event for an educated audience to the provinces and the working class, Cobb plays on traditional prejudices. As Capt. Wilmot asks of Charlotte's maid, "But tell me, Kitty, how did this *rage* for English Readings reach a town so far from London?" (5). The fact that the contest grows out of a long-standing conflict between a retired shoemaker (Bootekin, Charlotte's father) and a retired Irish mantua-maker (Mrs. Poplin) adds an element of misogyny to the class and regional prejudices. Apparently Mrs. Poplin's pretensions are routinely imitated by Bootekin, "And now the whim of burlesquing a rational and elegant amusement—giving *Readings,* has siez'd her ladyship—he is to have the same on a more extensive scale of absurdity" (6).

The character of Bob Bootekin ridicules the aspirations of artisans and their self-improvement programs. Bob belongs to a London disputing society at which he argues points like "Whether the lady who has *black, blue,* or *grey eyes,* is likely to make the best wife?" or "Upon Charlotte's first introduction to Werter, did not she behave rather ungenteelly, in not offering him a dish of tea?" (14). But it is the fact that his current opponent is an old woman that gets his goat: "I never read but two books in my life—my *cash-book,* and my *journal*—but I'm resolved to like reading now, from mere opposition—What the devil, an't I a better gentleman, by a *hundred* a year,

than any man in the neighbourhood?—and shall a paultry mantua-maker—
a walking *pincushion*—a *remnant* of old tabby, pretend to give *Readings,* when
I hardly know whether I can read or not?" (8).

Bob has prepared an evening on the model of Sheridan's Attic
Entertainment: it begins with an overture for two orchestras (to be played
by one fiddler, Sam Scrape), then a reading of "John Gilpin" (which he mis-
attributes to Sterne), then more music, and finally the contest with Mrs.
Poplin. Bob is feisty in approaching the contest: "I'll meet the lady,
Captain—let her chuse her subject, from Johnny Gilpin up to Milton—
prose, rhyme, or blank verse, all the same to me—I read 'em all alike" (18).
She, however, prefers sentimental readings: "You must know I like to chuse
for myself, Mr. Stately.—The pathetic is my forte—A sentimental story
makes one so charmingly miserable.—Oh, I love to touch the feelings—and
my voice has great power, Mr. Stately" (22). In the end, they decide to read
from *Romeo and Juliet*—but in editing the piece for the performance, Bob
has scratched out all of Juliet's speeches. The contest degenerates when the
two read louder and louder, at the same time: "Now, *lungs,* do your office,"
says Bob (25). Obviously, James Cobb's targets are multiple, including the
pretensions of a newly literate artisan class and the false sensibility of an old
woman. Workers, and especially women, should not claim the position of
reader/orator. Significantly, our heroine, Charlotte, does not expose herself
by reading in public.

Although James Cobb modeled his farce directly on Sheridan's performances, there were others as well. Perhaps the most prominent among
these were readings by the French actor Le Tessier (sometimes spelled Le
Texier). Le Tessier read French plays, in French and in his home, limiting
his audience to the educated, what Boaden called "a dressed and refined
party."[34] The visitor passed through Le Tessier's library to the reading room
and was served tea by a servant; the goal was evidently to lend the air of a
private occasion. Le Tessier sat as he read, using little gesture except to
wave his hand to mark a character's exit. But commentators praised the
way he altered his voice for each character so that there was never doubt as
to who was speaking. In addition to public readings like Sheridan's and
semiprivate ones like Le Tessier's, there were also "reading parties." Betsy
Sheridan (Thomas's daughter) describes one she went to in March 1785, at
the salon hostess Elizabeth Vesey's, at which her father read from Milton.
And Maria Edgeworth offers a fictional reading party in her 1801 novel,
Belinda. Here a French count (presumably modeled on Le Tessier) visits the
hostess to plan the evening, which includes his reading of all the parts of a
French play.[35]

Among women, the only successful public reader was, not surprisingly,

Sarah Siddons. Soon after Siddons became famous in the London thea
she was named "Preceptress of English Reading" to the royal princesses. 1
position did not involve teaching the princesses but, rather, frequent readings to the royal party at Buckingham House and at Windsor. These readings continued after her retirement: Siddons writes of a series of command
performances in 1813, at which the first night she read from Shakespeare
(*Henry VIII, Merchant of Venice, Hamlet*), the second poetry (*Paradise Lost,*
Gray's "Elegy," and Scott's "Marmion"), and the third again Shakespeare
(*Othello*).[36] These readings are remarkable, in part, for enabling Siddons to
read male parts she was not likely to enact. (Siddons had occasionally played
Hamlet, but never in London.) That is, we must infer that reading was felt
to be different from, and safer than, enacting. It was more distanced, involv-
ing less sympathetic identification.

After she retired from the stage, Siddons gave readings of Milton and
Shakespeare to private parties at Oxford and Cambridge and in her home,
and to a public, paying audience at the Argyle Rooms. Campbell describes
the format of these readings:

> In front of what was the orchestra in the old Argyle Rooms, a reading-desk
> with lights was placed, on which lay her book, a quarto volume, printed with
> large letter. When her memory could not be entirely trusted, she assisted her
> sight by spectacles, which, in the intervals, she handled and waved so grace-
> fully that you could not have wished her to be without them. A large red
> screen formed what painters would call a background to the person of the
> charming reader. She was dressed in white, and her dark hair, *à la Grecque,*
> crossed her temples in full masses. There was something remarkably elegant in
> the self-possession of her entrance, and in the manner in which she addressed
> the assembly. Her readings were alternately from Milton and Shakspeare [*sic*].
> I have already made free to confess my conviction that the works of the for-
> mer poet are too spiritual and undramatic to be susceptible of any improve-
> ment from human elocution. But, about her readings of Shakspeare, I can only
> say that, to my understanding, no acting I ever witnessed, nor dramatic criti-
> cism I ever read, illustrated the poet so closely and so perfectly. (243)

What struck Boaden was the challenge for a woman to read all the male
parts—it was more difficult, he says, than for a man like Le Tessier to read
the female roles. As he says, "There is, therefore, an almost awkward effort
of an elegantly dressed female to assume the vehement passions, coarse
humours, and often unguarded dialogue of every variety of manly character."[37] But Boaden emphasizes that Siddons succeeded in performing the
poetry without any risk of impropriety; she was governed by "the reserve
of her sex" (319). In such a case, the performer must, again, privilege text,
"the enthusiasm of poetry rather than the feelings of nature.... The

3. "Mrs. Siddons" by Thomas Lawrence (1804). Her
inspiration comes through her fingers from the open
book. (Tate Gallery, London/Art Resource, N.Y.)

witches of Mrs. Siddons, accordingly, were poetical creations" (319). As in
her acting, then, it was the emphasis on the text that created a "safe" space
in which Siddons could retain her dignity.

These public readings must have been in some ways the perfect performing situation. Siddons had absolute control over the "set" and the

"script"; there were no compromises to be negotiated with the[?] agers or fellow actors. True, they were exhausting, like all solo per[?] (at Windsor, Siddons tells us, she took several breaks). But this [...] been more than compensated for by opportunities for full control and for playing a range of roles, including male parts. In these readings, Siddons could express her full majesty; they were the perfect expression of her public persona. As portrayed in a painting by Thomas Lawrence, the inspiration for that majesty, which is so strongly evident in Siddons's eyes, derives from the open book to which she points. Siddons has no "voice" in this painting; her lips are closed. Whatever she expresses originates in the text.

Siddons's Performance in Speech

Before leaving Sarah Siddons, I would like to turn, briefly, to her private speech, which is described in many surviving representations as much less powerful than her public performances. We need to repeat the usual caveats about the accuracy of these representations. No doubt, Siddons was a competent user of language, able to match her speech to contexts formal or informal. People who knew her repeat that she was merely shy, and that with people with whom she felt comfortable, she was as lively as anyone. Most of the surviving representations describe formal or public occasions, and many of them are by witnesses meeting Siddons for the first time. So, as always, we cannot assume that these representations capture more than one facet of Siddons's range of discourse competence. But the consistency in these representations does convey what witnesses felt was most salient in her speech.

Many of the representations have as their theme Siddons's miscalculations in bringing her "tragic" voice into everyday situations. Campbell recounts one peculiarity, in which the dramatic intrudes on the domestic:

> [She had] the habit of attaching dramatic tones and emphasis to commonplace colloquial subjects. She went, for instance, one day, into a shop at Bath, and after bargaining for some calico, and hearing the mercer pour forth a hundred commendations of the cloth, she put the question to him, "*But will it wash?*" in a manner so electrifying as to make the poor shopman start back from his counter. I once told her this anecdote about herself, and she laughed at it heartily, saying, "Witness truth, I never meant to be tragical."[38]

Commentators meeting Siddons at social occasions reiterate this point. For example, when Washington Irving met Siddons at a dinner party in 1813, he said, "It was a rich gratification to see the queen of tragedy thus out of her robes. Yet her manner even in the social board still partakes of the state and gravity of tragedy. Not that there is an unwillingness to unbend, but that there is a difficulty in throwing aside the solemnity of long-acquired habit." And Sydney Smith claimed that, while Siddons laughed heartily at his jokes, she "never got out of tragedy even in common life. She used to *stab* the potatoes; and said, 'Boy, give me a knife!' as she would have said, 'Give me the dagger!' "[39]

Even more telling are occasions on which Siddons's speech is explicitly linked to text. For example, Walter Scott caught Siddons slipping into iambic pentameter. According to his son-in-law and biographer John Gibson Lockhart, "Scott (who was a capital mimic) often repeated her tragic exclamation to a footboy during a dinner at Ashestiel,—'You've brought me water, boy.—I asked for beer.' Another time, dining with a Provost of Edinburgh, she ejaculated, in answer to her host's apology for his *pièce de résistance,*—'Beef cannot be too salt for me, my Lord!' "[40]

In all of these representations, Siddons remains in her public persona as tragic actress, where commentators expected her to speak as a private woman. We must remember, though, that the discourses on middle-class women's speech in this period concentrated on two modes: the empty loquacity of the speaker of woman's language and the silence of the modest domestic woman. Siddons evidently refused to enact either of these roles. The representations of her silence (such as the encounter with Arthur Wellesley discussed above) are especially meaningful in this context. Unlike the silence of other women, Siddons's was an occasion for criticism.

William Smellie, we remember, linked women's loquacity to the needs of child-rearing: infants required the mother's chatty responsiveness. Especially significant, then, are the representations of Siddons as a silent *mother*—an oxymoron pointing to the difficulty of bridging the public/private distinction. In a letter to a Bath friend, Thomas Sedgwick Whalley, Siddons herself describes a scene in which her son managed to stump her into silence:

> Harry has just puzzled me very much. When going to eat some filberts after dinner, I told him you desired I would not eat them; "but," says he, "what would you have done if Mr. Whalley had desired you would?" I was at a stand for a little while, and at last he found a means to save me from my embarrassment, by saying: "but you know Mr. Whalley would not desire you to eat them, if he thought they would hurt you." "Very true, Harry," says I; so it ended there.[41]

Again, of course, what matters is not that Siddons was momentarily speechless, but that this was thought significant enough to be included in a biography. Siddons's silence mattered.

Siddons's silence often took the form of a refusal to abide by normal conversational norms. Politeness, we recall, is theorized in terms of maintaining another's face; politeness is supremely concerned with the interaction that occurs during speech. But the surviving representations of Siddons's speech depict her as specifically impolite, as a star who intends an effect *on* an audience rather than interacting *with* a conversational partner. This is epitomized on an occasion when Siddons had unwanted visitors, women who barged past her servant.

> I felt extremely indignant at such unparalleled impertinence; and before the servant had done speaking to me, a tall, elegant, invalid-looking person presented herself (whom, I am afraid, I did not receive very graciously), and after her four more, in slow succession. A very awkward silence took place; when presently the first lady began to accost me, with a most inveterate Scotch twang, and in a dialect which was scarcely intelligible to me in those days. She was a person of very high rank: her curiosity, however, had been too powerful for her good-breeding. "You must think it strange," said she, "to see a person entirely unknown to you intrude in this manner upon your privacy; but you must know, I am in a very delicate state of health, and my physician won't let me go to the theatre to see you, so I am to look at you here." She accordingly sat down to look, and I to be looked at, for a few painful moments, when she arose and apologized; but I was in no humour to overlook such insolence, and so let her depart in silence.[42]

There was rudeness on both sides here, and a modern reader is probably most struck by that of the intruders. Siddons, we may believe, reacted appropriately to the implication that she was available at any time as an object to be observed; we would allow her to resist the gaze. Still, what is typical of Siddons here is that her own face-threatening gesture is one of majestic silence. Silence, as I argued above, accrues multiple meanings in different contexts and cultures; we saw that the silence of Quaker women was accepted by observers (that is, not seen as face-threatening). Observers of Sarah Siddons, though, linked her silence to the odd predicament of an actress without a text. Frances Burney commented on Siddons's stiffness, then wrote, "Whether fame and success have spoiled her, or whether she only possesses the skill of representing and embellishing materials with which she is furnished by others, I know not; but still I remain disappointed."[43]

Siddons's silence, then, reinforced her public persona; in her stateliness, she was as far as possible removed from the loquacious speaker of woman's language. But Siddons was equally far removed from the other allowable mode, the modest (silent) woman. The silence of the modest woman is deferential; she allows others to control the conversation, to hold the floor. The representations of Siddons's speech, on the other hand, emphasize her ability to hold the floor *through* her silence. When Siddons is silent, no one else dares speak. The artist Benjamin Robert Haydon described Siddons's visit to his studio in 1820:

> Everybody seemed afraid, when in walked, with all the dignity of her majestic presence, Mrs. Siddons, like a Ceres or a Juno. The whole room remained dead silent, and allowed her to think. After a few minutes Sir George Beaumont, who was extremely anxious, said in a very delicate manner: "How do you like the Christ?" Everybody listened for her reply. After a moment, in a deep, loud, tragic tone she said: "It is completely successful."[44]

Even within the family circle, Siddons's silence ruled. When a young Frances Kemble was being scolded by her commanding aunt, only the child was brave enough to break the ensuing silence. Kemble wrote much later, "The tragic tones pausing, in the midst of the impressed and impressive silence of the assembled family, I tinkled forth, 'What beautiful eyes you have!' . . . Mrs Siddons set me down with a smothered laugh."[45] Here, of course, Siddons breaks character a bit. But even in this most private, family scene, Siddons's silence holds the floor. She is still the "public" woman, the actress, even where other women might play a more domestic role. Her silence is never the deferential yielding of place that characterizes the "good" modest woman.

Of course, not all the surviving representations emphasize Siddons in her public role, and especially not those by people who knew her well. Amelia Opie, for one, describes Siddons nursing a new baby and sounding like an "ordinary" mother: "The baby is all a baby can be, but Mrs. S. laughs, and says it is a wit and a beauty already in her eyes."[46] And Hester (Thrale) Piozzi corrected an acquaintance who found that

> at times, in private company, [Siddons] gave one a notion of a wicked, unhappy Queen, rather than of a purely well-bred gentlewoman.
>
> When I made some such remarks as these to Mrs Piozzi, she said I was partly right; but that her friend, Mrs Siddons, could be infinitely comic when she pleased, and was among her intimates; though anything but a comedian on the boards. She then added a very amusing description of her having a family party, ordering the parlour-door to be made fast, and proceeding to perform most of the part of Sir Anthony Absolute, with astonishing spirit and pleasantry.[47]

Of course, while Piozzi rejects the notion that Siddons can only be tragic, she still describes her as always theatrical; enacting a male character behind a closed door seems especially linked to the transgression of the public (male)/ private (female) boundary. Significantly, Siddons has chosen *The Rivals* as her text but does not enact the stereotypically female Mrs. Malaprop.

Polite conversation, we remember, occurs in semipublic spaces: the salon, rather than either the theater or an intimate family room. Let me end, then, with an example of Siddons's speech in a salon setting that, like the conversation with Mary Knowles (Introduction), has come down to us in three separate representations. The event was a December 1782 party at the home of the literary hostess Mary Monckton. In 1785, Richard Cumberland published a satirical account of the evening in his collection of essays, *The Observer*. After a rather mean-spirited attack on the Bluestockings as false pedants, and after a brief appearance by a young novelist who must be Frances Burney, Cumberland represents Siddons's conversation in this way:

> I now joined a cluster of people, who had crowded round an actress, who sat upon a sopha, leaning on her elbow in a pensive attitude, and seemed to be counting the sticks of her fan, whilst they were vying with each other in the most extravagant encomiums.
> —You was adorable last night in Belvidera, says a pert young Parson with a high toupee; I sat in Lady Blubber's box, and I can assure you, she and her daughters too wept most bitterly—but then that charming mad scene, by my soul it was a chef d'oeuvre; pray, Madam, give me leave to ask you, was you really in your senses?
> —I strove to do it as well as I could, answered the actress.
> —Do you intend to play comedy next season? says a Lady, stepping up to her with great eagerness.
> —I shall do as the manager bids me, she replied.
> —I should be curious to know, says an elderly Lady, which part, Madam, you yourself esteem the best you play?
> —I always endeavour to make that which I am about the best. (224–225)

As in the scene with the Scottish lady, Siddons here is victimized by her celebrity: she is the object of attentions she undoubtedly would have termed impertinent. But celebrity does entail being gracious to one's fans (we might call this a particular kind of "conversational work"). And every response Siddons makes is a small put-down of her questioner, discounting the question and indicating her displeasure by the brevity of her answers. Siddons had no small talk—or, more properly, that is what struck people who expected something else.

A second representation, by Frances Burney, portrays a very different Siddons: not one whose silence controls the room, but rather one who is silenced:

> A lady who sat near me then began a dialogue with Mr. Erskine, who had placed himself exactly opposite to Mrs. Siddons; and they debated together upon her manner of studying her parts, disputing upon the point with great

warmth, yet not only forbearing to ask Mrs. Siddons herself which was right, but quite overpowering her with their loquacity, when she attempted, unasked, to explain the matter.[48]

Burney herself was a very shy person, and it is possible that she had insights into Siddons's shyness that other witnesses missed. Certainly this representation of Siddons as powerless in conversation is unique.

Siddons gave her own version of this evening in her "Memoranda," which Campbell reproduces. She calls Cumberland's version "accurate," and explains that she had been invited under false pretenses, having been promised that only a few mutual friends would be there, "for I had often told [Miss Monckton] very seriously, that it suited neither my studies nor my inclinations to be engaged in parties, from which I begged most earnestly to be excused; for, to say the truth, I had been forewarned how eagerly any notorious person was pursued for exhibition."[49] But receiving assurances, Siddons came early and "very much in undress," and accompanied by her young son, "whom she desired me to bring with me, more for effect, I suspect, than for his *beaux yeux*" (99). Siddons thus presents herself in her bourgeois maternal role, the very opposite of the glamorous celebrity. Unfortunately for her, after a pleasant interlude, a great crowd does appear, which

> counteracted every attempt that I could make for escape . . . and if it had not been for the benevolent politeness of Mr. Erskine, who had been acquainted with my arrangement, I know not what weakness I might have been surprised into, especially being tormented, as I was, by the ridiculous interrogations of some learned ladies, who were called *Blues,* the meaning of which title I did not at that time appreciate, much less did I comprehend the meaning of the greater part of their learned talk. . . . Glad enough was I at length to find myself at peace in my own bed-chamber. (99)

The representations of Siddons's speech highlight the gap between the powerful effect she created on stage and her perceived inability (or refusal) to engage in ordinary conversation. Her performances derived their power from an analysis of text and of character; they did not involve the give-and-take of conversational interaction. Thus Siddons's tactic of relying on correctness to lay claims on both power and modesty seems to have worked less well in this arena than it did on the stage. The representations of her speech by a wide range of commentators tend to link her speech to text and consistently critique her avoidance of polite face-saving gestures. That this need not be critiqued, we saw in Chapter 2; that women speakers could negotiate positions of strength within the polite norms, we will see in Chapter 5.

Sarah Siddons was obviously exceptional in her ability to position her-

self as both great actress and domestic woman; doing so involved developing a "safe" place for her stage work and an insistence on her committed
motherhood. For the rest of this chapter, I would like to turn toward less
exceptional women. Since acting highlights the connections between reading and speaking, looking at how bourgeois educators and women viewed
their own performances will move us toward the reading of literary texts
that will concern us in Chapters 4 and 5. First, however, let us consider the
degree to which acting and (especially) reading could be framed in terms of
women's accomplishments.

Accomplished Reading: The Wanderer

In the late eighteenth century, at the same time that admonitions to
silence were promulgated in the conduct literature, norms for display were
being articulated in the discourse surrounding women's "accomplishments."
This discourse was highly contradictory and colored by class considerations.
The criticisms made that one could no longer distinguish the classes by their
speech could be applied here as well: training in accomplishments allowed
middle-class girls to mimic the gentry. One of the standard criticisms was
that women no longer learned useful skills like cooking and keeping the
household accounts; now they were only taught to chirp in Italian, to net
screens, and to draw "a little." That is, they imitated a leisure class.[50] Moralists along a political spectrum from Hannah More to Mary Wollstonecraft
attacked the devotion to accomplishments as a false education, one that
would ill prepare women either for domestic life or for the hereafter. In his
Dictionary, Samuel Johnson had defined "accomplishment" as embellish-
ment or ornament, explicitly distinguishing it from moral excellence.

The cultivation of accomplishments was generally associated with the
marriage market. Whether or not women aspired to marry "up," accomplishments allowed them to display their talents in ways that were codified
and thus proper. Ann Bermingham argues that the fact that the accomplishments were usually abandoned after marriage demonstrates that their
purpose was primarily to attract suitors. She stresses the performative aspect
of accomplishments, maintaining that they transform the performing subject
into the object of the (male) observer's judgment. Through the cultivation
of accomplishments, women were transformed into commodities.[51] (The
economic metaphor is present in the way that accomplishments are always
something that is "acquired.") It is, of course, the uselessness of accomplishments that lends them cultural capital: they indicate that women have
the leisure to pursue them instead of performing domestic labor. (In *Pride*

and Prejudice, Mrs. Bennet gets downright huffy when Mr. Collins praises what he presumes to be her daughters' cooking; she assures him they perform no such chores [*P&P* 65].) Accomplishments allowed women to display their taste and education (that is, cultural capital) in ways that were bound by rules, and thus safe.

One of the most explicit discussions of accomplishments in the contemporary literature takes place in *Pride and Prejudice,* in a scene at Netherfield. The easily pleased Mr. Bingley thinks "all" young ladies are accomplished because they can perform the very useless work of painting tables, covering screens, and netting purses. The less agreeable Mr. Darcy, however, requires more to call a woman accomplished. His "faithful assistant," Miss Bingley, can call a woman accomplished only if she has "a thorough knowledge of music, singing, drawing, dancing, and the modern languages . . . ; and besides all this, she must possess a certain something in her air and manner of walking, the tone of her voice, her address and expressions, or the word will be but half deserved" (39). Yet for Darcy this is still not enough: "and to all this she must yet add something more substantial, in the improvement of her mind by extensive reading" (39).

Elizabeth doubts that any woman can meet this standard. Yet in this extensive list of criteria for accomplishment, Darcy may be alluding to James Fordyce's *Sermons to Young Women,* which was one of the most important conduct books of the period, and which is mentioned elsewhere in *Pride and Prejudice.* Fordyce had organized accomplishments into three categories: domestic, elegant, and intellectual. Under domestic accomplishments, Fordyce recommends frugality in household management; about half of this section consists of verses from the biblical book of Proverbs. Fordyce's second category, elegant accomplishments, includes the kinds of aesthetic display that Johnson and Mr. Bingley refer to: dancing, needlework, drawing, and music.

The third category, intellectual accomplishments, includes the study of history, geography, astronomy, and so on, and (more surprisingly) oral reading. Especially notable here is the general sense, consistent with Fordyce's overall point, that transforms intellectual achievement into "accomplishment." For Fordyce, study is not an end in itself: "Your business chiefly is to read Men, in order to make yourselves agreeable and useful. . . . Nevertheless, in this study you may derive great assistance from books" (124). Fordyce recommends that women read to each other while they do needlework, and he summarizes the standard advice of the elocutionists: begin with plain prose works, which are easiest because they are closest to conversation; attend to the sense of an author to plan proper emphasis, and so on (132–33). But his advice is framed not in terms of the elocutionists' affective persuasion, but rather in terms of acquiring "a very valuable and pleasing accomplishment" (132). And, typically, "all this should be practised in the frequent hearing, and under the kind animadversion, of an experienced judge" (133).

Fordyce may be exceptional in including reading as an accomplishment; certainly we are more used to thinking of decorative arts than of intellectual ones. Moreover, as we will see in Chapter 4, many commentators discouraged the notion that women should read aloud in company; no matter how rule-bound the reading was, it was so closely associated with oratory that to read was to claim a position of power. But reading could be acceptable if it was framed the way Siddons's acting was framed: in terms of correctness. And if elocution can be an accomplishment, it serves to demonstrate the education and taste of the reader, and to offer her performance for the judgment of the hearer.

A fine example of the discourse on accomplishments appears in Frances Burney's last novel, *The Wanderer* (1814). Here, a nameless, positionless heroine survives for a time by revealing her worth through the display of accomplishments. The society she enters is, of course, not entirely welcoming, and her patrons are eager to discover her family connections. But in the meantime, she is able to live on the cultural capital of her class: her refined speech and manners make invitations possible; she extends her welcome by displaying her skill in playing, singing, and drawing.

This portion of *The Wanderer* extends the consideration of accomplishments when the heroine is drawn into her patrons' private performance of Colley Cibber's *The Provok'd Husband* (chapters 8–11). The late eighteenth century was a great period for amateur theatricals. Perhaps just because of figures like Sarah Siddons, acting became respectable enough for some women to engage in it, though within strict boundaries. Between 1780 and 1810, many aristocratic households built theaters on their properties and staged elaborate theatricals, performed by upper-class amateurs aided by professional actors. These would not be open to any paying customers, but they were not exactly intimate: each performance might have 150 invited guests.[52] The playwright Frederick Reynolds describes, among others, a performance at Blenheim Palace in 1787. Here, the theater was built in a greenhouse and could hold two hundred; enacted were Kelly's *False Delicacy* and Cowley's *Who's the Dupe?;* the performers were members of the aristocratic Spencer and Russell families. What comes out of Reynolds's description is the mixture of envy and disdain that professional theater people felt for these aristocratic amateurs: Reynolds was sitting next to the somewhat fidgety Miles Peter Andrews (a popular dramatist) and "Being, myself, unable to hear one line out of twenty, which these *really private* actors uttered, I expressed a wish that some friendly person would hint to them, that the entertainment of their audience would not be diminished, if they would condescend to speak audibly." Andrews, however, disagrees: "If you knew anything of the matter, Sir, you would be aware, that *not to hear them* is our only chance of getting through this tiresome evening."[53] The food is apparently the most enjoyable thing of all, and Andrews doesn't hesitate to inform his host that the theater was too cold, the play dull and obsolete, and the acting execrable.

Reynolds and Andrews might have been even more disdainful of the performances of middle-class amateurs. Frances Burney described several performances she herself participated in, in 1771 and 1777; as she tells it, they were marred by the stage fright that caused her to lose her voice. In one, "I was fool enough to run off quite overset, and unable to speak. I was really in an agony of fear and shame!"; in another, "Not once could I command my voice to any steadiness."[54] Burney describes various degrees of controlling her stage fright, and she seems to have enjoyed the performances at times. But we can also sense her ambivalence about being on display. She reports that a fellow actress "called to the audience *not to clap again; for it was very impertinent*" (1:129, italics in original). After a later theatrical, she was invited to meet the audience, "but I begged to be excused as I knew none of the party, and had been pertly stared at enough" (1:179).

In *The Wanderer,* Burney attributes similar feelings to her heroine, who must be gradually led to display, as her modesty is only slowly overcome. The heroine (who at this point is called Ellis) first agrees only to be the prompter and even there begins modestly. At first her tones are "languid" and her pronunciation "inarticulate" (80), until she is gradually involved in the endeavor. When the temperamental woman who was to play Lady Townly backs out, Ellis first reads the part, then agrees to perform it. Again, she begins haltingly and inaudibly, gradually enters into the spirit of the part, and finally triumphs. Throughout, Burney consistently emphasizes Ellis's dependence on text.

The Wanderer's discussion of accomplishments reaches its climax with Ellis's performance of literature. Here, the heroine's reading has exactly the same effect as a more traditional accomplishment, the performance of music. I quote it at length to show how Burney uses the same vocabulary for reading and for music. Being asked to play the piano,

> Ellis instantly went to the instrument, and there performed, in so fine a style, a composition of Haydn, that Mrs. Howel . . . was struck with wonder, and

congratulated both her young guest and herself, in so seasonable an acquisition of so accomplished a visitor. . . .

Nor ended here either their surprise or their satisfaction; they soon learnt that she played also upon the harp; Lord Melbury instantly went forth in search of one; and it was then . . . that Ellis completed her conquest of their admiration; for with the harp she was prevailed upon to sing; and the sweetness of her voice, the delicacy of its tones, her taste and expression, in which her soul seemed to harmonize with her accents, had an effect so delightful upon her auditors, that . . . Lady Aurora was enchanted, was fascinated. . . .

Eager to improve these favourable sensations, Ellis, to vary the amusements of Lady Aurora, in this interval of retirement, proposed reading. And here again her powers gave the utmost pleasure; whether she took a French authour, or an English one; the accomplished Boileau, or the penetrating Pope; the tenderly-refined Racine, or the all-pervading Shakespeare, her tones, her intelligence, her skilful modulations, gave force and meaning to every word, and proved alike her understanding and her feeling.[55]

In *The Wanderer*, reading is consistently linked with music as an appropriate accomplishment for women to display. Reading and music are similar in that both require the performer to bring a written "score" to life. Burney emphasizes the parallel by using parallel descriptive language: both singing and reading show off Ellis's "tones," her reading voice has "modulations," and so on. Most important, both serve the function of accomplishments by revealing Ellis's class position and personal worth. The general reluctance to include reading as an accomplishment must be related to the association of reading and power, and to the putative dangers of sympathetic identification, both of which work less powerfully in the case of music. But again, when framed as a matter of correctness, the performance of reading becomes more thinkable for women.

Silence and Display in Mansfield Park

If *The Wanderer* articulates the most positive outcomes of women's display, Jane Austen's *Mansfield Park* (published in the same year, 1814) is much more ambiguous. Since this novel evokes discourses on elocution, theater, reading, and speech, and especially since it situates concerns about display within norms schematized by class and gender, it offers us a useful summary for this chapter. Modern critics have focused especially on this novel's exploration of the risks of amateur theatricals; many critics feel that the Mansfield theatricals, while occupying only a small part of the novel, are its central event. What is puzzling, however, is that although Jane Austen's family enthusiastically produced theatricals when she was a child, the novel itomizes "the antitheatrical prejudice" of conservative evangelicalism. More generally, the novel seems to endorse conduct-book behaviors that are criticized elsewhere in Austen's works. For most readers, the silent, modest heroine is much less approachable than wits like Elizabeth Bennet (*Pride and Prejudice*); as Lionel Trilling said long ago, "Nobody, I believe, has ever found it possible to like the heroine of *Mansfield Park*." Because Fanny Price is so unlike other Austen heroines, critics disagree over whether Austen meant to support the conservative ideology she exemplifies or to demonstrate its failures.[56]

For the purposes of this chapter, however, I would like to put aside questions of authorial intention and focus on the degree to which this novel engages the language of elocution and connects elocution's influence on acting and on speech. While Fanny Price is, obviously, no Sarah Siddons, her acting and her speech reflect similar discourses. Rather than offering a literary interpretation, then, I would like to utilize *Mansfield Park* to support a historical argument: to show how tightly connected were the discourses on various kinds of display—accomplishments, reading aloud, theater, and speech—and how they all were inflected by gender. This will anticipate, in part, the argument of Chapter 5, that reading aloud was understood as a way of practicing speech.

The elocution movement permeates the text of *Mansfield Park*. Since the hero, Edmund Bertram, is ordained, he is a member of the elocutionists' first target audience. In one scene, he and Henry Crawford explicitly consider the increased attention paid to correct reading, in terms that reflect the elocution movement's concerns:

> The subject of reading aloud was farther discussed. The two young men were the only talkers, but they, standing by the fire, talked over the too common neglect of the qualification, the total inattention to it, in the ordinary school-system for boys, the consequently natural—yet in some instances almost unnatural degree of ignorance and uncouthness of men, of sensible and well-informed men, when suddenly called to the necessity of reading aloud, which had fallen within their notice, giving instances of blunders, and failures with their secondary causes, the want of management of the voice, of proper modulation and emphasis, of foresight and judgement, all proceeding from the first cause, want of early attention and habit; and Fanny was listening again with great entertainment.
>
> "Even in my profession"—said Edmund with a smile—"how little the art of reading has been studied! how little a clear manner, and good delivery, have been attended to! I speak rather of the past, however, than the present—There is now a spirit of improvement abroad; ... in every congregation, there is a larger proportion who know a little of the matter, and who can judge and criticize." (*MP* 339–40)

Elocution, in this account, operates in the male realms of public speech and in addition provides the occasion for (male) prerogatives of judging and criticizing. Immediately after this, Edmund and Crawford reinforce the emphasis on correctness by analyzing individual passages in the church service, discussing "the properest manner in which particular passages in the service should be delivered" (340).[57]

Edmund becomes a churchman largely at his father's urging, and it is to the father that we must look for the purest articulation of conservative norms. Sir Thomas Bertram is, for Austen, an unusually active patriarch, utterly unlike the lax or absent fathers of the other novels. When he is away, his children judge their own behavior by what Sir Thomas would wish; when he is present, he tolerates no disobedience to his rule. Having adopted Fanny (his wife's niece) when she was a child, he exerts increasingly powerful control over her, even sending her away so that she might regret having refused Henry Crawford. Sir Thomas expects Fanny to be "free from wilfulness of temper, self-conceit, and every tendency to that independence of spirit, which prevails so much in modern days, even in young women, and which in young women is offensive and disgusting beyond all common offence" (318). We may take Sir Thomas, then, as the spokesman for conduct-book ideology.

Even though Sir Thomas is abroad when his children begin to stage the theatricals, it is his disapproval that is most at stake, and the project ends the moment he returns. The patriarchal home had been literally and figuratively altered by the creation of a theater; Sir Thomas wastes no time in returning his house to its former state, going so far as to burn the actors' copies of the play they had been rehearsing. But while Austen offers us a range of reasons why the theatricals were improper, it is clear that to Sir Thomas, they were especially improper for women. Edmund is his mouthpiece when the older son, Tom, tries to justify the theatricals on the basis that their father had encouraged their practice in "anything of the acting, spouting, reciting kind" (126) and had had them perform bits of Shakespeare for them. Edmund makes a distinction based on gender: "It was a very different thing.—You must see the difference yourself. My father wished us, as school-boys, to speak well, but he would never wish his grown up daughters to be acting plays. His sense of decorum is strict" (127). We should note, again, the echo of the elocutionists' claim that reciting and acting serve to improve speech. Amateur acting, like reading, could be beneficial for men, "if it only gives a good emphasis, and improves the *speaking* of those who are to be our Senators."[58] Since women were not to become Senators, though, acting might be harmful in teaching them to speak with authority.

Again, what's at stake is the dictate that women be modest in speech.

The Mansfield theatricals were inspired by rehearsals at an aristocratic household that a guest of theirs had been visiting, and the conflict over private theatricals can be understood in part as a class conflict: aristocratic women were put on display as a matter of course; for the bourgeoise, the injunction to modesty was much stronger. In adopting the conservative morality of the conduct books, Sir Thomas participates in the "embourgeoisement" of the gentry (discussed in Chapter 1). For him, display is unseemly for women. In this, he agrees with commentators who argued that display is at odds with women's social function. In his "Remarks upon the Present Taste for Acting Private Plays" (1788), Richard Cumberland pointed to the conflict between acting and (bourgeois) maternal duties: the "Andromache of the Stage may have an infant Hector at home . . . ; he may be sick . . . and the maternal interest in the divided heart of the actress may preponderate over the Heroine's."[59] As Catherine B. Burroughs says, "Cumberland warned that this fashion 'should be narrowly confined to certain ranks, ages, and conditions in the community at large,' and that 'young women of humble rank and small pretensions should be particularly cautious how a vain ambition of being noticed by their superiors betrays them into an attempt at displaying their unprotected persons on a stage, however dignified and respectable'" (151). Thomas Gisborne, a conservative conduct-book writer, articulated the risks of women's display in strong terms:

> For some years past the custom of acting plays in private theatres, fitted up by individuals of fortune, has occasionally prevailed. It is a custom liable to this objection among others; that it is almost certain to prove, in its effect, injurious to the female performers. . . . What is . . . the tendency of such amusements? To encourage vanity; to excite a thirst of applause and admiration . . . ; to destroy diffidence, by the unrestrained familiarity with persons of the other sex, which inevitably results from being joined with them in the drama; to create a general fondness for the perusal of plays, of which so many are unfit to be read; and for attending dramatic representations, of which so many are unfit to be witnessed.[60]

While Sir Thomas is absent, Fanny and Edmund voice the conservative fears about women acting in theatricals. Fanny in particular is shocked that *Lovers' Vows,* a play that seems to justify affairs of the heart, "could be proposed and accepted in a private Theatre! Agatha and Amelia appeared to her in their different ways so totally improper for home representation—the situation of the one, and the language of the other, so unfit to be expressed by any woman of modesty, that she could hardly suppose her cousins could be aware of what they were engaging in" (137).

In considering amateur theatricals, conservative moralists noted that the enacting of passions could, through sympathetic identification, stamp those passions into women's characters. In the prologue to a play she wrote for a school performance, Hannah More cites this danger:

> And shall we then transplant these noxious scenes
> To private life? to misses in their teens?
> The pompous tone, the masculine attire,
> The stilts, the buskin, the dramatic fire,
> Corrupt the softness of the gentler kind,
> And taint the sweetness of the youthful mind.
> Ungovern'd passions, jealousy and rage,
> But ill become our sex, still less our age;
> Whether we learn *too well* what we describe,
> Or *fail* the poet's meaning to imbibe,
> In either case your blame we justly raise,
> In either lose, or ought to lose, your praise.
> How dull, if tamely flows th'impassion'd strain!
> If well—how bad to be the thing we feign;
> To fix the mimic scene upon the heart,
> And keep the passion when we quit the part![61]

This is, of course, just what happens in *Mansfield Park:* the intimacies among the characters of the play help develop illicit intimacies among the actors.

But if the theatricals threaten the health of Mansfield Park, a second form of display is treated as somewhat less dangerous: reading aloud. Authors like Mary Wollstonecraft, who acknowledged the harmful effects of women's acting, argued that reading aloud might be beneficial for them:

> Females are not educated to become public speakers or players; though many young ladies are now led by fashion to exhibit their persons on a stage, sacrificing to mere vanity that diffidence and reserve which characterizes youth, and is the most graceful ornament of the sex.
> But if it be allowed to be a breach of modesty for a woman to obtrude her person or talents on the public when necessity does not justify and spur her on, yet to be able to read with propriety is certainly a very desirable attainment.[62]

Yet Sir Thomas, ever the most conservative voice, clearly only encouraged his sons (and certainly not Fanny) to "spout." In this novel, reading is another suspicious form of display, reserved for men. Fanny performs domestic work by reading to amuse her languid aunt, but she does so only when no one else is present. When the men come in, she puts her book aside and Henry takes over.

A third kind of women's display is also suspect in this novel: accomplishments. As we saw above, many educators contrasted the acquisition of accomplishments with more solid forms of learning. In *Mansfield Park,* as well, accomplishments are forms of display that our heroine does *not* practice. Her Bertram cousins laugh at Fanny because her low status had prevented her from acquiring accomplishments; Mary Crawford is less rude to Fanny, but she clearly plays the harp primarily to gain Edmund's admiration. Accomplishments here represent the decadence of idleness. At the end of the novel, after the Bertram girls have both eloped (one adulterously), Sir Thomas blames himself for having had them educated in accomplishments rather than principled behavior: "To be distinguished for elegance and accomplishments—the authorized object of their youth—could have had no useful influence that way, no moral effect on the mind."[63] Here as always, Sir Thomas represents conduct-book norms.

Finally, in this novel Austen seems to extend her critique of display to women's speech as well, particularly Mary's, which is witty and self-serving. In this novel, unlike Austen's others, wit and judgment are incompatible, and the heroine is characteristically silent. Sir Thomas, again, serves as a touchstone for conservative morality, someone who is so hostile to women's speech that his own daughters cannot communicate with him. Sir Thomas awes and silences Fanny as well, even when he invites her comments: Fanny wishes she could tell him that Henry Crawford is unprincipled, "but her heart sunk under the appalling prospect of discussion, explanation, and probably non-conviction" (317). Fanny's deference and her preference for silence have made her a less approachable heroine than one like Elizabeth Bennet. We are so used to measuring worth by "air-time," it is hard to value a heroine who regularly listens to others' long speeches, answering briefly if at all. Even with her beloved Edmund, Fanny rarely speaks fully; "to sit silent and unattended to" is "her favourite indulgence" (223).

One sign of Austen's interest in Fanny's silence is that she represents it as so overdetermined. We can imagine that Austen was exploring the many causes of women's silence, along with its consequences. First of all, Fanny is (like Sarah Siddons) simply naturally shy. Unlike her blood sisters or her cousins, Fanny is fearful of new situations and prefers to remain in the background. In this, she hardly changes from her earliest childhood through the end of the book. Because other women in the novel are so unlike Fanny in this respect, we must understand this as a "merely" personal quality.

Second, Fanny is silent because of her youth; she is not "out." Early in the novel, Mary wonders whether Fanny is "out" and initiates a discussion of how girls who are and are not "out" speak differently. Mary claims that "A girl not out . . . looks very demure, and never says a word. You may smile—but it is so I assure you—and except that it is sometimes carried a little too far, it is all very proper. Girls should be quiet and modest. The most objectionable part is, that the alteration of manners on being introduced into company is frequently too sudden" (49). Henry agrees, with an anecdote about a girl from whom he could not drag a word, until she was "out" and "stared me out of countenance, and talked and laughed till I did not know which way to look" (50). Edmund, generally a spokesman for plain sincerity, replies that both modes are mere poses; "such girls are ill brought up." (50). But while we cannot imagine that Fanny's silence indicates that she is merely playing the role of a demure young girl, Austen does invite us to recognize youth as one factor in women's silence.

Third, if Fanny's silence results in part from her personal shyness and her youth, it also reflects her sense of her class position and her dependency on her wealthy relations. This sensitivity has been reinforced by her aunt Norris, who is keenly aware of "the nonsense and folly of people's stepping out of their rank" (221); she advises Fanny "not to be putting yourself forward, and talking and giving your opinion as if you were one of your cousins" (221). Even where the social situation might call for Fanny to do the conversational work, and even when Edmund criticizes her, Fanny resists asserting herself as an equal to the Bertrams:

"—You are one of those who are too silent in the evening circle."

"But I do talk to [my uncle] more than I used. I am sure I do. Did not you hear me ask him about the slave trade last night?"

"I did—and was in hopes the question would be followed up by others. It would have pleased your uncle to be inquired of farther."

"And I longed to do it—but there was such a dead silence! And while my cousins were sitting by without speaking a word, or seeming at all interested in the subject, I did not like—I thought it would appear if I wanted to set myself off at their expense, by shewing a curiosity and pleasure in his information which he must wish his own daughters to feel." (198)

Fanny's class position is in the middle, somewhere between the baronetcy of the family she lives with and the vulgarity of her birth family; Fanny's is the "middle" class of the conduct books. Fanny becomes especially conscious of bourgeois norms for women's speech when she visits her birth family in Portsmouth and is shocked at the way people shout all at once, interrupt, squabble, and curse. Her birth home is "the abode of noise, disorder, and impropriety" (388). Her disdain for noise reflects both class and gender considerations: gentility expresses itself with restraint, and women especially should not speak in the "fearless, self-defending tone" (379) on which Fanny's sister Susan relies. As the narrator remarks, "The elegance, propriety, regularity, harmony—and perhaps, above all, the peace and tranquillity of Mansfield, were brought to her remembrance every hour of the day, by the prevalence of everything opposite to them *here*. The living in incessant noise was to a frame and temper, delicate and nervous like Fanny's, an evil which no superadded elegance or harmony could have entirely atoned for. It was the greatest misery of all" (391). Among the Portsmouth family, representing a lower social stratum, "the men appeared to [Fanny] all coarse, the women all pert, every body underbred" (395).

At the other end of the scale, equally distant from Fanny's silence, is the witty and insincere speech of Mary Crawford, representing the world of fashion, which we glanced at in Chapter 2. Mary Crawford enacts the failings against which the conduct books warned. In her and in the Bertram sisters, with their serious moral lapses, the novel links the criticisms of display for women in all its forms—accomplishments, reading, acting, speech. Fanny refuses all of these forms of display, eventually earning the approval of our conduct-book ideologue, Sir Thomas. But just as Sir Thomas plays a more active part than do other Austen patriarchs, he is the only one whose moral development is highlighted. By the end of the novel, Sir Thomas has realized his error and regrets having silenced his daughters and his niece.

We return, then, to the problem articulated at the beginning of this chapter: how can a woman display without losing decorum? In *Mansfield Park,* Austen offers us a decorous heroine who avoids display and several selfish young women who do not, but (in contrast to her usual practice) she does not provide a model of the perfect middle. In other novels, Austen does create heroines who manage to speak, read, and play without losing their good sense or becoming immodest. *Mansfield Park,* though, makes the strongest argument that the discourses applied to display in musical and theatrical performance and in speech are inextricable. As we saw, many observers felt that Sarah Siddons's "everyday" speech had been colored by the roles she played on stage. That is, just as acting theorists feared that the passions you performed became a part of you (for better or for worse), the pronunciation of text influenced one's everyday linguistic practice. In Part II of *Speaking Volumes,* I will argue that the reading of literature was also performative and also contributed to the development of women's skill in speech.

PART II

Reading and Speech

CHAPTER 4

Reading and Domesticity Among the Burneys and Other Families

To the writer of fiction alone, every ear is open.
—A. L. Aikin (Barbauld), *Miscellaneous Pieces in Prose*

When Frances Burney published her first novel, *Evelina*, she was twenty-five years old and unusually self-effacing. Her letters and diaries, naturally enough, describe the unlooked-for success of the novel at great length, with a tone varying from shyly triumphant (The account begins, "This year was ushered in by a grand and most important event!"[1]) to genuinely apprehensive of potential criticism of the novel's quality or of her own presumption in publishing it. Burney writes not only of the book's reception in her immediate and extended family, but also of booksellers' gossip, published reviews, and the reactions of eminent figures in the literary world. Moreover, Burney records *how* her book was read, shared, and discussed. She describes at least six separate performances of the novel, and mentions many more, in an account that occupies more than fifty printed pages. That such a detailed account was written and preserved, we owe of course to Burney's stake as author. But while that explains the recording of these readings, the representation of the readings themselves is not "tainted" by that unusual circumstance. Most of the readers Burney describes did not know she was the author of the anonymous *Evelina* and did not read with especial attention or personal interest. Thus, Burney's account seems a reasonable representation of how a popular new book was read, shared, and discussed among the literate middle class in the late eighteenth century.

And the readings documented by Burney are, for the most part, *oral* readings, domestic performances interrupted by commentary on the text. The readings she describes were embedded in bourgeois domesticity: in caring for an invalid, in providing amusement during a long evening at home, in enjoying the shared privacy of the marital bedroom. These readings develop and support relationships among family and friends. Yet they also participate in the discourses about oral performance that we looked at in Chapter 3. Domestic reading adopted the techniques of the elocutionists, but tamed their goals. In schools and through manuals, young readers were trained to read "with propriety," that is, to perform a text correctly. But whereas the ostensible focus of the elocutionists, public reading, had as its goal persuasion, in domestic reading we see that reading functions to support new conceptions of familial relations.

The goal of this chapter is twofold: to offer a new account of the experience of literature during this period, and to examine the ways in which reading was a part of domestic relationships. I center the chapter around the Burney family because their reading is so well documented, but it is not my intention to add to the Burney biography. Rather, I use the Burney material as evidence for a more general argument; I assume that in its very richness it represents the many ways in which the oral performance of literature could function in bourgeois domestic life. This chapter will not consider, except in passing, the silent solitary reader who has been central to much scholarship on the period. The figure of the solitary reader—especially the woman reader—is an essential eighteenth-century trope, frequently cited in conflicts over domestic authority. The woman reader evokes anxieties surrounding large-scale social change and represents new uncertainties in class and gender relationships. But while the trope of the woman reader is meaningful, it does not convey the full range of actual practice. Instead, by reducing the variety of practices to one stereotype, the trope and the attention paid to it serve to establish the kind of falsely coherent category, "woman," that we have already seen describing "the" woman speaker.[2]

Accounts of "the" woman reader highlight what was most striking to contemporary observers, and most threatening, but other kinds of evidence demonstrate a wide range of reading experiences. Surviving diaries and letters, like those of the Burney family, show that reading could be silent and solitary or could be shared in the family circle; could be merely for amusement or for moral instruction; could (and did) have as many varied means and ends as reading does today. For example, Anna Larpent, the wife of the Inspector of Plays, left a seventeen-volume diary written between 1773 and 1828. According to John Brewer, the diary shows that Larpent read daily and voraciously; she was a confident critic of imaginative literature, a sub-

missive student of nonfiction, and a devout reader of pious works. Her religious devotions included solitary, intensive reading. Other works were discussed with family and friends. Still others were read aloud by members of
the household and by guests. In other words, Larpent read some works
intensively, others not; some privately, others aloud; and positioned herself
as reader or critic differently at different times.[3] Anna Larpent, like the
Burneys, was perhaps unusual in the prominence that literature took in her
life. But the range of her reading experiences reminds us to distinguish the
figure of the woman reader, discursively important as that is, from reading
as practiced by specific individuals.

In seeking to situate reading within domestic relationships, I will focus
primarily on the educated middle class and on the novel. In so doing, I recognize that I partially reproduce the limitations of both the trope of the
woman reader and the ensuing scholarship about her. Most accounts of
eighteenth-century literature explain the growth of new genres, like the
novel, as largely owing to the growth of a new reading audience.[4] Although
literacy rates at the end of the century remained low by our standards, contemporaries certainly perceived them as growing at an alarming rate. Much
commentary survives that expresses an anxiety about the extension of literacy—and the leisure to read—to middle-class women; like the discourse
about women's speech, part of what was at stake was a sense that class distinctions were being erased. Conversely, much of the suspicion expressed
about novels in the period arose from the awareness that novels addressed
concerns of the middle class and that, because the novel is not a learned
form, it could be written and read by those (like women) who had not received a classical education. The fact that so many novels celebrate middle-
class girls "marrying up" helps explain the conservative fears linking class,
gender, and genre.

The novel and the middle class offer rich evidence and relative clarity
regarding important issues about women, reading, and speech. Upper- and
lower-class reading have by contrast been neglected, though they, too, offer
many insights. Upper-class women had opportunities and positions of
authority that must skew our overly fixed notions of women's confinement.
And the discourse about lower-class readers demonstrates a heightened anxiety about the newly literate, particularly during the turmoil surrounding
the French Revolution, when radical texts could be read by potential riot-
ers. In *Village Politics,* for example, Hannah More instructs workers who are
reading Thomas Paine that they had better let the gentry do the reading for
them; when Jack asks Tom what he is reading and why he looks so grim,
Tom says, "Why I find here that I'm very unhappy, and very miserable;

which I should never have known, if I had not had the good luck to meet with this book." Even when not directly connected to revolutionary activity, lower-class reading is suspect. As More comments in her *Strictures on the Modern System of Female Education,*

> May the author be indulged in a short digression while she remarks, though rather out of its place, that the corruption occasioned by [novels] has spread so wide, and descended so low, as to have become one of the most universal, as well as most pernicious sources of corruption among us. Not only among milliners, mantua-makers, and other trades where numbers work together, the labour of one girl is frequently sacrificed, that she may be spared to read those mischievous books to the others; but she has been assured by clergymen who have witnessed the fact, that they are procured and greedily read in the wards of our hospitals! an awful hint, that those who teach the poor to read, should not only take care to furnish them with principles which will lead them to abhor corrupt books, but that they should also furnish them with such books as shall strengthen and confirm their principles.[5]

At the same time that Sunday schools were being founded to offer literacy to the working poor, the more privileged hoped that their reading would be limited to "appropriate" texts. Only a bookseller like James Lackington truly celebrated the opportunities offered to the newly literate (or at least, the new market for his wares):

> The sale of books in general has increased prodigiously within the last twenty years. . . . The poorer sort of farmers, and even the poor country people in general, who before that period spent their winter evenings in relating stories of witches, ghosts, hobgoblins, &c. now shorten the winter nights by hearing their sons and daughters read tales, romances, &c. and on entering their houses, you may see Tom Jones, Roderick Random, and other entertaining books, stuck up on their bacon racks, &c. If *John* goes to town with a load of hay, he is charged to be sure not to forget to bring home "Peregrine Pickle's adventures;" and when *Dolly* is sent to market to sell her eggs, she is commissioned to purchase "The history of Pamela Andrews." In short, all ranks and degrees now READ.[6]

While working-class reading deserves more study, I address the middle class for several reasons. One is evidentiary: as the site of contestation in the eighteenth century, the middle class attracted the bulk of the commentary and was the audience for quantities of treatises and works of literature. In addition, as Virginia Woolf reminds us, "towards the end of the eighteenth century a change came about which, if I were rewriting history, I should describe more fully and think of greater importance than the Crusades or the Wars of the Roses. The middle-class woman began to write."[7] That writing offers us access, however mediated, that is not available into the lower class, whose thoughts about themselves were less likely to be recorded.

But most important, I address the middle class (broadly defined, to exclude only the aristocracy and the poor) because of my interest in the link between reading and domesticity. Many scholars have argued that the eighteenth century saw the development of new forms of domestic relations—or at least new ways of describing them, characterized by an increasing emphasis on bonds of affection. The new focus on domesticity was associated with, though not limited to, the middle class and lower gentry; it was defined in opposition to the perceived moral failures of both the aristocratic world of fashion and the squalor of poverty. Over the course of the century, childhood began to be recognized as a separate and special time, for example, and descriptions of childhood are increasingly sentimental. It became less acceptable to send one's children out to nurse; motherhood began to be fetishized. At the same time, fathers were also expected to take more interest in their children and to participate more fully in domestic life. And expectations about marriage changed, so that prudential considerations had to be balanced with bonds of affection (this is, of course, what's at stake in so many novels). Scholars disagree about whether or not the nuclear family was a product of the late eighteenth century, but there is no question that discourse about family and private life became privileged in this period. In this chapter, I will call this ideology "domestic" or "bourgeois" or loosely "middle-class"; it should be emphasized that domestic ideology could be adopted by people of any social class.[8]

Since Foucault, scholars have tended to stress the negative aspects of an internalized domestic ideology: that the social obligation to marry or to care for children, for example, now entailed feeling specific emotions. What Lawrence Stone celebrated as "companionate marriage" has seemed to others a coercive intrusion into the soul (though they wouldn't use that word). Furthermore, scholars like Nancy Armstrong have argued that novels and other discursive forms were important means by which the values of domesticity were ingrained.

In this chapter, it will be important to keep both the coercive and the positive aspects of intimacy fully present. In the late eighteenth century, I will argue, family reading was a part of the development of bourgeois domesticity and participated in the struggles over power and intimacy that characterize domestic life. Reading together enabled family members to have a shared intellectual life; reading novels opened a forum for discussing the social and moral aspects of family life. But the reader was also in a position of power, a position that evoked the elocutionary orator. The reader (in

mixed company, generally a man) could censor texts and guide their interpretation, protecting his audience from the "dangers" of fiction.

Reading is a diverse activity that resists categorization. Reading is situated in a web of social life, bound by conventions shaping who can read and
when, what they seek in their reading, with whom they share it, and with
what meanings they invest it. Solitary reading in the eighteenth century
figured the escape from parental authority and, as such, attracted much
commentary. My interest is, rather, in family reading, for which there is
equal evidence and different insights to be gained. This chapter will address
three aspects of domestic reading: first, how the principles of elocution were
applied to family reading; second, how reading together fostered domestic
relationships; and third, how domestic reading affected the experience of literary texts. In this chapter, the consideration of women's speech will be
somewhat muted. My discussion of reading and domesticity rests on the
assumption that reading was a specific kind of oral performance, governed
like speech by gender norms; the more explicit connection between reading and speech will be made in Chapter 5.

Elocution Domesticated

If the discourse on the silent woman reader is articulated in the periodical press, that on domestic, shared reading comes to us through the elocution movement. In practical terms, the elocution movement attained its
widest influence not in the oratory of the pulpit or the bar, but in the reading practices of the bourgeois family. The goals and methods of the elocutionists directly influenced family reading: not only were the specifics of
how to read transmitted via schoolbooks to ordinary readers, but the person
of the reader accrued some of the authority and persuasiveness of the orator. Elocution shaped both the techniques of the reading of literature in the
home and the meanings assigned to the performance. Elocution began the
move into the home because the elocutionists' focus on natural speech led
them to recommend the reading of belles lettres; their theories were then
incorporated into lessons on belles lettres in schoolbooks. These schoolbooks reflect both the elocutionists' attention to the reader's position of
power and their specific advice regarding how texts should be read. Thus,
the elocution movement helped construct the figure of the domestic reader
and the oral performance of texts within the home. In this section, I will
describe the relation between elocution and domestic reading in general
terms; in the next sections, we will see how this functioned in the Burney
household and in other families.

The elocutionists considered themselves rhetoricians who happened to emphasize one branch of traditional rhetoric, delivery. We have seen that Sheridan's *British Education,* for example, argued that an improvement in English oratory would benefit all of society; Sheridan placed his argument in the context of classical oratory and civic virtue. But the elocutionists' examples and their instructions focus almost exclusively on the performance of texts written by others—on reading. This is not to say that elocution is not linked to larger issues in the philosophy of language: elocutionists do address questions that are recognizably modern, like "where does meaning lie?" and "how do we infer the author's intention?"[9] Sheridan, of course, also situated himself within a conversation going back at least to Plato, about whether written or oral language was superior. But for all of his emphasis on the "living" voice, Sheridan's advice (like that of all the elocutionists) concerns not oratory, but reading—not debate nor impromptu speech nor even the composition of speeches, but solely the reading of texts prepared by others.

The elocutionists thus blur the distinctions between reading and speaking. We see in many of their texts a slippage between the two words. In a chapter of his *Liberal Education* entitled "On Learning to Speak or Read with Propriety," Vicesimus Knox said bluntly, "Under speaking I comprehend reading" (1:191). This slippage is especially typical of the many schoolbooks that adapted the elocutionists' ideas, in which "speaking" may mean public speaking or ordinary conversation. For example, one of the most widely used school anthologies was William Enfield's *The Speaker* (1774). This is a collection of extracts from modern literature and from Shakespeare, with a few selections translated from Latin originals. The student is to prepare and perform these texts aloud. But Enfield's prefatory "Essay on Elocution" treats reading primarily as simply the easiest way to practice speech. He begins by reiterating "a very plain truth, that to be able to speak well is an ornamental and useful accomplishment. . . . Every one will acknowledge it to be of some consequence, that what a man has hourly occasion to do, should be done well" (v). Enfield sometimes is clear that his interest in reading is secondary to that of speaking; he offers a set of rules for reading his selections, which he considers "best adapted to form a correct and graceful Speaker" (vii). At other times, reading and speaking are jumbled together and the terms used interchangeably, for example, when he says, "In executing this part of the office of a speaker, it will by no means be sufficient to attend to the points [punctuation] used in printing" (xxi).

Since reading was the best way to practice speech, the elocutionists stressed the extent to which reading should imitate a "natural" speaking voice. One of their favorite targets was what they called "reading with a tone," a kind of chanting or sing-song voice that too many relied on both in reading the church service and in reading literature aloud. To combat reading with a tone, the elocutionists urged practitioners to read literary texts that were closer to ordinary language. In one of the earliest and most-quoted elocution texts, John Mason said, for example, "it will be advisable to begin with those Books that are written in a familiar Stile, that comes nearest to that of common Conversation; such as the *Pilgrim's Progress,* the *Family Instructor,* or some innocent *Novel.*"[10] Because of its claim to "naturalness," the novel was favored as a means to excellent reading and speaking. In his *Introduction to the Art of Reading with Energy and Propriety* (1765), John Rice, like many others, faults "unnatural" or declamatory reading: "Reading may, with Propriety, be called artificial Speaking; as it is, indeed, the Imitation of natural Eloquence. Hence, like all other imitative Arts, its End is defeated by every Appearance of Study, Habit, or Affectation. Any Peculiarity of Tone and Manner of Reading, therefore, must be disgustful, as it is unnatural" (9–10). Like Mason, Rice urges the reader to begin with texts that are closest to "natural" speech: narration first of all, then description, public speaking, and theatrical declamation.

The elocutionists' use of belles lettres invited the introduction of elocutionary ideas into schoolbooks. By the last quarter of the eighteenth century, the principles of elocution were widely taught and indeed dominated the teaching of reading in the schools. Of course primers had always linked reading and pronunciation, as they do today. What is interesting is how elocution was codified for older students and for literary texts. Sheridan, never one for modesty, took credit for the dissemination of elocutionary principles. Addressing "All Masters and Mistresses of Academies and Boarding Schools," he claims that since he first published his thoughts on elocution, "you have all, in your several advertisements, made the teaching of the art of reading and speaking English correctly, a material branch of your profession."[11] Advertisements for schools consistently linked reading with speaking, with "reading" always understood to mean "reading aloud." One school's advertisement stated that its students "are engaged in reading or hearing the best Authors in Divinity," while others promised to teach students to "speak, read, and write, with Propriety of Style."[12] Toward the end of the century, dozens of anthologies were compiled expressly for use in schools; these also tend to equate reading and speaking. We have already seen this in William Enfield's widely used *The Speaker;* his second anthology was called *Exercises in Elocution.*

As used by the elocutionists and the anthologists, the very term *reading* almost always meant "reading aloud." As John Rice put it, "the Art of Reading consists in conveying to the Hearer the whole Meaning of the Writer."[13] Furthermore, the anthologists participated in the patriotic enterprise that characterizes Sheridan's writing. English reading was to stand beside Latin—and "reading" here means both the delivery and the very choice of the selection. Because the most conversational texts were the best to practice reading, the anthologies gave a new kind of seriousness to English literature. Occasionally Latin was compared unfavorably to English as a language for practice in reading. James Buchanan argued that Latin education was useless. Furthermore, as a result of neglecting English, "A young gentleman who has had this education cannot read. For, to articulate the words, and join them together, I do not call reading, unless one can pronounce well, observe all the proper stops, vary the voice, express the sentiments, and read with a delicate intelligence."[14]

As Barbara M. Benedict has shown, eighteenth-century anthologies functioned to shape readers' taste and critical faculties. In contrast to early miscellanies, which offered a variety of texts and invited the reader to participate in the critical process, later eighteenth-century collections present a unified, depoliticized taste with which the reader is expected to concur.[15] Benedict bases her case primarily on anthologies of verse, but her claim is equally true of the prose collections that will be of interest here. Works like Enfield's *The Speaker,* William Scott's *Lessons in Elocution,* or Lindley Murray's *The English Reader* all reprinted the same sort of selections from Shakespeare, Blair, or Sterne, in effect creating a canon of English literature. Moreover, in a period in which English literature was still viewed with some suspicion, the anthologists guaranteed that their selections were "safe" and would improve morality. The naughty bits of Sterne were, needless to say, not included; by offering only sanitized extracts of longer works, the anthologies teach that we read for the "beauties," the moral and aesthetic touchstones of literary works. One popular work was explicit in this goal: *Beauties of Eminent Writers, Selected and Arranged for the Instruction of Youth in the Proper Reading and Reciting of the English Language,* by William Scott (1793).

To be sure, educators as different as Mary Wollstonecraft and Hannah More argued that reading for the "beauties" was superficial at best. For my purposes, what is most salient is that reading for "beauties" is closely associated with oral performance. The anthologies (at least those designated for schools) explicitly offered practice for (oral) reading and for speech, naming this purpose in their titles, in their prefaces, and in the arrangement of extracts. Their selections were organized into categories that reflected not content, but the performing situation. For example, Joseph Dana divided *A*

New American Selection of Lessons, in Reading and Speaking (1792) into two broad categories, "Lessons in Reading" and "Lessons for Reading and Speaking." The first includes short moral pieces from Blair, the *Spectator,* Goldsmith, and so on. In the second group are three subcategories (orations, dialogues, and poetry), which were felt by the elocutionists to have an especially strong oral quality. Similarly, William Scott's *Lessons in Elocution* was an anthology of pieces divided into two sections, "Lessons in Reading," which included mostly prose essays, and "Lessons in Speaking," which was entirely composed of speeches, either oratorical or theatrical. Yet both types of selections were intended to be recited by the student. Both of Enfield's schoolbooks, *The Speaker* and *Exercises in Elocution,* were divided into seven sections: narrative pieces, didactic pieces, argumentative pieces, orations and harangues, dialogues, descriptive pieces, and pathetic pieces. In his *Principles of Elocution,* John Wilson not only adopted similar categories but also prefaced each section with specific instructions on how narrative pieces, instructive pieces, poetry, and so on should be read.

Wilson's instructions are unusually explicit and will be considered again in Chapter 5. More commonly, the school anthologies were prefaced by general instructions on reading, usually reprints or adaptations of sections from elocutionists like Mason, Sheridan, Blair, or Walker. Mason and Sheridan had established the categories for the criticism of oral reading, which included loudness, pace, intonation, articulation (pronunciation), pauses and emphasis, and gesture. These provided the basis for all the later eighteenth-century advice and were generally codified into simple rules. As John Walker said, "The art of reading is that system of rules, which teaches us to pronounce written composition with justness, energy, variety, and ease."[16] William Enfield offers eight typical rules as a preface to *The Speaker,* with explanations, "as appear best adapted to form a correct and graceful Speaker" (vii):

1. Let your Articulation be distinct and deliberate. [Here he warns against non-standard pronunciations, against "cluttering," complex sounds, and against speaking too rapidly.]
2. Let your Pronunciation be bold and forcible. [The student should practice deep and vehement breathing.]
3. Acquire a compass and variety in the height of your voice. [Enfield warns against monotony and advises using a voice appropriate to the character and situation.]
4. Pronounce your words with propriety and elegance. [This partially reiterates rule 1, against provincial dialects.]
5. Pronounce every word consisting of more than one syllable with its proper ACCENT.

6. In every sentence, distinguish the more significant words by a natural, forcible, and varied EMPHASIS. [Since the elocutionists felt that emphasis conveys meaning, this was a key rule and required that the reader prepare the text ahead of time.]
7. Acquire a just variety of Pause and Cadence. [Enfield warns against overreliance on punctuation, which may mark grammar, not pronunciation.]
8. Accompany the Emotions and Passions which your words express, by correspondent tones, looks, and gestures. [Enfield avoids codifying gesture the way others had; he urges students to study nature.] [viii–xxvi]

Enfield's rules emphasize the kind of "correctness" that we considered in Chapter 3. They imply that every word and every text has one correct pronunciation and that the student need only determine the author's meaning to plan the corresponding tones, looks, and gestures. What is odd is that Enfield's rules are so disembodied. In the acting/elocution texts, the reader's goal is to mediate between two others: the author and the audience. The performer takes on the character and authority of the author in order to persuade the audience. But in Enfield's instructions, the author is referred to rarely and the audience not at all. Persuasion has been abandoned as a goal, in favor of the correct performance of abstract text. The emphasis on correctness may have served a similar function for students that it did for Sarah Siddons, emphasizing their dependent position.

Correctness is less crucial, and author and audience are more visible, in an essay reprinted in several schoolbooks, the chapter called "Pronunciation, or Delivery" from Hugh Blair's *Lectures on Rhetoric and Belles Lettres*. The specifics of Blair's advice are similar to Enfield's and the other authors', but he frames it in terms that evoke the rhetorical situation: "For, let it be considered, whenever we address ourselves to others by words, our intention certainly is to make some impression on those to whom we speak."[17] Blair asserts that the speaker/reader has two goals: "first, to speak so as to be fully and easily understood by all who hear him; and next, to speak with grace and force, so as to please and move his audience" (viii). He categorizes all the traditional rules under one or the other of these two goals. Simple understanding has four "chief requisites . . . a due degree of loudness of voice; distinctness; slowness; and propriety of pronunciation" (viii). Insufficient loudness and distinctness were often criticized, sometimes as "low" or "mumbling" speech. What Blair terms "precipitancy of speech" was also much criticized; although it is possible to read at an annoyingly slow pace, "the extreme of speaking too fast is much more common, and requires the more to be guarded against, because, when it has grown up into a habit, few errors are more difficult to be corrected" (ix). Under "Propriety of Pronunciation," Blair condemns both regional accents and errors of accentuation. He warns against overusing accents, as other elocutionists had; in his *Lectures on the Art of Reading,* Sheridan had complained that "there are few who either read aloud, or speak in public, that do not transgress this law of accent, by dwelling equally upon different syllables in the same word; such as fór-túne, ná-túre . . . &c" (1:125–26). The correctness implied by Blair's first four categories, then, asserts that the "best" English, the most "natural" English, is that spoken by the gentry of the south of England; and furthermore, that this pure English is required for one to be understood.[18]

Blair's next four subjects, "Emphasis, Pauses, Tones, and Gestures," are less about correctness than about exploiting the voice and body to move an audience. We have already seen these subjects explored in the elocution/acting texts, particularly Sheridan on acting and Burgh on expressing the passions (Chapter 3). What is notable is that these theatrical modes of speaking are now reproduced in schoolbooks; they are percolating down to domestic readers. In some of the schoolbooks, commonplace examples are enlivened for students: the standard example of the importance of emphasis (in Sheridan, "Shall you ride to town tomorrow?") is rendered as "Did the Englishman deserve to die?" in one text.[19] But beyond these details, Blair's essay recapitulates the paradox that students must be trained to express a text naturally. For him, as for Sheridan and others, "The signification of our sentiments, made by tones and gestures, has this advantage above that made by words, that it is the language of nature. . . . Words are only arbitrary, conventional symbols of our ideas" (vii). Since we persuade by convincing an audience of the sincerity of our emotions, it is essential to use tones and gestures correctly: "The speaker endeavors to transfuse into his hearers his own sentiments and emotions; which he can never be successful in doing, unless he utters them in such a manner as to convince the hearers that he feels them" (xiii). Where Enfield's rules are fairly abstract, Blair's essay brings the rhetorical aspect of elocution to the forefront; unlike Enfield's, Blair's reader is in a position of power.

As we noted in Chapter 1, elocutionary rhetoric is one of sentiment: the orator persuades by demonstrating his own sentiments and arousing those of his audience. This aspect of reading moved easily into the domestic sphere and the performance of literature. Overtly sentimental selections were among the most popular in the anthologies; perhaps the most popular of all was "Maria," a pair of excerpts from Laurence Sterne about the narrator's pity for a lovelorn maiden. Enfield used an illustration of Maria as the frontispiece for *The Speaker;* Mrs. Poplin of James Cobb's *English Readings* loved "Maria" best of all her performing texts. The reading of "Maria" could epitomize attitudes toward the vogue for sentimental fiction. In 1791, for example, Hester (Thrale) Piozzi recalled her daughters' reaction to it: "I remember many years ago, when Susan & Sophia came home one Time from Kensington School—Mrs Cumyn's; they used to repeat some Stuff in an odd Tone of Voice, & laugh obstreperously at their own Ideas—upon Enquiry we found out that 'twas the pathetic Passages in *Sterne's Maria* that so diverted & tickled their Spleen." And "Maria" is included in an anonymous 1799 text, *The Reader, or Reciter,* whose author explicitly contrasts his plan for excellent reading with the elocutionists' rules:

> The principal object of those who have hitherto written upon the subject, appears to have been that of marking the several points of punctuation with an equability of pauses, pointing out the emphatic word, and in fact labouring to make the reader uniformly accurate, while the spirit and animation of elocution are entirely neglected. To amend this defect, or rather to perform that which has been unattempted by them, is the intent of the following sheets. There is a certain glow and spirit of expression to be found in most of the productions of English Authors of eminence, that if kept alive in the delivery, a sentence will be thereby impressed upon the mind with irresistible effect; but if neglected, . . . although correctness be strictly attended to, still all will seem dull, tame, and insipid.[20]

Interspersed with the text of "Maria" (and all his selections), the author gives instructions like "There must be a melancholy simplicity breathe throughout your expression in reading whatever Maria says" (99) and "your delivery of [these lines] must bear strong marks of genuine and unfeigned sincerity" (100). The performance of sentimental passages like these was especially closely connected to the affective function of family reading.

Through schoolbooks and anthologies, the principles of elocution became widely known among those who had access to education. We saw in Chapter 3 that Jane Austen assumed the reader of *Mansfield Park* could follow a discussion of elocution. In other texts, the more absurd features of elocution were etched in comedy. Laurence Sterne included a parody of elocution in *Tristram Shandy,* in which Corporal Trim reads a sermon he happened to find in a book to Tristram's father, his uncle Toby, and Dr. Slop (the man-midwife) while Tristram's mother is in labor. Like much of Sterne's book, the scene and its targets are ambiguous. The passage begins with an excessively detailed description of Trim's stance while reading, a scene that Hogarth illustrated at Sterne's request. Trim holds the sermon in his left hand, has most of his weight on his right leg, and leans toward his audience, left leg bent. His right arm is at his side, palm open, ready to be waved about at climactic moments. Sterne is often mystifying, and it is not quite clear why so much attention is paid to this (the description is several pages long) nor what Sterne's attitude toward it is. Probably, he is teasing about the kinds of formal rules about the oratorical stance that were illustrated in some elocution texts.

Corporal Trim is the epitome of the sentimental reader who would later be described by Blair. At the very beginning of his reading, he is reminded of his brother, who has been a captive of the Inquisition for fourteen years. The story of the brother interrupts the reading, and Trim's emotion affects his audience: "——The tears trickled down *Trim's* cheeks faster than he could well wipe them away:—A dead silence in the room ensued for some minutes.——Certain proof of pity!" (1:144). But Trim gets most involved when the sermon refers directly to the Inquisition. He drops the text in agony, moving all three members of his audience. He tries to begin again, but finds he cannot, and so Tristram's father carries on. Though Trim's emotional stance makes reading impossible, it becomes a matter for praise:

> Thou hast read the sermon extremely well, *Trim,* quoth my father.—If he had spared his comments, replied Dr. *Slop,* he would have read it much better. I should have read it ten times better, Sir, answered *Trim,* but that my heart was so full.—That was the very reason, *Trim,* replied my father, which has made thee read the sermon as well as thou hast done; and if the clergy of our church, continued my father, addressing himself to Dr. *Slop,* would take part in what they deliver, as deeply as this poor fellow has done,—as their compositions are fine (I deny it, quoth Dr. *Slop*) I maintain it, that the eloquence of our pulpits, with such subjects to inflame it,—would be a model for the whole world. (1:164–65)

Trim's performance exemplifies sentimental reading and its effect on both performer and audience. Also notable for my purposes, however, is the way behavior is gendered here. This is a stag affair. It occurs, we remember, while Mrs. Shandy is upstairs going through labor; the spatial separation reflects the division into separate spheres. She is doing what is most female (giving birth), while they are doing what is typically male (engaging in a shared intellectual exercise). What is most humorous about this scene is the way the men constantly interrupt Trim to comment either on the quality of his performance or on the sermon's content. Trim has only gotten through one sentence when Walter Shandy breaks in with, "Certainly, *Trim,* . . . you give that sentence a very improper accent; for you curl up your nose, man, and read it with . . . a sneering tone" (1:143). Much time is also devoted to the theological import of the sermon, with Dr. Slop (a Catholic) pointing out every possible heresy, and the others defending the Protestant position. As the person of lowest status in the group, Trim can rarely hold the floor for very long. Instead, his performance is the occasion for the others to

4. Trim reading (1761). Engraved by Hogarth for *Tristram
Shandy*. (Harry Ransom Humanities Research Center,
The University of Texas at Austin)

comment and to debate (at least until Dr. Slop falls asleep). Reading is presented as an active, participatory, critical—and male—activity.

   We cannot be surprised that the figure of the orator as described in the
elocution texts is male, nor that schoolbooks by and large assume a male
audience. The elocutionists generally mentioned women only as the first
teachers of sons; since their explicit concern was with the public speech of

ite, the pulpit, and the bar, women could safely be ignored. The ...ooks also generally direct their attention to boys. To give only a few examples, Vicesimus Knox thought boys should begin to practice public speaking at age thirteen; his chapter "On the Literary Education of Women" does not mention oral performance. John Walker's detailed description of how to stand while reading includes illustrations—of adolescent boys. The pieces anthologized in William Scott's *Lessons in Elocution* under "Lessons in Speaking" are either speeches by men or dramatic scenes with only male characters; the book is most appropriate for boys.[21] Given the social hierarchies of the day, we would expect that the reader, like the orator, is generally configured male. But Sterne shows us not only a male orator but a male audience, active, commenting, critical. This audience is engaged in a shared intellectual enterprise that serves both to individuate the participants and to bind them together.

It is against this background that the figure of the solitary woman reader becomes meaningful. If Sterne's portrait typifies male reading (however humorously), the discursive figure of the female reader posits its binary opposite. Men read serious moral or intellectual material and discuss it critically; women read low-status works and keep no critical distance. As Elizabeth Long puts it, the solitary woman reader "finds her ideological place in a binary opposition that associates authoritative men with the production and dissemination of serious or high culture, and even privileged women with the consumption and 'creation' of ephemeral or questionable culture." Or, in Ina Ferris's words, "The striking thing about the characterization of female reading is that it makes reading an act of the body rather than the mind."[22] Diaries like those of Anna Larpent demonstrate that educated women in fact read much serious literature and that their reading practice was varied both in the works they read and in the ways they approached those works. Still, while the trope of the solitary female reader in no way captures the range of actual practice, let us look at it for a moment to highlight the ways it contrasts with reading as taught by the elocutionists.[23]

The criticisms of the woman reader were widespread in the eighteenth century, but they harp on the same few themes. One of these was that women were neglecting their duties if they spent time reading. The growth of capitalism both enabled this practice and can account for the hostility to it. On the one hand, women who only a generation before might have spent their time working in the domestic economy (raising pigs, canning, etc.) now did have more leisure time for more "genteel" pursuits. On the other hand, it was the fear of this rising class that may have motivated some of the criticism. But it is notable that the fear was articulated primarily against women. Not uniformly, of course: Johnson's critique of novel-readers as "the young, the ignorant, and the idle" was gender-neutral.[24] But most of the attacks were against women. Sterne's example reminds us that women should be bearing children, not reading. Women's reading is typically imagined in places of leisure. One frequent complaint is that women read while having their hair dressed, so that the next reader finds hair powder between the pages. A reviewer in the *Monthly Review* notes "that nothing is more common than to find hair-powder lodged between the leaves of a novel; which evinces the corresponding attention paid to the inside as well as to the outside of a modern head."[25] Women readers are portrayed as idle, just killing time. Literary representations of women's reading often take place in resort areas, especially Bath, the setting for George Colman's *Polly Honeycombe,* Sheridan's *The Rivals,* Smollett's *Humphry Clinker,* and Austen's *Northanger Abbey,* all of which mock silly women readers.

Another theme of the criticisms was that women read badly: they read bad literature (that is, novels); they skimmed through what they did read; they misinterpreted; they were incapable of maintaining a critical distance from the text. In each of the works set in Bath (above), and in others like *The Female Quixote* by Charlotte Lennox, women are portrayed as bad readers because they have poor judgment about the texts. Most frequently, the fear expressed is that women imagine that novels accurately represent reality and thus that novels instill unrealistic expectations about the kind of suitor a woman will attract. The heroine of *The Rivals* insists that her lover must be a "romantic" ensign; she rejects the suitor chosen for her by her guardians in favor of the poor Beverley. (Luckily for her, Ensign Beverley turns out to be the approved suitor in disguise.) In other cases, the fear expressed is that women will be seduced by men who resemble novelistic heroes. Rousseau, famously, declared in the preface to *La nouvelle Héloïse,* "Jamais fille chaste n'a lu de romans" ("No chaste girl ever read novels"); he seems to have meant this quite seriously.[26] George Colman puts it more comically in the prologue to *Polly Honeycombe:*

> 'Tis not alone the Small-Talk and the Smart,
> 'Tis NOVEL most beguiles the Female Heart.
> Miss reads—she melts—she sighs—Love steals upon her—
> And then—Alas, poor girl!—good night, poor Honour! (xv)

The novel-reading woman was exposed to moral danger because she granted authority to texts that had not been approved by her parents; these texts might inculcate a moral code different from the one in which she was brought up. In the late eighteenth century, this threat is focused on the choice of a marriage partner exactly because custom was shifting from parental choice to allowing the partners to choose for themselves. But the problem is more general and has to do with hermeneutical practices. Had women been "better" readers, they would have been inoculated against any potential harm. The danger lies as much in the reader's lack of judgment as in the texts themselves.

The reading of literature involves both sympathetic identification and critical judgment. In the late eighteenth century, it was the former that was seen as troublesome, because readers were thought to identify excessively. The quality of sympathetic identification was essential to eighteenth-century moral theories like those of Hume and Smith: when we feel the emotions of an other we are most likely to enact virtue. Sentimental literature works by arousing our emotions, but sympathetic identification raised questions about the boundaries or fluidity of the self. In discussions of literature, the risk was always portrayed as the loss of self or loss of critical distance. Catherine Gallagher argues that midcentury writers like Lennox and Johnson believed that sympathy would be limited to the time during which one was actively engaged with the text, that it would have no permanent effect. Later the situation changed: "The sentimental reader came to be portrayed not as an affective speculator, capable of entering and abandoning emotions, but as an emotional addict, craving fictional identification and powerless to disengage from it."[27]

The best-known examination of the dangers of sympathetic identification—paired with a spirited defense of the novel as genre—is in Austen's *Northanger Abbey*. Catherine Morland, the novel's heroine, becomes a devoted reader of gothic novels while staying in Bath, chaperoned by an inattentive family friend. With no parental oversight, Catherine is guided in her reading by another young woman, Isabella Thorpe, who turns out to be both a bad reader and an insincere friend. But before the break between them, the two women read and discuss all the latest works of horror. Catherine's obsession with gothics is dramatized when she visits the home of the Tilney family, the titular abbey, and imagines that she is in a location replete with mystery and even, perhaps, murder. Catherine's imaginings have been encouraged not only by her own reading, however, but by the hero, Henry Tilney, who teasingly leads her to expect that Northanger Abbey will resemble a gothic castle—then berates her when she has done so.

But as every good reader realizes, Austen's target is not novels themselves, nor even gothic novels, but bad readers of novels. Lest the reader miss the point, Austen includes her most direct defense of the novel, in a brief digression responding to criticism of the genre by both (male) critics and (female) novelists and readers. She imagines a "typical" female reader who is caught reading a novel:

—"And what are you reading, Miss—?" "Oh! it is only a novel!" replies the young lady; while she lays down her book with affected indifference, or momentary shame.—"It is only Cecilia, or Camilla, or Belinda;" or, in short, only some work in which the greatest powers of the mind are displayed, in which the most thorough knowledge of human nature, the happiest delineation of its varieties, the liveliest effusions of wit and humour are conveyed to the world in the best chosen language. (*NA* 38)

More important, the most admirable characters are also avid readers of novels, including gothics. Henry Tilney claims to have read "hundreds and hundreds" of them and to have especially enjoyed the gothics of Ann Radcliffe: "The Mysteries of Udolpho, when I had once begun it, I could not lay down again:—I remember finishing it in two days—my hair standing on end the whole time" (106). Henry can read with the sympathetic identification required to enjoy the horrors of a gothic novel. But he can also recognize the boundaries that must keep novelistic and realistic expectations separate. What Henry and his sister can do is to balance sympathetic identification and critical judgment. We see how this is achieved in the conversation that follows, which moves from gothics to language to history to aesthetics, and in which Henry and Miss Tilney demonstrate their taste and judgment. If "bad" reading results from too much sympathetic identification, "good" reading habits can incorporate potentially dangerous texts by placing them within a wider critical context.

The same function can be served by the elocutionary performer. The reader of Austen's time, trained in elocution, would have conceived of himself as a figure of power, taking the place of the orator, and interpreting the text for his audience. Through his reading and his discussion, he could protect his family from dangerous texts.

Patriarchal Reading

Whether performed silently or aloud, alone or in company, reading is a social practice, its meanings influenced by cultural constructions. In shifting from the public realms considered by the elocutionists to the domestic circle, we must retain something of the authority and power of the orator, but combine that with self-consciously companionate relationships. That is, domestic reading could partake of both the disciplinary force of the patriarch and the kinds of intimacy that were sought by bourgeois families of the

late eighteenth century. Reading together could tame the potentially harmful effects of imaginative literature, including novels, by guiding the interpretation of fiction and by interrupting sympathetic imagination.

The reader was imagined by the elocutionists as someone in a position
of authority, using his rhetorical skills to persuade his audience in the senate, the pulpit, or the bar. In the reading of literature in the home, "persuasion" becomes more a matter of "affecting" or "moving." But the position
of reader still retained its connotations of authority. The reader held the
floor, as feminist linguists say, commanding attention from listeners who
were in the more passive position. Poor Corporal Trim, in *Tristram Shandy,*
is the comic inversion of the authoritative reader: he is the person of lowest
status in the room and is interrupted incessantly. We must infer that the
more normal pattern was just the opposite: the reader would be of high status and consequently rarely interrupted.

It is certain, and not surprising, that in mixed company the reader was
almost always a man. In Austen's novels, Mr. Collins, Mr. Elton, Mr. Martin,
Henry Crawford, and others read to women; and in Austen's family, her
father and her brother James. Austen does frequently mention women reading in her letters, but only when no men are present. Women usually read
only among themselves: as I mentioned in Chapter 3, in *Mansfield Park,*
Fanny Price reads Shakespeare to her aunt, but puts the book aside when the
men come in, and Henry continues the reading (*MP* 336–37). Similarly, in
Walter Scott's *Antiquary,* the heroine's father asks her to read, but she and the
other men present completely ignore the request, and three possible (male)
readers are considered before the hero is drafted. Even Mary Wollstonecraft
expresses doubt that a woman should ever read to a man. In a review of a
novel, she says the authoress claims to have read her work to a celebrated
clergyman, who criticized it and whom Wollstonecraft imagines urging the
authoress to throw it into the fire. Yet even so, says Wollstonecraft, "She has
not sufficient judgment—we had almost said modesty—to follow such
sound advice, or she could never have written, and afterwards read (to a
man) the unnatural tragi-comic tale we have just been laughing at."[28]

Because the position of the reader represented a kind of authority,
domestic reading could reinforce the patriarchal relationship. Much of the
fear of literature's effect derived from the risk of sympathetic identification;
this risk was reduced when literature was read aloud in the family circle. As
listener, rather than reader, a young woman was another step removed from
the text. She experienced the text in a mediated form, interpreted by an
authority figure who might interrupt his reading to comment on the text
(further disrupting sympathy) and whose reading itself necessarily involved

interpretation. Domestic reading, as influenced by the elocution movement, could thus be understood as protecting women against potentially dangerous texts while it reinforced the bonds of intimacy and discipline that characterize family life.

The process of guiding the reception of literature while fostering intimate relationships is perhaps best demonstrated with reference to younger children. Eighteenth-century educators did not, of course, press parents to read to their children with the same urgency that parents hear today. But the impulse was rather the same. Here, for example, is the introduction to *Evenings at Home; or, the Juvenile Budget Opened,* an anthology for young people compiled by John Aikin and Anna Laetitia (Aikin) Barbauld; it is worth quoting at length:

> The mansion-house of the pleasant village of *Beachgrove* was inhabited by the family of Fairborne, consisting of the master and mistress, and a numerous progeny of children of both sexes. Of these, part were educated at home under their parents' care, and part were sent out to school. The house was seldom unprovided with visitors, the intimate friends or relations of the owners, who were entertained with cheerfulness and hospitality, free from ceremony and parade. They formed, during their stay, part of the family; and were ready to concur with Mr. and Mrs. Fairborne in any little domestic plan for varying their amusements, and particularly for promoting the instruction and entertainment of the younger part of the household. As some of them were accustomed to writing, they would frequently produce a fable, a story, or dialogue, adapted to the age and understanding of the young people. It was always considered as a high favour when they would so employ themselves; and after the pieces were once read over, they were carefully deposited by Mrs. Fairborne in a box, of which she kept the key. None of these were allowed to be taken out again till all the children were assembled in the holidays. It was then made one of the evening amusements of the family to *rummage the budget,* as their phrase was. One of the least children was sent to the box, who putting in its little hand, drew out the paper that came next, and brought it into the parlour. This was then read distinctly by one of the older ones; and after it had undergone sufficient consideration, another little messenger was dispatched for a fresh supply; and so on, till as much time had been spent in this manner as the parents thought proper. Other children were admitted to these readings; and as the *Budget of Beachgrove Hall* became somewhat celebrated in the neighbourhood, its proprietors were at length urged to lay it open to the public. They were induced to comply; and have presented its contents in the promiscuous order in which they came to hand, which they think will prove more agreeable than a methodical arrangement. (1–3)

Aikin and Barbauld offer a frame story within which the reader should contextualize the pieces of their anthology. We are in the realm of the domesticated gentry, owners of a mansion house but whose lives center on the education of their numerous children. Even guests are linked to the project of domestic education and willingly contribute their efforts. However, what Aikin and Barbauld draw our attention to is not the contributed writings themselves, but rather how they are protected from promiscuous use, being read only under highly controlled circumstances. We note that Mrs. Fairborne reads the pieces first (no doubt to ensure they include no indelicacy), then "deposits" them in a box as if they are cash; using the old-fashioned term "budget" for the box that held the manuscripts makes explicit the link between family reading and bourgeois (economic) virtue.

The readings themselves are highly ritualized, taking place only during holidays when the whole family is gathered. The younger children may only draw the pieces out of the box; the older ones read it "distinctly" (presumably any mumbling is corrected) and then the piece is discussed. The domestic reading that is modeled here is shared with neighboring families, and then with the purchaser of the volume in hand. Thus the reading is embedded in layers of both discipline and intimacy. The only room for serendipity is in the random order with which the young children pull the stories out of the budget; the author's highlighting of this "promiscuous order" serves only to reinforce the extent of the control of the reading.

In *Evenings at Home,* the reader is not an established authority figure but a child being trained for that role. More usually, to repeat, the reader was a mentor of some kind—a parent and a guardian of moral values. Reading "with" children and adolescent girls was often recommended to mothers, again both to shape the children's understanding of the literature and to maintain an intimate relationship. Thus, the reader exerted control both over the text and over the listener. The late eighteenth century saw an increasing number of works of children's literature, which were presumably guaranteed to be inoffensive. The advice books concentrate, rather, on the potentially harmful fiction (that is, novels) that older children and adolescents might read. Mary Hays urges a mother to read "with" her daughters, contrasting *reading* with the word usually reserved for silent reading, *perusal:* "Yet do not mistake me, nor suppose that I mean to recommend the indiscriminate perusal of romances and novels; on the contrary, I think with you, that the generality of works of this kind are frivolous, if not pernicious." But reading "with" children helps them develop the critical distance that disrupts sympathetic identification:

> Accustom your daughters by a cheerful and amiable frankness, to do nothing without consulting you; let them read with you, and let the choice of their books be free. Converse with them on the merits of the various authors, and

accustom them to critical and literary discussions. They will soon be emulous of gaining your approbation by entering into your ideas, and will be ashamed of being pleased with what you ridicule as absurd, and out of nature, or disapprove, as having an improper and immoral tendency.[29]

Mary Hays's advice to let a daughter read anything as long as you guide her reading is typical of the more liberal educators. In his *Plan for the Conduct of Female Education in Boarding Schools,* Erasmus Darwin argued that reading together is even more effective than censorship. Expunged texts may serve to arouse the reader's curiosity; "it is therefore perhaps better, when these books are read to a governess, that she should express disapprobation in a plain and quiet way of such passages" (37). Mary Wollstonecraft also recommended that girls' reading be guided, rather than censored:

> The best method, I believe, that can be adopted to correct a fondness for novels is to ridicule them: ... if a judicious person, with some turn for humour, would read several to a young girl, and point out both by tones, and apt comparisons with pathetic incidents and heroic characters in history, how foolishly and ridiculously they caricatured human nature, just opinions might be substituted instead of romantic sentiments.[30]

The advice of Hays, Darwin, and Wollstonecraft assumes that the reader can control unruly works of literature. By contrast, more conservative authors may recommend simply denying access to potentially dangerous texts, an approach exemplified by the lists of "approved" books appended to conduct books. For example, Austen demonstrates Fanny Price's conduct-book modesty by her reluctance to choose: when she dares to subscribe to a circulating library, she is "amazed at her own doings in every way; to be a renter, a chuser of books!" (*MP* 398). But reading "with" a daughter reinforces not only literary taste but the bonds of intimacy and of discipline that characterize domestic relations.

The tension between discipline and intimacy is especially evident in the discourse about the authority of fathers within a domestic ideology. Where Lawrence Stone celebrated the "affective individualism" that he argues supported a newly dominant nuclear family, other scholars take issue with two of Stone's major points, either setting the dominance of the nuclear family further back in time or (of more relevance here) questioning the whiggishness of Stone's narrative. For these scholars, "affective individualism" merely internalized the disciplinary functions of earlier modes, but was at least as coercive. As the sole property owner and legal head of the household, the father's power was absolute throughout the eighteenth century; the new attentiveness to bonds of affection could not but be tangled with coercive and disciplinary forces. In fact, as Caroline Gonda argues, theorists like Locke described affective relations as the best way to maintain parental authority. This stress on "the tactical importance of inculcating filial love" remained prominent in conduct books; in the words of James Nelson, "At the same time that the Authority of Parents is to be maintain'd above every other Consideration, Children should be taught to love them to a superlative Degree. This Love in Children to their Parents, will naturally make them fly to them on every Emergence; and thus Obedience will become a Pleasure."[31]

The tension between parental authority and bonds of affection is amply demonstrated in the literature of the period, where (to repeat) plots often crystallized around the choice of a marriage partner. In the middle of the century, the question for Richardson's *Clarissa* is, do women have the right to refuse the partner chosen by their parents? Later, as in Austen, the burden has shifted to the younger generation, and the question often becomes, can a woman find a marriage partner of whom her parents will approve? Yet eighteenth-century literature is also replete with scenes that directly emphasize the father-daughter relationship, in ways that sound mawkish or even shockingly close to incestuous to modern ears. In Burney's *Evelina,* the first meeting between father and daughter entails the physical manifestations of sensibility like fainting, wailing, and embracing, yet this is also a tale that is preeminently about paternal authority and responsibility. Patriarchal reading, as influenced by the elocution movement, participated in the sentiment, intimacy, and authority portrayed in these works.

Let us return for a while to the Burney family, whose papers capture the complexity of bourgeois domesticity and reading's role in its maintenance. Charles Burney (Frances's father) was in some ways the very archetype of the "new" reader, the beneficiary of mid-eighteenth-century print culture. The son of an impecunious musician and painter, Charles suffered an unsettled childhood and humble education, but was determined to succeed through his talents and began a program of self-education. He was well along in his program when, while apprenticed to the composer Thomas Arne, he came to the attention of the aristocratic Fulke Greville, who had asked his harpsichord maker to produce a musician who was "fit company for a gentleman."[32] Though Burney remained with Greville for a relatively short time, he made important acquaintances during this period and began his march of upward mobility. After beginning his career in London, Burney was forced by ill health to move to King's Lynn (Norfolk) for what would turn out to be nine years. During this period, he continued his self-education, initiated a correspondence with another self-made man, Samuel Johnson, obtained an introduction, and on his return to London was admitted to Johnson's circle. Burney eventually reached his goals, becoming the first eminent music historian and transforming himself into a man of let-ters. Much as Sarah Siddons would her acting, Burney successfully trans-formed a talent that formerly would have relegated him to the status of an exalted servant into great respectability (the notion that a musician should be a genius was still a few years in the future).

Burney, then, epitomizes bourgeois industry and self-improvement, in the context of the development of modern professional culture. We are for-tunate that he, like his daughter, left ample written records of his project. His descriptions often sound Franklin-esque: he records the impression made upon him by someone who told him, "When I was a young man, I determined never to go to bed at night, till I knew something that I did not know in the morning."[33] While riding the long distances to the homes of his music students, he studied the works of Dante and Petrarch, carrying the volume of poetry in one pocket and a dictionary he had copied out for himself in the other.[34]

A supremely sociable person, Burney also pursued his self-improvement program in ways that were situated firmly within his domestic life. While waiting for his wife to join him in King's Lynn, he wrote her a long poem, in rhyming tetrameter, describing how the two of them would improve themselves. In her *Memoirs of Doctor Burney,* Frances Burney includes the poem to convey "some idea of the sympathy and the purity of his marriage happiness, by the rare picture which these lines present of an intellectual lover in a tender husband" (1:91). Here are some sections:

> Come, my darling!—quit the town;
> Come!—and me with rapture crown.
> . . .
> [Burney describes some future amusements, then continues.]
> If these delights you deem too transient,
> We modern authors have, or antient,
> Which, while I've lungs from phthisicks freed,
> To thee with rapture, sweet, I'll read.
> . . .
> To humanize and mend the heart,
> Our serious hours we'll set apart.
> . . .
> We'll learn to separate right from wrong,
> Through Pope's mellifluous moral song.
> If wit and humour be our drift,
> We'll laugh at knaves and fools with Swift.
> . . .
> [Burney refers to other English authors, then continues.]
> May heaven, all bounteous in its care,

These blessings, and our offspring spare!
And while our lives are thus employ'd,
No earthly bliss left unenjoy'd,
May we—without a sigh or tear—
Together finish our career! (1:91–93)

In King's Lynn, the Burneys were part of "a bookish little coterie that assembled weekly at Mrs. Stephen Allen's" (1:117–18). Burney read Johnson's *Rambler* and *Idler* essays to this group in an exercise combining self-improvement and friendship. In these readings, Burney "became" Johnson, performing with the elocutionary skill and sincere emotion that arouse sympathy in his audience. As Frances Burney described it,

> the charm expanded over these meetings, by the original lecture [that is, reading] of these refined and energetic lessons of life, conduct, and opinions, when breathed through the sympathetic lips of one who felt every word with nearly the same force with which every word had been dictated, excited in that small auditory a species of enthusiasm for the author, that exalted him at once in their ideas, to that place which the general voice of his country has since assigned him, of the first writer of his age. (1:118)

Shared reading, shared taste, and a shared moral sense work together to bind these friends in their personal relationships and to link them to a growing national readership.

As Charles Burney and his wife raised their children, reading together was a large part of their domestic life. Frances's mother died when Frances was only ten, but her readings were remembered fondly. Many years later, Frances described watching and listening as her mother read with her elder sister:

> Your mind, my dearest Esther, was always equal to literary pursuits. . . . I have often thought that had our excellent and extraordinary OWN mother been allowed longer life, she would have contrived to make you sensible of this sooner. I do not mean in a common way, for *that* has never failed, but in one striking and distinguished; for she very early indeed began to form your taste for reading, and delighted to find time, amidst all her cares, to guide you to the best authors, and to read them with you, commenting and pointing out passages worthy to be learned by heart. . . . Well I recollect your reading with our dear mother all Pope's Works and Pitt's *Aeneid*. I recollect, also, your spouting passages from Pope, that I learned from hearing you recite them before—many *years* before I read them myself. But after you lost, so young, that incomparable guide, you had none left.[35]

Reading together fosters domestic relationships, but the disciplinary aspect of family reading is at least as prominent in the Burney family papers, particularly in interactions between Charles and Frances. This father-daughter relationship epitomizes the power of affective bonds within a patriarchal system. Frances was the perfect daughter, dedicating her works to Charles, copying his out (she had to disguise her hand in copying her own *Evelina* lest the printer recognize her as the author), and later editing the papers he had left into his *Memoirs*. Some critics have faulted Frances Burney for being too much the perfect daughter, too concerned with propriety. Betty Rizzo argues that propriety was so essential to Charles and Frances for two good reasons: on the one hand, because their position in society was so fragile and entirely based on merit; on the other, because their family had so many skeletons to hide, including illegitimate births and incest.[36]

Charles's affectionate authority over Frances was expressed in many ways. For example, she agreed, for the sake of the family, to accept a position at court and to remain there for several years in a situation that was stifling to her and that led to a serious illness. But another example demonstrates more directly the authoritarian aspect of domestic reading: Charles's censorship of a play Frances wrote soon after her success with *Evelina,* a comedy evoking the ridiculous aspects of the Bluestockings, entitled *The Witlings.*

Always aware of the precariousness of his social position, Charles seems to have squelched the play because it might have offended socially prominent people like the Bluestockings (it involved characters like "Lady Smatter" and "Mrs. Voluble," who speaks stereotypical woman's language); it is also possible that he was himself offended by a character he may have read as an attack on himself. In any case, what is important here is that his censorship is so closely tied to oral reading. Charles had apparently already read and approved of the first three acts of this five-act comedy. Parts of the manuscript had also been read and praised by the dramatist Arthur Murphy and had been read aloud by Frances to Hester Thrale. But when the manuscript was complete and Frances wanted to read it to her "second" father, Samuel Crisp, Charles insisted on taking it himself and performing it solo.

According to Frances's sister Susanna, the reading was in general a success, with Samuel Crisp remarking "It's *funny*—it's *funny* indeed" and another sister, Charlotte, laughing "till she was almost black in the face." But Susanna's description of the reading gives an inkling of Charles's reaction:

> The fifth [act] was more generally felt—but to own the truth it did not meet all the advantages one could wish—My Father's voice, sight, & lungs were tired . . . & being entirely unacquainted with what was coming not withstanding all his good intentions, he did not always give the Expression you meant to be given— Yet he exerted himself . . . to give it force & Spirit—& except this Act, I believe only yourself would have read the play better.[37]

After this reading, Charles turned absolutely against the play and insisted that Frances abandon it, convincing her it was not worth saving. In this instance Charles exemplifies the moral authority of the position of the reader, in which the role of public orator is partly manifest in the domestic situation.

If reading aloud was the best way to determine whether or not a work was a moral one, reading could also "improve" texts. When reading to his family, the reader could simply skip over or alter dangerous passages. As a very young woman and again as a parent, Frances Burney praises readers who censor texts as they read. She says, for example, "It is not possible for a man to make a better husband than Mr. Rishton does. . . . He is reading Spencer's 'Fairy Queen' to us, in which he is extremely delicate, omitting whatever, to the poet's disgrace, has crept in that is improper for a woman's ear."[38] Years later, Burney's husband also censors, this time a novel: while reading *Gil Blas* to their young son, the "excellent Father judiciously omits or changes all such passages as might tarnish the lovely purity of his innocence by any dangerous impressions."[39] This censoring may imply that the text is already known to the reader, that he has already judged it acceptable if one makes a few alterations. More important, it implies that the experience of the text is mediated by familial relationships. The reader feels he has a duty to shape the text for his audience; the listeners receive a text that is fitted to their situation.

Censoring the text is only the most extreme form of mediation. The simple act of reading, as the elocutionists framed it, always and inevitably involved interpretation. The reader had to choose his tone, emphasis, and so on, guided by his sense of authorial intention. In the context of family reading, the text was also interpreted by an ongoing discussion. The many descriptions of family reading frequently imply that the readings were interrupted for commentary, either by the reader or by his audience. The interruptions Trim suffers may be comical, but they are not incredible. We have seen above that educators particularly urged that the reading of novels be guided by the commentary of an older, more powerful reader—often, a patriarchal reader.

Patriarchal reading is beautifully documented in a series of letters Susanna Burney wrote to her sister in May through July 1778, in which she describes two readings of the recently published *Evelina*. In the first, Charles Burney reads to Mary Hales and her daughter, Catherine Coussmaker. These women were not afraid of novels and even mocked a "formal old maid . . . who would think it destruction for a girl to read a novel." Still, they adopted the subservient role in that they allowed Charles to choose the book and sat silent while he read it. In fact, they are totally dependent on Charles's reading. When they are to leave town before he has finished, "he has made them promise not to open the book but in his presence, which tormenting as it is Miss Coussmaker says she regrets the less because *Dr. Burney* DOES *read it so well!*" As a reader, Charles is conscious of his audience. Susanna doesn't accuse him of censoring the text, but when Charles feels there might be too much of a vulgar character, she suspects the reason is that "you read with fine ladies."[40]

In the second reading that Susanna describes, Charles Burney reads the novel aloud to his wife, in the early mornings, in their bedroom. Here again, the reading combines aspects of discipline and of intimacy. Susanna gives a firsthand account of this reading; she began to eavesdrop when she heard laughter from her parents' bedroom and listened whenever she could. Like Mary Hales and Catherine Coussmaker, Susanna praises Charles's reading as a performance and his acting out of the various characters. But most of all, she quotes his commentary. From her description, it seems that he interrupts himself almost between every phrase ("Not a period of it did he pass over unnotic'd"). Often, he is admiring the craft of the author, whom he knew to be Frances. In other places, his commentary is interpretive. The listeners must always know the moral worth of the various characters, when the reader says things like, "'tis such a dog, that Sir Clement," "*that man is* ALWAYS *right*," "a true, *fashionable, unprincipled Man of the World!*," "this Character seems to me a *model* for a young man,"[41] and so on. Meanwhile, Susanna does not report anything said by Charles's wife. It may be that Susanna didn't care what her stepmother said, or didn't think Frances would. Or, it may be that the reading and the interpretation were totally controlled by Charles. If the danger of solitary reading was that the reader would come up with the wrong moral lesson, that danger was obviated here.

Charles Burney epitomized the patriarchal reader. A good example of a father failing to perform his duty as reader and upholder of standards is provided in a little play by an anonymous "Authoress," *Half an Hour after Supper* (1789), which like *English Readings* (Chapter 3) was performed at the Haymarket. This time, there are *two* planned elopements, by the two daughters of a bourgeois household. The father, Mr. Sturdy, reiterates the commonplaces about the corrupting power of novels: his daughter "Bet" now prefers to be called the more literary "Eliza"; his family wasn't moved to charity by poor Bob Martin and his family because "their distress wasn't elegant" (9). The girls and their maiden aunt seek to enact a novel. The risk for Mr. Sturdy's daughters, he knows, is that "they will fly from my authority and protection into the arms of a couple of scoundrels" (9). But this is not a warning about reading in the closet. The titular "half an hour after supper" is time spent in family reading, with the aunt reading a sentimental novel aloud. And what does Mr. Sturdy do? He sleeps at the table, then toddles off to bed. After the usual complications, the intended elopements get botched, and order is restored when one of the fiancés decamps, while the other is invited to work in Mr. Sturdy's countinghouse. So, in the end, the father is a good bourgeois patriarch. But he risks suffering the dangers of novels precisely because he fails to perform his office. He lets the women read and experience dangerous sympathetic identification, when he should have disrupted it by his reading and commentary.

Other Kinds of Domestic Reading

I have been arguing that reading together helped sustain sentimental domestic relations, both in their intimate and in their disciplinary aspects. I would like to move out from the parental dynamic for a moment, to glance at other kinds of relationships that reading helped to maintain. Foremost among these is the heterosexual romantic relationship. The notion that reading together fosters intimacy is not, of course, new in the eighteenth century; indeed, the trope of reading lovers is at least as old as Dante. In canto 5 of *The Inferno* (the circle of sexual sinners), the shade of Francesca relates how her sin originated in an act of reading. As she and Paolo read of Lancelot and Guinevere, they enacted their wish for their own adulterous affair:

> . . . One day, for pleasure,
>   We read of Lancelot, by love constrained:
>   Alone, suspecting nothing, at our leisure.
> Sometimes at what we read our glances joined,
>   Looking from the book each to the other's eyes,
>   And then the color in our faces drained.
> But one particular moment alone it was
>   Defeated us: *the longed-for smile,* it said,
>   *Was kissed by that most noble lover:* at this,
> This one, who now will never leave my side,
>   Kissed my mouth, trembling. A Galeotto, that book!
>   And so was he who wrote it; that day we read
> No further.[42]

Scenes that eroticize reading are not uncommon in eighteenth-century literature. One of the best known is in Austen's last novel, *Persuasion:* after Louisa Musgrove's accident, when she is confined to bed, the melancholy Captain Benwick reads poetry to her, and the two fall in love. But there are many examples. In *The Monk,* by Matthew Lewis, the hero, Don Raymond, agrees to read romances to his beloved's aunt for several hours a day, hoping to ingratiate himself so that she will permit his union with her niece. Unfortunately, his plan backfires when, after he finishes reading *The Loves of Tristan and the Queen Iseult,* the aunt confesses her own passion for him.

In a lighter mode is a 1788 ditty, "The Turf, and Reading Made Easy." The narrator describes a spring day when "I met with my jewel a going to School,/With her Turf and her Reading made easy" (6). She smiles at him and asks him to teach her a lesson (*Reading Made Easy* was a popular primer). Though the narrator is only a wandering beggar, and the fact that the heroine carries a bit of turf for fuel indicates her rustic simplicity, the scene becomes a version of Dante's:

> I soon did comply, I could not deny,
> We sat where the primrose were sprining,
> Beneath a green tree where none could us see,
> While sweetly the birds they were singing;
> I shew'd her a colume she thought 'twas a volume,
> While soft killing transports did seize me,
> I kiss'd her she smild, then I said my dear child,
> Pray shut up your Reading made easy. (7)

The narrator seduces his beloved by promising to marry her, then leaves for eight months. The song has a happier ending than Dante's tale, though: when the narrator returns to find the girl pregnant, her father is willing to pay him sixty pounds to marry her; he now is industrious and prosperous. This seduction has little to do with either shared literary tastes or the powerful performance of poetry; this young couple merely work through a primer. But the ditty shows how naturalized the topos of eroticized reading had become.

Reading is also eroticized in Mary Shelley's novella, *Mathilda* (written 1819). Mathilda's mother having died after childbirth, Mathilda has been brought up by a stern aunt, until her father reclaims her when she is sixteen. Their relationship is affectionate but troubled; eventually he confesses his incestuous desire for her, and the story ends in tragedy. The crisis is foreshadowed by a scene of shared reading. When the father and daughter stay at his childhood home:

> We walked together in the gardens and in the evening when I would have retired he asked me to stay and read to him; and first said, "When I was last here your mother read Dante to me; you shall go on where she left off." And then in a moment he said, "No, that must not be; you must not read Dante. Do you choose a book." I took up Spenser and read the descent of Sir Guyon to the halls of Avarice; while he listened his eyes fixed on me in sad profound silence.[43]

Here, the father's powerful and ambivalent feelings are concretized in the choice of a text. He wishes to, but knows he must not, allow his daughter to replicate Francesca/her mother.

Since the topos of eroticized reading nearly always pictures a man reading to a woman, it reinscribes the power relations depicted in patriarchal reading. However companionate an eighteenth-century marriage, there was still an ample residue of hierarchical relations. In scenes of reading, there is often some power relation. We see this kind of dynamic in Burney's *Evelina,* when the heroine reads with her older and much higher-status suitor. This comes late in the novel, when Evelina is a guest in the same house as Lord Orville, and she is commenting on how attentive he is. In addition to walking together, "when we read, he marks the passages most worthy to be noticed, draws out my sentiments, and favours me with his own" (296). Their reading is part of his gentle courtship, yet he always retains the position of mentor. The same topos is expressed in Radcliffe's *The Mysteries of Udolpho* (1794), which includes several scenes of reading together. Late in the book, the heroine reminisces: "here she had often sat and worked, while he conversed, or read; and she now well remembered with what discriminating judgment, with what tempered energy, he used to repeat some of the sublimest passages of their favourite authors; how often he would pause to admire with her their excellence, and with what tender delight he would listen to her remarks, and correct her taste" (585).

In Frances Burney's descriptions of her own reading with her beloved husband, though, there are few remnants of hierarchical relations. In her journals, she made lists of the books she read each year: alone (very few), with her son Alex, and with her husband. Most of her reading was shared, and when she details these readings, it is the shared sentiment she dwells on. For example, when she and d'Arblay read a journal of the French Revolution, one section "makes the most soul-piercing scene, & stopt us from all reading a considerable time,—frequently, indeed, we have been obliged to take many minutes respite before we could command ourselves to go on.— But the last Scene with the royal family—the final parting—& it tore us to pieces!——'tis the most heart-breaking picture that ever was exhibited."[44] Reading together is an experience that allows the couple to share emotions. The sentiment is heightened when Burney reads from her own diaries while nursing her husband in his last illness:

> I began reading to my dear General The Hermite de la Chaussée d'Antin, in the intervals of his pains, & we were mutually charmed with its really Adisonian excellence: it came in turn with the lecture of my juvenile Journals, which were commenced when I was fifteen, & continued till my marriage—my blessed

Marriage! He dearly loved to hear them—Oh what loved he NOT that had sympathy with his Wife—her thoughts—her feelings, her life, her conduct?—[45]

Burney's reading with her husband, with its shared sentiment, reinforced the bonds of affection between them. Other texts, less sentimental in tone, recommend reading together as a painless way to enact the companionate marriage. Hester Chapone gives advice for companionate marriage in *A Letter to a New-Married Lady* (1777). When the couple are alone in the country, "conversation will hardly supply sufficient entertainment; and, next to displeasing or disgusting him, you should of all things dread his growing dull and weary in your company. If you can prevail upon him to read with you, to practise music with you, or to teach you a language or a science, you will then find amusement for every hour; and nothing is more endearing than such communications" (16–17). This advice was standard enough that it can be used in a comic inversion. In *An Essay on the Art of Ingeniously Tormenting* (1753), Jane Collier recommends tormenting a husband by ignoring his reading:

> The same indifference, also, may you put on, if he should be a man who loves reading, and is of so communicative a disposition, as to take delight in reading to you any of our best and most entertaining authors. If, for instance, he desires you to hear one of Shakespeare's plays, you may give him perpetual interruptions, by sometimes going out of the room, sometimes ringing the bell to give orders for what cannot be wanted till the next day; at other times taking notice (if your children are in the room), that Molly's cap is awry, or that Jackey looks pale; and then begin questioning the child, whether he has done anything to make himself sick. If you have needle-work in your hands, you may be so busy in cutting out, and measuring one part with another, that it will plainly appear to your husband, that you mind not one word he reads. If all this teazes him enough to make him call on you for your attention, you may say, that indeed you have other things to mind besides poetry; and if he was uneasy at your taking care of your family and children, and mending *his* shirts, you wished he had a learned wife; and then he would soon see himself in a gaol, and his family in rags. Fail not to be as eloquent as possible in this subject; for I could bring you numberless precedents of silly and illiterate wives, who have half talked their husbands to death, in exclaiming against the loquacity of ALL women, who have any share of understanding or knowledge.[46]

Jane Collier contrasts the stereotypical loquacity of women with the role they ought to assume in the reading situation: the woman should be the recipient, the audience for the man's display. Insofar as the reader assumes the person of the author, he of course becomes authoritative. But because reading itself was a learned activity, it could demonstrate the reader's taste and judgment. It could also reveal his sensibility. Austen's Marianne

Dashwood can criticize poor, dull Edward and praise her Willoughby by contrasting their readings (*S&S* 17–18). On the other hand, in Edgeworth's *Belinda,* reading becomes a test of virtue: only if Clarence Hervey can read a poem about a betrayed woman without self-consciousness will Belinda believe in his worth (350–51).

But if reading gives men an opportunity to display, it also becomes a figure for the silencing of women, for putting them into the passive position. The women read to by Charles Burney are certainly silent. The same is true in a conduct book by Ann Murry, *Mentoria; or, The Young Ladies Instructor* (1778), in which the title character is a governess to two upper-class sisters, Lady Mary and Lady Louisa. When an occasion arises for oral reading, an up-to-then irrelevant brother is brought in to perform. There are many other representations of this phenomenon.

Still, if the norm was that women listened passively, the literature also offers examples of strategic responses to this norm. One might instigate a reading in order to free one's mind or to avoid the worse imposition of bad conversation. In this case, the audience simply ignores the reader. Frances Burney used this tactic: "M. La Blancherie . . . now comes here perpetually, & nearly wears us out with his visits. Of late we have agreed, since we cannot get rid of him, to make him read. He has given us Corneille's Rodugune, which I found less exquisite than when I read it with my Susan. . . . This is surely the best thing we can do with the man."[47] Jane Austen provides a fictional corollary in *Emma:* when Mr. Elton's fidgeting distracts Emma while she is taking Harriet's likeness, "It then occurred to her to employ him in reading. . . . Mr. Elton was only too happy. Harriet listened, and Emma drew in peace" (46–47). A less polite strategy was to simply interrupt the reader: Lydia's ungovernable tendencies, in *Pride and Prejudice,* are figured in the scene in which she interrupts Mr. Collins while he is reading a conduct book aloud (68–69).

Given the inevitable power relations in mixed-sex scenes of reading, reading when only women were present had a special kind of intimacy. In stark contrast to the antisocial and trivialized figure of the silent woman reader, scenes of women reading together emphasize the way reading fosters supportive relationships. Reading together was certainly part of the intimacy between Jane Austen and her sister. Austen read *Pride and Prejudice* to Cassandra, secretly, before she read it to the rest of the family. She read her niece Anna's novel thus, too, then wrote to her: "I hope you do not depend on having your book back immediately. I keep it that your G[rand]Mama may hear it—for it has not been possible yet to have any public reading. I have read it to your Aunt Cassandra however—in our own room at night, while we undressed—and with a great deal of pleasure."[48]

Reading together is part of the erotic intimacy described in the journals of Eleanor Butler and Sarah Ponsonby, the so-called Ladies of Llangothen, who eloped and lived together in Wales for many years. Butler's published journal describes a life of rural retirement and the pleasures of domestic life. Shared reading was an important component of these pleasures. She writes, for example, "Reading Rousseau to my Sally. She drawing her map upon Vellum, made a great mistake in one of the tropics which spoil'd her morning's Work . . . Incessant rain the entire evening. Shut the shutters, made a good fire, lighted the Candles. . . . A day of strict retirement, sentiment, and delight." Or: "My beloved and I went to the new garden. Reading. Drawing. Read 'Davila.' Then my beloved read 'La Morte d'Abel.' Nine till twelve in the bedchamber reading. . . . A day of sweet and delicious retirement."[49] Far from being a solitary activity, reading is an integral part of a life of domestic intimacy.

But the intimacy fostered by reading need not have an erotic component. Both autobiographical and fictional material from the eighteenth century demonstrate that reading together was an important part of relationships among the literate middle class. We have already noted the way Charles Burney framed reading with his wife and with his friends in King's Lynn. Reading together was a project of shared self-education and both revealed and nurtured shared taste. We get hints of the role reading together played in the life of Mary Brunton in the "Memoir" published by her husband after her death in 1818. Mary Brunton was the author of two novels published during her lifetime, *Self-Control* (1811) and *Discipline* (1814). Born in Orkney in 1778, she was the daughter of an officer, married a clergyman at age twenty, and lived with him in East Lothian and in Edinburgh. She cared for two young wards of her husband, then died following the stillbirth of her only child. In his "Memoir," Alexander Brunton focuses on the development of his wife as an author. He includes outlines of her work and letters discussing it; letters describing a journey they took to England are segregated out into a later part of the book in which the "Memoir" and miscellaneous unfinished works were published. Thus, while the "Memoir" is not Mary Brunton's own account of the growth of her mind, it is the record of someone sympathetic to her work.

In the early part of the "Memoir," especially, what we are given is a record of Mary Brunton's reading and how her reading attached her to other people. Brunton had very little disciplined education, we are told, having had no governess and a mother who was accomplished rather than educated. She did spend a short time at a school in Edinburgh, but for the most part she seems to have been left alone with her books: "as a great part of her training was still left to herself, her love for reading spent itself on poetry and fiction. They helped to people for her that world of her own, which the day-dreams of youth called up in her solitude" (viii).

Alexander Brunton begins his description of their marriage with an account of their reading: "Her time was now much more at her own command. Her taste for reading returned in all its strength, and received rather a more methodical direction. Some hours of every forenoon were devoted by her to this employment; and, in the evening, I was in the habit of reading aloud to her, books chiefly of criticism and Belles Lettres" (ix). Like Anna Larpent's, Mary Brunton's reading was wide-ranging and by turns solitary and social. Her husband recognizes that there was an asymmetry in the reading they did together. During their early married life, in East Lothian, "Few literary people were within our reach. It was chiefly with me that she talked of what she had read; and, as some of the subjects were new to her, she contracted, far more than enough, the habit of speaking as a pupil" (xv). Reading with her husband, then, sustained intimacy while solidifying the hierarchy of their relationship.

Their circle of friends became wider when they moved to Edinburgh, and Alexander notes Mary's mingling with more educated people. At this time, Mary developed a friendship with a Mrs. Izett, with whom she kept up "the only close and confidential correspondence, beyond the bounds of her own family, in which Mary ever engaged" (xvii). Significantly, Alexander describes this friendship in terms of the literary life that Mary and Mrs. Izett shared:

> But the circumstance which, more than any other beyond the range of her own domestic intercourse, tended both to develope her intellect, and to establish her character, was an intimacy which she formed, soon after her removal to Edinburgh, with a lady in her immediate neighbourhood. They were indeed so near, that it was easy for them to be much together. They read together—worked together—and talked over, with confidential freedom, their opinions, from minuter points to the most important of all. In their leading views of human life and human duty, they were fully agreed. But whether they agreed, or whether they differed, they benefited each other essentially—either mutually confirming each other in the truth, or mutually leading each other towards it. (xvi–xvii)

As Alexander Brunton tells it, it was to fill the time available when Mrs. Izett was engaged that Mary Brunton began writing her first novel. The friendship was essential in her development as a thinker and a writer. And it was reading together and discussing what they read that fostered this friendship. Her husband recognizes that no youthful influence, not even his own, was as significant in her literary and moral life.

Experiencing the Text

Thus far, I have been arguing that reading together was an important part of bourgeois domesticity and that even while reading fostered intimacy, the association of reading and power functioned within the family to reinscribe hierarchical relationships. In the last section of this chapter, I would like to look at domestic reading from another angle: how did the norms of family reading affect the experience of the text? One of the frequent criticisms of reader-response theory is that it has tended to be ahistorical, to assume that readers in the past experienced literature in the same ways we do now. This often entails imagining a highly educated reader (like the critic) reading alone and silently. But since family reading was common in the eighteenth century, eighteenth-century readers would have had a very different reading experience from that of the modern critic or from that imagined for the solitary woman reader in her closet. Far from being alone with her text, directly experiencing the author's (metaphorical) voice, she was hearing the (literal) voice of an interpreter. Her experience of literature was mediated by the relationships in which it was situated and by the practical consequences of oral performance. Let us turn now to some of the specific practices that shaped that performance.

I begin with a caricature by James Gillray, in which three women sit around a table listening to a fourth woman read a novel. The women are dressed in the fashionable garb of the turn of the century, with revealing chemises and vaguely Greek hairstyles; their faces, however, are quite plain. They are leaning forward, eyes agog. The time is a quarter to one in the morning; the novel is *The Monk*. Most of Gillray's caricatures were political and aimed at men, but this is one of a number of "satires on persons and manners" that mock women's foolish indulgences. But after all, we might ask, what is so foolish about reading *The Monk* aloud? What rules are these women breaking?

To answer this, let us turn back for a moment to *Northanger Abbey* and its hero reader, Henry Tilney. As mentioned earlier, far from scorning popular gothics, Henry tells us that he could not lay *The Mysteries of Udolpho* down, indeed that he read it with his hair standing on end the whole time. But we also learn *how* he read *Udolpho*. His sister says, "I remember that you

5. "Tales of Wonder!" (1802). Gillray mocks women reading a gothic novel together. (© Trustees of the British Museum)

undertook to read it aloud to me, and that when I was called away for only five minutes to answer a note, instead of waiting for me, you took the volume into the Hermitage-walk, and I was obliged to stay till you had finished it" (*NA* 107). Henry acknowledges in his next speech that his behavior was rude, "in my eagerness to get on, refusing to wait only five minutes for my sister; breaking the promise I had made of reading it aloud, and keeping her in suspense at a most interesting part, by running away with the volume" (107). Henry's knowing rudeness reveals just how compelling this gothic novel is: one cannot wait, one cannot read it aloud. It is best read silently and alone.

Silent and oral reading differ in concrete ways that are illuminated by Henry's experience. First of all, oral reading is *slow*. This increases attentiveness to textual details such as irony or the characters' idiolects, especially if a skilled reader enacts the different voices. Second, oral reading is *discontinuous*: either one stops to discuss the reading (as we saw in Sterne and the Burney diaries), or one must work around miscellaneous interruptions (as described by Jane Collier and Miss Tilney). Third, oral reading is *mediated* by its situatedness: the social relations between reader and audience necessarily affect the experience of the text. The gothic novel is inappropriate for shared reading because each of these experiential features diminishes the pleasure of the gothic. One wants to read gothics quickly, without interruption, and with full identification. We saw above that reading was considered dangerous for naive (women) readers because they overindulged in sympathetic identification. It was precisely here that patriarchal reading functioned to make texts harmless. As Elizabeth Montagu said, "Interruptions and intrusions of other objects are fatal to sympathy, and Fiction fades away in the importunate solicitations and presence of Realities."[50]

However, it is not clear that eighteenth-century authors of other kinds of works (that is, besides gothics) made the absolute link between sympathy and coherent, complete plots that modern readers tend to make. Many eighteenth-century novels do not rely at all on the kinds of coherent plots that we think necessary. For example, the works of Laurence Sterne in no way demand a front-to-back reading. On the contrary, his novels are composed of a series of tableaux barely attached to a frame. It is no coincidence that excerpts from Sterne are so often to be found in the school anthologies; they are easily detachable from the surrounding wholes. Even novels like Austen's, whose plots some readers (myself included) believe are perfect, were not necessarily read as a "whole" in the eighteenth century. There is much evidence that eighteenth-century readers read for "beauties," for gems they could memorize or copy into their commonplace books.

In *Mansfield Park,* for example, Henry Crawford's reading of Shakespeare reveals the power of the reader on display. But it also demonstrates that family reading would not necessarily be a front-to-back affair, but could involve skipping from passage to passage. As Henry reads, Fanny at first tries to ignore him:

> But taste was too strong in her. She could not abstract her mind five minutes; she was forced to listen; his reading was capital, and her pleasure in good reading extreme. To *good* reading, however, she had been long used; her uncle read well—her cousins all—Edmund very well; but in Mr. Crawford's reading there was a variety of excellence beyond what she had ever met with. The King, the Queen, Buckingham, Wolsey, Cromwell, all were given in turn; for with the happiest knack, the happiest power of jumping and guessing, he could always light, at will, on the best scene, or the best speeches of each; and whether it were dignity or pride, or tenderness or remorse, or whatever were to be expressed, he could do it with equal beauty. (337)

In this situation, the reader exerts the same kind of control over the text that the anthologists did: he picks out excerpts, giving a heavily edited, discon-

.nuous version of a well-known text. I do not think Austen's terminology (Fanny "was *forced* to listen") is coincidental: Crawford is using his power here, imposing his will and his interpretation. The text that his listeners experience is one that is cut into "beauties," and far from increasing sympathetic identification, the performance has a distancing effect.

And here is the problem with Gillray's readers. As I have suggested, Frances Burney and Jane Austen both document many shared oral readings, but both suggest that gothics are best read silently and alone. Burney feels that she didn't enjoy *Udolpho* because of how she read it: Radcliffe's "writings are all best calculated for lonely hours & depressed spirits. I should probably have done more justice to Udolpho if I had read it in one of my solitary intervals."[51] If family reading was fatal to sympathy, it was certainly fatal to the horror and suspense at the heart of gothic fiction. The readers in Gillray's caricature are foolish not only because ugly women have no right to be titillated, but because they are reading inappropriately.

Let us return, finally, to the readings of *Evelina* documented in the Burney papers. Both the plot of *Evelina* and its writing and publication history are centrally concerned with the affection and discipline of the bourgeois family. The titular heroine's actions are motivated by a powerful ambivalence about whether or not to demand that her legitimate and wealthy father recognize her. Frances, as we have already noted, had to disguise her hand because it was so closely associated with her father's works; in the poem prefaced to the novel, her father is addressed almost as a god. This novel and its history are deeply embedded in the struggles of affective families. And so were the readings that Frances Burney described in such detail. We have already seen that when Charles Burney read *Evelina* to his wife, in their bedroom, his performance was peppered with commentary that guarded against possible misinterpretations of the text. This commentary was an important part of the experience of family reading. But let us turn, in closing, to the feature most salient to the concerns of this book, the connection of oral performance with speech.

Burney shows us how talk about books entered the conversations of her family friends. But she documents more than readers' comments about the book; if her report is at all accurate, readers could retrieve very specific details, quote fairly long sections, and imitate the characters' language. The situation of family reading creates an "intensive" reading of a different sort than that described by Engelsing: the oral performance enlivens the text and makes it more memorable, and the interruptions and discussions fix the text in the audience's mind. The pace of the reading, the enactment, the interruptions, the situatedness all serve to help the audience engage with the text even as they disrupt the negative possibilities of sympathetic identification.

We see all of these features in the account of a reading by Frances's aunt Anne and a visitor, Hannah Humphries, to her cousin Richard, who was then recovering from illness. True to her diffidence, Burney is most interested in whether or not the readers will guess that she is the author; she is astonished when they guess the author to be a man. More relevant here is the way that the reading is situated in the domestic situation, the women reading to care for an invalid, and spending several days at it. Burney records the women's rather empty commentary ("How pretty that is!") and Richard's more acute criticism of the heroine's bashfulness. And she conveys the intensity of the reading experience: "I never went to Brompton without finding the third volume in Richard's hands; he speaks of all the characters as if they were his acquaintance, and praises different parts perpetually. Both he and Miss Humphries seem to have it by heart, for it is always *à propos* to whatever is the subject of the discourse, and their whole conversation almost consists of quotations from it."[52] Even allowing for an author's flattered exaggeration, it is clear that this family was deeply engaged in the text. And the novel achieved the moral effect that so many authors claimed to strive for. Burney comments on Richard's engagement with his

> favourite Lord, whose character he studies every day of his life; with whom he seemed so struck, that we all fancied that he meant to make him his *model,* as far as his situation would allow. Indeed, not only *during* his illness he penetrated us by his patient and most amiable behaviour, but since his recovery, he has more than kept his ground, by having wholly discarded all the foibles that formerly tinged his manners, though they *never,* I believe, affected his heart.[53]

Frances's sister Susanna recorded a similar engagement in her description of Charles's reading to Mary Hales and her daughter, Catherine Coussmaker. In her version of the ladies' response to the novel, Susanna represents an audience so involved in the reading that they can imitate the characters' language and repeatedly compare people they meet with figures from *Evelina.* As they ride through London, they are reminded of people and places from the book. But they are particularly struck by the novel's dialogue and the way idiolects are sustained. At dinner one night, they border on rudeness to the French governess, and Catherine's brother later asks them whom they were laughing at.

> "Gracious me!" cried Lady Hales, "Kitty, that book will certainly get us into a scrape!—for I never can hear poor Mad^e de Ferre open her mouth now with-

out its putting me so in mind of that Mad^e Duval, so that I am ready to die with laughing."

"No," said Mr. Coussmaker, "I don't think so—Mad^e de Ferre is very different. . . ."

"Why that's very true—but her *never noting,* and her blunders in conversation, are so ridiculously like, that they always remind me of each other."[54]

According to Susanna, the ladies could describe sections of the novel in great detail, explaining each character's proposal for a bet, for example. One senses the shared pleasure of the mother and daughter at a reading so different from the hurried skimming while one's hair is powdered or the solitary reading in the closet, topoi that typified "the woman reader." One cannot separate the pleasure of the reading from the pleasure of the text; both serve to bind the family together in a shared experience. In this spirit of intimacy, Catherine Coussmaker suggests that she and Susanna should read together.

> "But," said [Susanna], " 'twill be too recent in y^r memory."
> "Oh, I should like to read it all over again, for the sake of the language immediately — but indeed I believe there is not a circumstance from the beginning to the end of the book that I do not perfectly remember — for we have read it in a most delightful manner — not hurried it over — but stopt to laugh and talk it over between almost every letter."[55]

Family reading was a specific kind of oral performance, governed by social norms just as spontaneous speech was. For the purposes of this book, let me reiterate that what struck readers of *Evelina* most forcibly were the ways in which this novel represents speech and the ways in which those representations were performed. Catherine Coussmaker anticipated many commentators when she said, "A great deal of it is conversation—such a variety of Characters 'tis amazing I declare," and she noted that "Dr. Burney does read the conversations, and mark the characters so well, 'tis quite delightful."[56] Burney's facility with dialogue led readers like Hester Thrale to encourage her to write for the stage.[57] In Chapter 5, I will argue that one consequence of the theatrical quality of novels like Burney's and Austen's was that the discourses about acting could be applied as well to the reading of fiction: that readers performing the text absorbed the author's ethos. For now, let me merely note the attention to Burney's dialogue and the impact it made on readers. If Mary Hales could imitate Mme Duval, "Miss Thrale and her mother seemed to have it by heart, and *quoted* in the course of the day several of the *Snow Hill phrases.*[58]

At the slower pace required by oral reading, one appreciates sentence-level pleasures: a particularly well chosen word, a bit of narrative irony, the accuracy of a character's voice in dialogue. These pleasures abound in the novels we associate with oral readings, like those of Austen, Dickens, and Joyce. But many eighteenth-century novels do not reward leisurely reading. The gothics parodied by Gillray are eminently skimmable. For example, with the exception of one or two low-comic figures, the characters' voices in *The Monk* are totally undifferentiated. Even Don Raymond's telling of his tale is completely unbelievable as oral narrative (it is ninety pages long and bridges two volumes). What is pleasurable in gothics is the drive of the plot, which is best appreciated through a fast and uninterrupted reading.

By contrast, *Evelina*'s pleasures have little to do with the drive of a plot and much to do with set pieces and with voice. A generation later, Jane Austen's niece said of her: "She was considered to read aloud remarkably well. I did not often hear her but *once* I knew her take up a volume of Evelina and read a few pages of Mr. Smith and the Brangtons and I thought it was like a play."[59] Austen could sensibly read just a few pages aloud because her audience already knew *Evelina*—but she probably *chose* those pages because they were like a play. Epistolary novels may focus only on the voice of a single letter writer, as in Goethe's *The Sorrows of Young Werther*. In *Evelina,* however, Burney took advantage of the voice of the reader by writing so much dialogue, in so many different idiolects. Like a play, this novel is best appreciated when it is performed. Let us turn now to the ways in which eighteenth-century discourse figures the effect of the reading on the reader.

CHAPTER 5

Reading Austen, Practicing Speech

Speaking, it is presumed, cannot be more successfully taught, than by
referring us to such rules, as instruct us in the art of reading.
—John Walker, *A Rhetorical Grammar*

Every reader remembers the opening line of *Pride and Prejudice:* "It is a
truth universally acknowledged, that a single man in possession of a good
fortune, must be in want of a wife." In that one sentence, the narrator of this
novel establishes herself as a wit and her novel as one that will certainly end
with a wedding. This opening sentence serves, in an unusually concise way,
to prepare the reader to interpret what follows as comedy. Without the
generic expectations of comedy, what immediately follows would not be
funny at all: it is a portrait of a sadistic husband baiting his wife and might
have been written to evoke anger or pain. Once the narrator has established
the comedic genre, though, she need hardly intrude at all to control our
interpretation of this scene; for two full chapters, we are given almost
entirely unadorned dialogue.

Unlike the novel's opening line, this feature is too often forgotten. *Pride
and Prejudice* is remarkable among novels of the long eighteenth century
(including Austen's own) in the way we are thrust directly into a scene presented in dialogue. More frequently, readers are given considerable background information before the action begins; many eighteenth-century
novels begin with a narrative account of the hero or heroine's birth and
childhood. Beginning in medias res is unusual enough; beginning with dialogue may be unique. But this unusual opening serves to establish the frame-

work for a concern crucial to *Pride and Prejudice:* the complex relation between speech and authority.

In a comic inversion, the opening dialogue perfectly illustrates what *not* to do in conversation. Let us look at the first few lines:

> "My dear Mr. Bennet," said his lady to him one day, "have you heard that Netherfield Park is let at last?"
> Mr. Bennet replied that he had not.
> "But it is," returned she; "for Mrs. Long has just been here, and she told me all about it."
> Mr. Bennet made no answer.
> "Do not you want to know who has taken it?" cried his wife impatiently.
> "*You* want to tell me, and I have no objection to hearing it."
> This was invitation enough. (*P&P* 3)

Mr. Bennet here violates the most basic rule of conversation: that of taking turns. It is the prime duty of one converser to respond to the other in a way that generates further conversation. Yet he pointedly ignores every invitation to respond and refuses to perform even minimal face-saving gestures. Still, no matter how rude Mr. Bennet may be, the reader tends to adopt his point of view because his wife is even worse: the epitome of the loquacious woman, for whom gossip is the highest form of discourse. Mrs. Bennet's impotence—her inability to gain her husband's respect or that of the reader—signals the issue at stake in this chapter, the difficulty with which women can claim authority in conversation.

Pride and Prejudice may be exceptional, even within Austen's own oeuvre, for the degree of its emphasis on speech and its attentiveness to the rules governing conversation. But, as I will argue, this novel exemplifies the concern with women's speech that has been the subject of this book. As we have seen, the eighteenth century was a time of increased theorizing about spoken language and its relation to print. Yet while the elocutionists developed methods for training orators and maintained that practice in reading inevitably created authoritative speakers, they showed little interest in realms of speech available to middle-class women. Conduct-book writers, on the other hand, tended to direct their efforts toward keeping these women silent. The question to be addressed here, then, is the role that fiction may have played in the discourse about women's speech and, specifically, how eighteenth-century women may have utilized literature to practice the various strategies required for linguistic competence.

In emphasizing the relation between reading and speech, this chapter will entail more textual analysis than did earlier portions of this book. However, my primary interest here is not the explication of Austen's texts.

Many scholars before me have examined Austen's use of dialogue and the oral qualities of her narration. Austen's skill in delineating her characters through their idiosyncratic speech has been demonstrated by scholars from Howard S. Babb (at a time when it was still felt necessary to defend Austen's greatness) to J. F. Burrows (whose computer analysis details Austen's consistent use of idiolect).[1] A second strain of Austen criticism has stressed her use of free indirect discourse (that is, the coloring of narration by the indirect voices of characters); Austen was among the very first in English to use free indirect discourse, and it gives an especially oral quality to her writing.[2] And very recently, there has been some attention paid to the ways Austen represents concerns of feminist linguistics.[3]

The point here, however, is not *that* Austen was a master of dialogue or free indirect discourse, though that is certainly true. My point is, rather, what her attention to dialogue meant for the *reader* of Austen's texts. I am concerned here with how the written text helped the reader to learn to speak, as that was articulated explicitly in pedagogical works and appears implicit in Austen's novels. That is, I wish to explore first, what it *meant* to read a text aloud, then *how* a text was read, and finally what the performance of this particular text invites. In this chapter, I turn away from the exceptional speakers of Chapters 2 and 3 and toward "ordinary" middle-class women who accepted the norms of polite conversation and forged identities within those norms. How might a novel like *Pride and Prejudice* have developed this reader's speech repertoire? And more generally, how, given the obstacles against it, might an "ordinary" eighteenth-century woman develop ethos as a speaker?

Given the spottiness of the historical record, the evidence for my argument will be somewhat indirect. Austen did not compile the kind of detailed records of her first readers' reactions that are found in the Burney diaries. Her extant letters do not record conversations at all, and since she was not a celebrity, no famous commentators collected even the traces of conversation that survive from Opie and Siddons. The few records we have indicate that Austen was not herself a great conversationalist; she was a delightful storyteller to children, but with adults she was if anything like Mr. Bennet, dangerously silent.[4] More important, if any "ordinary" contemporary readers described how *Pride and Prejudice* taught them how to speak, their accounts are not (yet?) to be found. My argument must rest, on the one hand, on treatises by elocutionists and educators describing how to read fiction and how oral reading affected the reader and, on the other, on a close reading of Austen's work that reveals how her texts engage the elocutionists' advice. I use *Pride and Prejudice* as a test case for the historical argument that fiction took the place of conversation manuals in teaching speech. Other works might have served the purpose nearly as well; indeed, my argument assumes that *Pride and Prejudice* is not unique except in its excellence.

This chapter will have four sections. First, I examine how the elocution movement's association of speech, reading, and ethos percolated down to a domestic audience. Second, I detail how students were instructed to read literary works of different genres and how authors like Austen prepared their texts for the oral reader. Third, I use *Pride and Prejudice* as a model text for the teaching of speech strategies. And fourth, I conclude with Austen's last completed novel, *Persuasion,* arguing that the later novel moves beyond the earlier concern with speech toward other modes of constructing identity. *Persuasion* returns us to the examination of silence with which this book began.

Ethos, Personation, and Practice in Speech

In earlier sections of this book, I utilized modern linguistic models to examine surviving representations of eighteenth-century speech. Let us go back, for now, to categories that would have been more recognizable to Austen, and examine the relation between conversation, character, and ethos. In Aristotelian rhetoric, *ethos* is that portion of persuasion that derives from the respect accorded a speaker as his character is revealed in speech; it is distinguished from *logos* (the logic of the specific argument) and *pathos* (the predisposition of the audience). The power of ethos was of prime concern in Austen's novels, most notably in *Persuasion,* which centers on the repercussions of the decision by a youthful heroine to yield to her mentor's judgment. While, years later, the heroine still feels her mentor's judgment was wrong, she never feels that she herself was wrong to be persuaded by ethos. Aristotle did not, of course, consider gender in his discussion of ethos. But Austen marks this as a gendered issue in a conversation in *Pride and Prejudice,* in which Elizabeth privileges ethos as a means of persuasion, while Darcy insists on logos. They are discussing a hypothetical case of a man who delays a trip when asked to do so by a friend. Darcy begins:

"... you must remember, Miss Bennet, that the friend who is supposed to desire his return to the house, and the delay of his plan, has merely desired it, asked it without offering one argument in favour of its propriety."

"To yield readily—easily—to the *persuasion* of a friend is no merit with you."

"To yield without conviction is no compliment to the understanding of either."

"You appear to me, Mr. Darcy, to allow nothing for the influence of friendship and affection. A regard for the requester would often make one readily yield to a request, without waiting for arguments to reason one into it." (50)[5]

In the context of the entire novel, one cannot claim that Elizabeth's method is any more successful than Darcy's—she is consistently led astray by attending to ethos when she has misjudged it; only over the course of the novel does she learn not to confuse ethos and charm. My point is rather that her preference for ethos is "typically" gendered. A proper woman of her period "should" yield to authority. However, Elizabeth's articulation differs from Aristotle's here: whereas Aristotle was concerned with the features of the rhetor's speech on a single occasion that inspire trust, Elizabeth emphasizes the trust and affection between friends that exist prior to the specific rhetorical occasion. Austen consistently utilizes ethos in this way. The mentor in *Persuasion*, Lady Russell, can influence Anne Elliot because of their lifelong relationship. Conversely, Elizabeth Bennet discounts just criticisms of the scoundrel Mr. Wickham because they come from a source, Miss Bingley, whom she has come to dislike. More than for Aristotle, then, ethos for Austen was embedded within ongoing personal relationships. It was salient not only in oratory but also in conversation.

Ethos was a central concern of eighteenth-century rhetorical theory, and its connection to reading comes through the elocution movement. Let us return to Hugh Blair's essay " Pronunciation, or Delivery" (discussed in Chapter 4) for a typical articulation. Blair's essay, to repeat, is especially important because it was widely reprinted in school anthologies; Blair, more than Sheridan or other elocutionists, would have been known to a domestic audience. Blair begins his essay with an ancient anecdote about Demosthenes: "when being asked, What was the first point in oratory? he answered, Delivery; and being asked, What was the second? and afterwards, What was the third? he still answered, Delivery" (vii).[6] Blair then describes the qualities needed for effective delivery (loudness, distinctness, and so on). But when he turns to consider how a student may best improve delivery, he turns away from technique toward ethos: "What stands highest in the order of means [for improvement in eloquence], is personal character and disposition. In order to be a truly eloquent or persuasive speaker, nothing is more necessary than to be a virtuous man" (xvi). Virtue, for Blair, rests in feeling proper sentiments, which are communicated to the audience: "love of justice and order," "love of honesty and truth," and so on. As is typical of moral systems based on sentiment, Blair's makes room for the "feminine" virtues: "Joined with the manly virtues, [the speaker] should, at the same time, possess strong and tender sensibility to all the injuries, distresses, and sorrows, of his fellow creatures. . . . Modesty is essential; it is always, and justly, supposed to be a concomitant of merit, and every appearance of it is winning and prepossessing" (xviii).

We come up short at the word "appearance," with its dual meaning of "semblance" and "instance." Does Blair mean that the speaker need only "seem" modest, or that he must truly "be" modest and instantiate that for his audience? This ambivalence is already present in ancient writings on rhetoric.[7] In the tradition going back to Isocrates, the speaker must truly "be" virtuous; as Quintilian put it, eloquence derives from "a good man speaking well." This tradition leans toward a belief in a "true" self that may be revealed or disguised by speech, and it is the view generally adopted by traditional Christians.

But a second tradition, epitomized by Aristotle's *Rhetoric* and more associated with secular modes, presents character as something constructed in and simultaneous with speech, rather than as a stable, essential self. For Aristotle, the audience responds to the speaker's character as it is presented in the speech; it is up to the speaker, then, to construct a speech that will demonstrate "good sense, good moral character, and good will . . . anyone who is thought to have all three of these good qualities will inspire trust in his audience."[8] In this tradition, rhetoric is *strategic,* a matter of matching means and ends. Commentators sometimes erroneously associate this view of rhetoric with hypocrisy or deviousness. Doing so implies the existence of a "true" self that one hides, when in fact fakery is beside the point. In the Aristotelian tradition, there *is* no self apart from the character that is continuously being constructed in speech.

This latter view of character is more consistent with much eighteenth-century ideology (and, obviously, with various forms of postmodernism) than is the stable self of Isocrates. Before Romanticism, the nature, even the existence, of the stable authentic self was by no means assumed. Christian theology might posit a stable "soul," but even it left a great portion of character dependent on social context. The tradition of Locke, which dominated eighteenth-century English philosophy, subordinated the self to its sensory perceptions. And in ordinary eighteenth-century usage, character was firmly situated in a social context and manifested itself through speech and action. As David Oakleaf points out, Johnson's *Dictionary* defines *character* first of all as " 'a mark; a stamp; a representation' rather than something revealed by such a sign."[9] As Oakleaf argues, the word *character* has multiple and overlapping meanings in the period, but it generally entails "public" character or reputation, what others say about us. Austen uses the term ambiguously. When Elizabeth fears that her flirtatious sister Lydia's "character will be fixed" if she is permitted to go to Brighton (*P&P* 231), *character* may mean either Lydia's moral being or her reputation—or both. What matters here is that *character* retained an Aristotelian nuance: character was constructed at least partly in speech, both in how others spoke about us and in how we presented ourselves to them.

Within this context, the elocution movement's attention to the *appearance* of virtue is less paradoxical than it seems. Because it focused on the performance of texts written by others—on reading—elocution takes the construction of arguments (logos) as a given, just as the predispositions of the audience (pathos) are. Only delivery is at stake; the only area of concern is how best to enact the ethos that is present in the text. The technical advice of the elocutionists on the pace of reading, emphasis, and so on, assumes that the reader must enter into the spirit of the author, reading as if the work were his own. John Mason said that "The great Design and End of a good Pronunciation is, to make the Ideas seem to come from the Heart; and then they will not fail to excite the Attention and Affections of them that hear us."[10] In that case, as Peter De Bolla notes, "the question over whose voice is heard aloud, the reader's or the author's as imitated by the reader, has clear ramifications within the eighteenth-century conceptualization of the subject."[11] De Bolla frames this as a power struggle between author and reader: "When the question being addressed is: should one become the person of the author, thereby relinquishing one's own personality, against the possible personation of the author, appropriating the person of the author to oneself, the stakes that are being played for are very high indeed" (240).

But the stakes are somewhat different if we soften the commitment to two stable selves, author and reader, fighting for dominance. The elocutionists' advice on attaining the appearance of virtues should be understood less as a matter of hypocrisy or even theatricality than as an indication that character, in this period, has more to do with how one seems to others than to one's faithfulness to a true self. In that case, the reader who embodies the qualities implied in a text *becomes* that character. It is this act of "personation" (to use the eighteenth-century term) that links reading, speech, and ethos.

In discussing personation, the elocution texts and schoolbooks present a range of ideas whose poles would be similar to those represented by Isocrates and Aristotle: that the reader uses strength from his own "self" to enliven the author's text, on the one hand, or on the other, that the reader "becomes" the author as he speaks the words of the text. But even those who don't take the purest Aristotelian position recognize the possibility that speaking a text—personating a character—will affect the reader. Educators were well aware of the formative power of pronouncing a text and the risk that students would be unduly affected by what they read; that is, that their speech would construct their characters. As we saw, some writers on acting theory feared that the actor might absorb negative qualities from the character he portrayed. Similarly, some elocutionists (especially schoolbook authors) warned students against possible consequences of oral performance. To counter this, William Cockin posited "that the warmth and energy of our delivery in reading, ought to be inferior to that used upon subjects in which we are immediately interested." Lindley Murray agreed. On the one hand, "It is essential to a complete reader, that he minutely perceive the ideas, and enter into the feelings, of the author whose sentiments he professes to repeat."[12] But to minimize risk, the student should keep a cautious distance from the text:

> In reading, let all your tones of expression be borrowed from those of common speech, but, in some degree, more faintly characterised. Let those tones which signify any disagreeable passion of the mind, be still more faint than those which indicate agreeable emotions: and, on all occasions, preserve yourselves so far from being affected with the subject, as to be able to proceed through it, with that easy and masterly manner, which has its good effects in this, as well as in every other art. (xx–xxi)

Younger children were especially vulnerable to the effects of personation. In her *Practical Education,* Maria Edgeworth criticized some textual details of Anna Laetitia Barbauld's *Lessons for Children* on the grounds that a child pronouncing them will be corrupted. Among these is the simple sentence, " 'I want my dinner.' . . . These and similar expressions are words of course; but young children should not be allowed to use them: if they are permitted to assume the tone of command, the feelings of impatience and ill temper quickly follow, and children become the little tyrants of a family." Of a later line, "Maid, come and dress Charles," Edgeworth says flatly, "this sentence for Charles should not be read [aloud] by a child."[13] Like educators of our time, eighteenth-century writers believed that children's moral imaginations were formed in large part by what they read. The earlier works differ, though, in emphasizing that that effect works much more powerfully when texts are read aloud. Reading aloud—personation—was like acting in its effect on the reader. As the reader pronounced a text, he enacted it, incorporating its passions into his character.

I use the masculine pronoun deliberately. Just as the elocution movement concerned itself with public speech, "in the senate, the pulpit, and the bar," so too the schoolbooks are overwhelmingly addressed to boys and their training for public life. And not only were women barred from public speaking and denied the training for it. The assumption of women's inferiority meant that they were "naturally" weaker in ethos. My reader surely noticed Blair's pronouncement that a persuasive speaker must be a virtuous "man." Aristotle was even clearer: in a section of the *Rhetoric* on the display of virtues, he notes in passing that "Virtues and actions are nobler, when they proceed from those who are naturally worthier, for instance, from a man rather than from a woman."[14] The sphere for women's speech was thus doubly limited: to the private realm of conversation, and with the presumption of inferior ethos.

How, then, might women learn to construct authoritative characters in speech? In phrasing my question so positively, I do not mean to diminish the power of the prejudices against women's speech that we have seen so often through this book. Smellie's mad mothers and Addison's female orators, along with many other representations of women's defective speech, form our constant background. The links forged between speech and character also disadvantaged women in focusing on public speech and male character. But let us turn, finally, to a realm in which women were included: in the link between reading and conversation, and in the possibilities for constructing ethos in everyday speech.

While the elocution texts theoretically meant "public speech" or "oratory" when they linked reading and speech, they often implied that reading would also improve the speech used in daily life. We remember that William Enfield described speech as something a man does hourly, clearly implying that he did not mean only oratory.[15] Occasionally, elocutionists were explicit about the effect that reading would have on speech. Here is John Walker:

> Reading is not ill defined by a late writer on the subject [John Rice], where he calls it, artificial speaking. It is an imitative art which has eloquent speaking for its model, as eloquent speaking is an imitation of beautiful nature. Reading, therefore, is to speaking, what a copy is to an original picture: both of them have beautiful nature for their object; and as a taste for beautiful nature can scarcely be better acquired, than by a view of the most elegant copies of it, speaking, it is presumed, cannot be more successfully taught, than by referring us to such rules, as instruct us in the art of reading.[16]

Similarly, in a "dissertation" appended to his *Course of Lectures on Elocution,* Sheridan relates oral reading to practice in private realms of speech, asserting that reading will improve manners and conversation.

Even when discussing elocution's effect on private speech, however, these books tend to consider only men. I have noted before that most of the school anthologies were explicitly designed for boys, using only boys in their illustrations and reproducing speeches of male characters. But there are a few exceptions, like Wollstonecraft's *The Female Reader* and Barbauld's *The Female Speaker*. When C. Short compiled an anthology of *Dramas for the Use of Young Ladies* (1792), she explained in her preface that "These little Dramas were written for a Society of Young Ladies, in whose welfare and improvement I am warmly interested; and as they have proved beneficial to this small circle, in promoting the habit of speaking with grace and propriety, I conceived they might be useful to others in similar situations, and therefore determined to present them to the public." A somewhat more ambitious goal is articulated in the preface to an American anthology by Samuel B. Morse, *School Dialogues . . . Calculated to Promote an Easy and Elegant Mode of Conversation Among the Young Masters and Misses of the United States* (1797). Morse addresses his volume particularly to young women and explains why his selections emphasize comedy:

> As in Schools, there is generally almost as great a number of one sex as of the other, the impropriety of neglecting females in regard to speaking is extremely evident. Single pieces are not so proper for them to speak; but well-chosen Dialogues, as the means of teaching the fair sex a graceful, easy, and elegant mode of conversation, will prove of the most extensive benefit. . . .
>
> It was thought best to select principally from Comic Writers alone; as the main design of these Dialogues is to improve youth in good elocution, and to teach them a natural and correct manner in conversation; to which end Tragedy is but very ill calculated. (iii)

Morse, like many elocutionists and anthologists, assumes that performing a text orally allows the reader to practice eloquent speech. "Single pieces" (that is, oratory) are improper for girls because they involve public speech, an authoritative mode that girls should not internalize. For Morse, comic dialogues are ideal in fostering elegance and grace within the realm of private conversation. Personating the characters of comedy is safe.

For my purposes, Morse's use of belles lettres has additional significance. By urging the performance of "literary" English, Morse and others offer us new implications for the extension of literacy among the middle class. For Helena Wells, we remember, practicing "literary" English was a means of upward mobility; this mobility in turn generated conservative reactions against the training that enabled middle-class girls to sound like duchesses. The class issues must remain salient especially in view of the association of literary forms like the novel with middle-class women readers.

But in addition to the dimension of class, the reading of belles lettres widens the linguistic range of conversational models for women. The many didactic texts advising women on their speech, both conservative and liberal, tended to ignore a central feature of linguistic competence: that no mode of speech is adequate in all contexts. Speech is radically contextual: the soccer stadium, the classroom, the analyst's couch—each requires its own special vocabulary, degree of formality, and style of interaction—what linguists call "register." The assumption that women should have only one mode of speech (or silence) assumes that women are limited to a single linguistic context. Conversation manuals and conduct books alike are inadequate guides because they are overly general, especially in their advice to women.

And yet here, I believe, is an opportunity for literature to serve the function of teaching speech. Fiction's very essence is to describe the specificity of experience—and thus of the many contexts of speech. The students who performed plays personated a single character in a range of specific contexts and learned how one person speaks in several registers. The lessons learned are greatly magnified in the performance of fiction like Burney's or Austen's. Here, *one* reader personates *all* of the characters, speaking in all their registers. The performance of fiction thus offers women practice in a much wider range of linguistic skills than do the conduct books or conversation manuals. By personating young and old characters, male and female, silly and wise, the reader learns how to construct a character in speech.

In short, the discourse of elocution in the late eighteenth century indicates that fiction took the place of conversation manuals in the teaching of speech. Elocutionists and educators argued explicitly that ethos was a function of speech and that readers personating literary characters internalized those characters' habits of speech. While women were generally excluded from practicing public speech, they were offered belletristic texts for the practice of conversational skills.

For the rest of this chapter, I would like to explore just how fiction could function in the teaching of speech. First, I will examine the details of how literary texts were supposed to be read and how the formal features of a text like *Pride and Prejudice* invited oral performance. With that background established, I turn back to the practice of speech and read *Pride and Prejudice* as a kind of conversation manual. Finally, I qualify my argument somewhat by looking at Austen's reservations about speech in her last novel, *Persuasion*.

Genres of Reading

The elocutionists' instructions on emphasis, pauses, and so on asked students to determine the author's meaning and plan their reading accordingly.

As we saw in Sheridan's analysis of the church service and Kemble's readings of Shakespeare, this task operated primarily at the level of the sentence. When students were asked to enact a text's "passions," they worked at a more general level, but one that was still local to the level of a paragraph or a page. Let us turn now, however, to a third level addressed by the elocutionists and schoolbook authors, the level of genre. In designing his text to assist in teaching elegant conversation, Samuel B. Morse favored one literary genre (comedy) over another (tragedy). Other authors developed more complex systems of genres of reading, which will operate in the reading of fiction that is at the heart of this chapter.

Elocutionists and schoolbook authors developed two kinds of categories of reading. In the first, authors specify hierarchies of effective reading practices; in the second, they attach reading practices to literary genres. Usually, however, these two systems overlap. For example, in an important treatise on rhetorical delivery, the Irish clergyman and educator Gilbert Austin offers a scale of reading, from easiest to most difficult, and attaches it loosely to genres. "Intelligible" reading has as its purpose the simple provision of information; it requires only proper articulation, pauses, accents, and volume, and is sufficient for clerks in public business when they read law writings or advertisements aloud. "Correct" reading adds emphasis, purity of pronunciation, and suitable demeanor; it is useful for reading public documents and parts of the church service. "Impressive" reading, which adds modulations of the voice and an expressive countenance, but little gesture, is required for reading the Liturgy and Scriptures. Next is "rhetorical" reading, useful for the sermon and for other public discourses, which adds gesture and forcefulness. Austin then shifts his ground, away from reading in church, and considers kinds of domestic reading of literature. His "dramatic" reading, used in the private reading of plays, requires personation of the characters. And Austin's highest category, the reading of epic poetry, demands that the performer be able to move easily through both the sublime descriptions and the ornamented and eloquent speeches that are typical of this genre.[17]

The association of literary genre and manner of reading is even stronger in a manual entitled *The Polite Lady; or, a Course of Female Education,* which was popular enough to go through eight editions before 1800. Like many conduct books, this one offers a survey of texts that are proper for young women to read. But *The Polite Lady* also gives advice on *how* to read these texts. After cautioning her (fictional) daughter against dramatic works that may be dangerous, the (fictional) mother suggests that there are proper ways to read:

> The truth is, all the several passions of the soul have certain tones of voice, which are peculiarly adapted to express them; and therefore whatever passion a speech or sentence contains, it should always be read with its proper and natural accent. This is one of the greatest niceties and beauties in reading, but in which, I am sorry to say it, most ladies are extremely deficient. They read a history, a romance, a play, a letter, an advertisement, every thing, with the same uniform, unmeaning tone: so that unless you attend to the sense, you shall not be able to judge by their manner what they are reading. (145)

This author not only slips unconsciously from "passions" to literary genres, but also suggests that reading styles of different genres are so different that one should be able to determine the text's genre without really listening to the performance. In the following pages, the mother contrasts two women reading plays aloud: in the first case, a woman reads a play full of "affecting scenes, and pathetic speeches" (145), but someone passing by mistakes it for literary criticism. The mother forgives him, for "in truth, from her insipid and lifeless manner of reading, he might as well have taken it for a book of cookery" (146). In the second example, a group of women saw a young lady sitting in an arbor reading and "began to form conjectures what might be the subject of the book. . . . Even before we came within reach of the sound, we all agreed that it must be some play" (147). The second woman is the better reader because her reading style is appropriate to the genre. That she reads alone, aloud, and outside, neither surprises the author nor elicits particular praise, nor is it her tone of voice that reveals the genre; rather, her gestures and facial expressions must somehow say "Shakespeare." Certainly she was reading "with great vehemence and emotion" (147). The author then explicitly states that the text's genre should be apparent from the style of reading, whether or not one hears the words:

> The truth is, you may judge from the air, manner, and gesture, of a good reader, or at most, from the inarticulate sound of her voice, though you should not be near enough to comprehend the sense, what is the general subject of the book. But with a bad reader, you must hear and understand the full sense and meaning of every word and expression, before you can know what she is about; otherwise you shall not be able to distinguish whether she is reading a play or an advertisement, the description of a battle or of a funeral procession. (148)

Among the literary genres, drama (not surprisingly) attracted the most commentary on personation and its effect on the reader. The issues here are slightly different from those affecting amateur theatricals, for here one reader enacts all the parts. Gilbert Austin mentions Le Tessier, whose public readings we considered in Chapter 3, as a probably unattainable ideal:

"His gestures, his voice and countenance change with every character often as successfully as rapidly. He does not name the persons, but then his performance is an absolute imitation of each, which is not to be looked for in private dramatic reading" (203). Austin does note a new "species" of dramatic reading, in which a group of readers each takes on just one of the characters. He implies that the norm was for one reader to perform them all, as we saw Henry Crawford and Charles Burney doing (Chapter 4).

But the same gesture of personation was required in the reading of all kinds of literature. Gilbert Austin, to repeat, thought epic was the most difficult genre to read, not only because it required such dignity, but because epic is a mixed genre, including narrative, description, and the speech of many characters. Thus, while the reader of oratory enacts the public speaker and the actor personates one character, the reader of epic—and its successor, the novel—must represent the author, the narrator, or any of a series of characters. John Rice noted a complication within dialogue that would be at least as challenging in reading fiction:

> In the Recital of mere Narratives, of Descriptions, and of argumentative or persuasive Discourses, the Reader stands in the Place, and speaks in the Person of the Writer; but in the Rehearsal of Conversation-Pieces, he must diversify not only his Mode of reciting, in Conformity to the Subject, but also in Conformity to the Character. Thus the same Narrative and Description, if spoken by different Personages, must be differently recited.[18]

If drama required that the reader shade narrative and description with nuances of personation, narrative fiction would accentuate this requirement. The early elocutionists, like John Mason, recommended the reading of novels simply because they afforded practice in reading in a conversational style. But by the turn of the century, by which time the novel was more firmly established as a respectable genre, authors recognized that novels were a "mixed" genre and required the reader to incorporate several genres of reading. As Gilbert Austin said,

> Novels, or modern fictitious biography, are so frequently the subject of private readings, and influence so much the taste of young people, that they demand some notice. . . . In reading these works aloud to the private circle, custom, arising from the eager desire of unravelling the story, has determined that the mere narrative should be read with unusual rapidity. The interesting scenes demand impressive reading, and many of the scenes, which are constructed like those in a regular drama, require to be read in a similar manner. (205–6)

Before we consider the ways that a novel could be written to take advantage of oral performance practices, let us turn briefly to the various kinds of reading that the novel as a mixed genre would require. As we saw above, the school anthologies were divided into categories that roughly delineated genres of reading. While most of the anthologies, like Enfield's *The Speaker,* give general instructions on reading as a preface to their selections, one published at the end of the century offers more specific instructions. In his anthology, *Principles of Elocution,* John Wilson prefaces each new generic category (narrative pieces, descriptive pieces, and so on) with advice on reading that genre. In his section on "eloquence of the bar and popular assemblies," his advice is reminiscent of that of earlier elocutionists: the reciter should "try to make the sentiments his own, to place himself in the situation of the original speaker, and to suppose a numerous audience attentive to all he utters" (203). But Wilson's advice becomes more attentive to complexities of personation in the literary sections. His "remarks on dialogue" echo Rice: "The reciter, in many kinds of composition, personates the writer; but in conversation-pieces, he appears as the speaker, and must suit himself, not only to the subject and occasion, but also to the character: for the same speech delivered by different personages, requires different modes of pronunciation" (351). Personation becomes even more complex in mixed genres, as when a character's speech involves description:

> Descriptions, in the *first* person, must be read differently from those in the *third:* for when joyous or sorrowful scenes are described by the happy or suffering subject, the reader is incapable of doing them justice, unless he counterfeit the feelings, and exemplify the tones of natural personation; but when the same scenes are described by a spectator, the emotions may be less vivid, the tones less varied, and the emphasis less forcible. (64)

Then there is full-blown fiction, which includes narrative, description, and dialogue. "When figures are introduced, the reader must always be directed by their own rules. For example, when personation is necessary, he must assume the situation, adopt the peculiarities, and exhibit the most striking features of the original character" (3).

By the end of the century, then, elocutionists had recognized the full complexity of attempting personation in a mixed genre like the novel: not only were there distinct ways to read narrative, description, and so on, but each of these must be read differently as they are spoken by different characters. It is not surprising that, at the same time, novelists who might expect oral performance of their works developed techniques that would take advantage of the reader's voice. As John Rice had said in his *Introduction to the Art of Reading,* "It is presumed . . . that the Observations contained in this Work, may be of some Service also to Writers, by inducing them to pay Attention to the Manner in which their Works may be recited; a Circumstance that will necessarily improve and meliorate their Stile, whether they compose in Prose or Verse" (6). But how, exactly, would the expectation of oral performance be concretized in a novel? Let us turn to Austen's *Pride and Prejudice* as an exemplary text.

In his "Biographical Notice" of his sister, Henry Austen wrote, "She read aloud with very great taste and effect. Her own works, probably, were never heard to so much advantage as from her own mouth; for she partook largely in all the best gifts of the comic muse."[19] Henry was not the only witness to praise Austen's skill as a reader, and her pleasure in reading aloud is hinted at by the numerous descriptions of readings in her novels and letters. When the first copy of *Pride and Prejudice* arrived from the printer, though they had a guest, the Austens "set fairly at it & read half the 1st vol. to her." Perhaps Jane was reading that night, for she was certainly happy with the performance. A week later, though, she wrote, "our 2d evening's reading to Miss Benn had not pleased me so well, but I believe something must be attributed to my Mother's too rapid way of getting on—& tho' she perfectly understands the Characters herself, she cannot speak as they ought."[20] A fine reader herself, a frequent one, and one with decided notions of what constitutes excellence, Austen almost certainly wrote her novels anticipating that they would be read aloud. In this section, I will examine ways in which the performance practice of reading informs important aspects of the text of *Pride and Prejudice*. I will hold a consideration of the text's effect on the personating reader for the next section.

There is little doubt that Austen knew of the elocution movement; we have already seen her utilize it in a scene in *Mansfield Park*, in the context of reading in the pulpit. Austen's father, also considered an excellent reader, was a clergyman, a member of the elocutionists' target audience; to supplement his income he took in students and may well have used one of the popular anthologies. Austen alludes to Blair's *Lectures on Rhetoric and Belles Lettres* in *Northanger Abbey* (108), and she pictures Mr. Martin reading to his family from *Elegant Extracts,* which was prefaced by the chapter from Blair's *Lectures* titled "Pronunciation, or Delivery" (*E* 29).

Several features of the text of *Pride and Prejudice* seem to respond to Blair's essay. We remember, for example, that Blair (like most elocutionists) devoted considerable effort to eliciting appropriate emphasis. Blair recommended that the speaker read over his text and rehearse it, marking the "emphatical" words. While he warns against emphasizing too many words, he promises that "On the right management of the emphasis, depends the whole life and spirit of every discourse" (x). But the reader of a novel would probably *not* prepare ahead of time; the careful close readings we saw in

Chapter 4 could not be absolutely counted on by the author. Therefore, it would be incumbent on an author expecting an oral reading to offer a text in which emphasis is already marked—a text that need not be rehearsed ahead of time. And indeed, Austen's use of italics can be understood as guides for the performer. The italics are nearly always in sections of dialogue, meant especially to be acted out. In some cases italics clarify rhetoric like that detailed in the schoolbooks, which provided examples for practicing emphasis in antithesis, enumeration, parenthetical remarks, and so on. For example, Austen clarifies Darcy's use of antithesis: "Mr. Wickham is blessed with such happy manners as may ensure his *making* friends—whether he may be equally capable of *retaining* them, is less certain" (92). Or, as Elizabeth says of Wickham's marital aspirations, "If *she* does not object to it, why should *we*?" (153).

In other cases, Austen's italics indicate shades of meaning that may not depend on standard tropes, but that similarly would not be obvious to a performer reading the text for the first time. The very first time Darcy looks at Elizabeth, he says, "She is tolerable; but not handsome enough to tempt *me*" (12). A reader who has not prepared this text beforehand would be most likely to stress "tempt," missing the point: Darcy's supposed arrogance. Later on, when Darcy has admitted to another flaw, Elizabeth replies, "*That* is a failing indeed! . . . Implacable resentment *is* a shade in a character. But you have chosen your fault well.—I really cannot *laugh* at it" (58). Without the italics, the unrehearsed reader would probably place the emphasis elsewhere, especially in the second sentence, with a loss of vigor.

A surprising number of the italicized words in *Pride and Prejudice* are personal pronouns. Deidre Shauna Lynch has argued that Austen's novels work, in part, by emphasizing the ways in which individuals stand out from their mundane surroundings; she points to Austen's use of free indirect discourse as one technique to that end.[21] The italicized words work in the same way, making that emphasis literal; the characters' sense of their own individuality is communicated by the reader. Darcy's "*me*" in the sentence above sounds self-centered. But he is just as likely to distinguish Elizabeth from the mediocrities around her: regarding living close to one's family, he says, "*You* cannot have a right to such very strong local attachment. *You* cannot have been always at Longbourn" (179). Similarly, he separates himself and Elizabeth from other people, at the end of the novel, when Elizabeth has thanked him for rescuing Lydia: "'If you *will* thank me,' he replied, 'let it be for yourself alone. . . . Your *family* owe me nothing. Much as I respect them, I believe, I thought only of *you*. . . . You are too generous to trifle with me. . . . *My* affections and wishes are unchanged, but one word from you will silence me on this subject forever' " (366). Thus, through her use of italics, Austen helps the performing reader to emphasize the individuality of her characters.

Another kind of emphasis is what Blair terms "emphatical pauses . . . made, after something has been said of peculiar moment, and on which we want to fix the hearer's attention" (xi). Blair warns the reader not to pause strictly according to punctuation, for punctuation often marks grammar, not pronunciation. On the other hand, an author like Austen, planning for unrehearsed oral readings, *could* punctuate the "emphatical pauses." The best example of this in *Pride and Prejudice* is of course the famous opening sentence, on which Austen certainly wants to "fix the hearer's attention," and which is followed by a paragraph break. Italics and paragraph breaks indicate emphasis for the silent reader as well, of course, but the absence of them in that case would not threaten the reading to the same degree. While the silent reader may always go over a text twice, the performer should not.

The marking of emphasis operates at the level of sentence construction; in many places, Austen seems to have indicated preferred readings for the benefit of someone reading *Pride and Prejudice* aloud without preparation, as her mother read it to Miss Benn. But did the performance practice of reading affect *Pride and Prejudice* on a larger scale? The writer who anticipates an oral reading will prepare a text that is easy to read aloud, that takes advantage of the benefits of oral reading, that minimizes sections that do not read well. If the author expects a professional or highly skilled reading, the text may include vocal flourishes. But in Austen's case, most probably, the expected reading was by an amateur who might not be very skilled and who, importantly, was probably female. In the following few pages, I will link this kind of reading with three features of Austen's novel: her use of dialogue and free indirect discourse, her domestic scale, and her reliance on women's voices.

DIALOGUE AND NARRATION

In his *Chironomia*, as we saw, Gilbert Austin articulated a hierarchy of good reading within the styles found in the novel: "mere narrative" is rushed through, to unravel the story, while "interesting scenes" are read impressively, and scenes in dialogue are read "like those in a regular drama." If "mere" narrative was customarily slighted by the reader, an author anticipating oral performance would have an excellent incentive to utilize dialogue. We have already seen this in the opening of *Pride and Prejudice*. But even where Austen uses narration, it is always highly personalized, in contrast to the neutral narration of authors like Ann Radcliffe (whose gothics, as I argued in Chapter 4, were best read silently). Indeed, in the domestic reading circle, it would be absurd to have an anonymous, neutral narrator. The narrative voice is literally the voice of someone one knows, perhaps one's own mother.

Austen's narrative is frequently enlivened even further by her use of free indirect discourse, which either she or Frances Burney (whose works, as we saw, were also read aloud) is often credited with inventing. Free indirect discourse presents characters' speech or thoughts within narration, without special punctuation but with vocabulary or "voice" that is felt to be the characters'. For example, instead of "She said, 'Oh! I am vastly pleased'" (direct discourse) or "She said she was vastly pleased" (indirect discourse), we may be given, "Oh! She was vastly pleased." Free indirect discourse encourages the reader to intersperse other voices with her own, even in snatches of a phrase here or there, where fully realized dialogue is not needed. While free indirect discourse is more prevalent in Austen's later novels, there are examples of it in *Pride and Prejudice*, such as this from chapter 3:

> An invitation to dinner was soon afterwards dispatched; and already had Mrs. Bennet planned the courses that were to do credit to her housekeeping, when *an answer arrived which deferred it all.* Mr. Bingley was obliged to be in town the following day, and consequently unable to accept the honour of their invitation, &c. *Mrs. Bennet was quite disconcerted.* She could not imagine what business he could have in town so soon after his arrival in Hertfordshire; and she began to fear that he might be always flying about from one place to another, never settled at Netherfield as he ought to be. (9–10, my italics)

Free indirect discourse allows the reader to make better use of her acting skills; in this passage, separate voices would contrast Bingley's formal politeness with Mrs. Bennet's petulance, and in each case, Austen has given the reader cues (shown here in italics) as to which voice to use in the sentence that follows.[22]

Both dialogue and free indirect discourse demand a very attentive reader. While Austen complained of her mother's inability to portray the characters in dialogue, she herself was skilled at this. As we saw, her niece Caroline thought that Austen's reading of *Evelina* was "like a play."[23] The simile is apt: the text of the novel is only a script, to be performed by the actor/reader. Austen fills *Pride and Prejudice* with dialogues that are almost like plays, connected by narrative passages enlivened by the voices of both narrator and characters. Very little is "mere narrative," to be diminished by being "read with unusual rapidity." On the contrary, the reader practices constant and flexible personation.

DIALOGUE'S DOMESTIC SCALE

If the novel is to be like a play, the author must not overreach the reader's virtuosity. Gilbert Austin's advice on reading dramatic texts suggests that the reader was to drop the attributions as much as possible, relying instead on changes of voice to differentiate the characters: "In the reading of plays [in mere private and family society], the names of the characters are sometimes read in a sort of dry under voice before the passages they are supposed to speak: but this awkward expedient should not be used except to prevent ambiguity. . . . A person of taste and judgment will feel when he may divest his reading of this incumbrance, and will know when he ought to submit to it" (202). Dropping the attributions increases the difficulty of reading a dramatic text; in choosing a scene to perform, the reader would recognize his or her limitations and choose one with few characters. The school anthologies always included dramatic dialogues, but almost never scenes with more than two characters: that is simply beyond the range of the amateur performer.

Austen's novel reflects this limitation. The scenes in *Pride and Prejudice* that are most like a play—the opening chapter, Mr. Collins's proposal, Elizabeth's confrontation with Lady Catherine, and so on—are dialogues between two characters. Austen has taken advantage of the personating reader, but not strained her abilities. This enforced intimacy determines the scope of the novel, virtually forbidding large public scenes in favor of private conversation.

For example, one long scene, which might have been the occasion for a large group discussion, is written, surprisingly, in a series of dialogues: the Netherfield ball (89–103). During the scene there are times when more than two people stand together, but almost never do more than two speak. Except for one brief interruption, when Elizabeth dances with Darcy their conversation is sheltered; Elizabeth's conversations with Miss Bingley, Jane, and Mr. Collins, in turn, are private. Until fairly recently, Austen's work was criticized for its domestic scale, its lack of grand public action. But Austen takes advantage of the limitation, making privacy essential in furthering the plot. In a private conversation with Elizabeth, Miss Bingly warns her against Mr. Wickham; her warning is easy for Elizabeth to discount because it is not verified by any third person. Even more telling is Elizabeth's dance with Mr. Darcy: the privacy allows a remarkably intimate conversation, in which she accuses Darcy of mistreating Wickham. Such a conversation would be unthinkable in a larger party. Yet Elizabeth and Darcy *are* in a larger party; Austen has simply chosen to limit the scale to ease the task of reading.

The many engagements in *Pride and Prejudice* are similarly announced only in private. Like a ball, an engagement announcement is inherently public, making Austen's choices odd unless we consider performance practice. The first engagement, Charlotte's to Mr. Collins, is broken to Elizabeth alone, in dialogue, before the public announcement, given in indirect discourse. In the second, Jane's to Mr. Bingley, Austen employs almost farcical entrances and exits: when Elizabeth breaks into their tête-à-tête, Bingley hurries out to ask Mr. Bennet's permission, leaving Jane to speak privately with Elizabeth; as soon as Bingley returns, Jane goes off, again leaving Elizabeth in a private dialogue. And finally, Elizabeth discusses her own engagement to Darcy, not with her family as a whole, but with Jane, her father, and her mother, in turn; the three characters all express incredulity, but their different reactions let us enjoy unhurriedly Jane's love of Elizabeth, Mr. Bennet's love of teasing, and Mrs. Bennet's love of money. The novelist has made choices that ease the performer's burden, and that consequently emphasize privacy, domesticity, and individual characterizations.

Performance practice may also explain why Austen utilizes a comparatively narrow range of speech. As Norman Page has observed, Austen makes no use of vivid dialect; her characters' speech exhibits no regional or class difference. A character like Mr. Martin in *Emma,* who is not a member of the gentry, may be given no speech at all.[24] The characters in *Pride and Prejudice* speak in voices as different as Lydia's slang and Mr. Collins's pomposity—but these differences are well within the experience of Austen's readers. Austen's most likely reader was someone like her mother: a middle-class woman, of limited education and experience, who may have understood the characters, but could not "speak as they ought." An author anticipating such a reader would make the best use of characters the reader could enact—women of her own station—and minimize her use of anyone different.

WOMEN PERFORMERS, WOMEN'S VOICES

As I argued in Chapter 4, the reader's role was typically gendered. It was customary for men to read to women; in fact, to protect women from immoral texts by choosing, censoring, and interpreting the novels they read. But Austen lived in a world populated almost entirely by women.[25] After her father died, her usual reading circle was female; the reading of *Pride and Prejudice* that Austen described in her letter was typical in this respect. It is not surprising, then, that Austen's novels favor female voices.

It would be foolish to suppose it impossible that a man should read a female role, or vice versa. A novel like *Evelina* was read aloud by both men and women (by Charles Burney and Jane Austen, for example), with no sense that that was inappropriate. But if cross-sexual readings were not absolutely forbidden, neither were they sought out. In the speeches and dramatic dialogues reprinted in school anthologies intended for boys, like Enfield's *The Speaker* or Knox's *Elegant Extracts,* nearly all of the speakers were male. Texts like Wollstonecraft's *The Female Reader* or Barbauld's *The Female Speaker* included a much larger proportion of women's voices.

In *Pride and Prejudice,* the liveliest speakers are women; the men are comparatively mute. Two sets of relatives are analogous in this respect: while Mr. Bennet and Elizabeth are both known for their enjoyment of laughing at their neighbors, Mr. Bennet provokes his wife primarily by his silence (as in chapter 1); Elizabeth's barbs are always in words. Similarly, Darcy and Lady Catherine are supposed, at first, to be alike. But during Elizabeth's stay at Netherfield, Darcy defends himself by his silence; Lady Catherine, in Kent and in Hertfordshire, by her piercing speech. Darcy's proposal to Elizabeth is told almost entirely in indirect discourse (which requires less acting ability); Lady Catherine's subsequent confrontation with Elizabeth is one of the liveliest dialogues in the novel. It has often been noted (perhaps not *quite* accurately) that in all of Austen's novels, there is not a single dialogue between men alone. Perhaps she avoided such dialogue not only because she wouldn't represent something she had never experienced (as some have suggested), but because she was thinking of the female performing voice.

Austen's preference for female voices signifies more than a concession to the limited abilities of her reader: it is arguably her greatest innovation. While Sheldon Sacks, writing prior to the feminist turn, showed that Austen was the first novelist to require real growth before granting her characters (of both sexes) their reward, Susan Morgan points out that Austen was the first to allow women to grow at all.[26] Austen's women are neither victims nor harlots; they are human beings with much on their minds besides their virginity. I would hesitate to argue that performance practice in any way "caused" Austen to consider women more seriously than previous authors had done. Rather, it presented her with resources (women's voices) and limitations (the demand for private conversations) of which she made excellent use.

Every performing medium has its limitations and its opportunities. Reading aloud will tend to characterize a narrator, to enliven dialogue, in sum, to make a novel more like a play. Other authors, anticipating different kinds of performances, have made choices other than those made by Austen. Charles Dickens, for example, made eloquent use of dialect and sociolect, and his characters people the entire universe of nineteenth-century England. Dickens revised his early novels, and wrote his later ones, to be performed by himself to a paying audience. Dickens was a virtuoso reader, and his novels show off his skill. But Austen's novels were performed in the family circle, by three or four women sitting together of an evening. Her novels do not demand of those readers that they personate characters or adopt roles that are foreign to them. Yet the novels demonstrate a range of speech strategies within those roles that provide a special kind of education. Let us turn now to the question of how Austen's attentiveness to conversation might affect the personating reader.

Reading Pride and Prejudice

As we noted above, feminist critics have argued that by the late eighteenth century, novels could serve the function of conduct manuals. Though eighteenth-century critics perceived the novel as a dangerous influence on young readers, modern ones have emphasized the extent to which novels reinforced patriarchal norms: authors presented a series of set scenes in which proper behavior was modeled, and readers internalized the norms portrayed. The evidence of elocution and education texts indicates that this process was also at work in the realm of speech: as the reader performed a text, she practiced both the speech strategies written as dialogue and the authority of narration. The conversation manuals that had been common earlier in the century were no longer widely used, and in any case they and the conduct books gave rather vague advice about "pleasing" or avoiding common conversational errors. But as we have seen, educators firmly believed that reading a text aloud helped the reader develop both an authoritative tone and a speech repertoire. The excerpts in school anthologies and the dialogues meant to be performed by students were chosen exactly for this purpose. And novels, with their depiction of specific situations and their layers of required personation, could instruct the reader in the subtleties of speech.

As critics have done about conduct-book norms, we may well wonder whether the speech norms instilled through reading were liberatory for women who may have had little access to formal education or whether they merely reinforced traditional linguistic hierarchies. In Chapter 1, we saw that a single prestigious form of English was coalescing during this period, one that was certainly aided in its development by the growing nationwide audience for belles lettres. If Helena Wells could teach her pupils to use a literary English through practice sentences, she would also expect them to learn the prestigious forms as they read and recited essays and fiction.

Fiction, in particular, would teach not only a literary prose style but the conversational strategies depicted in dialogue. This is not to claim that readers' speech lost the features of oral language that distinguish it from dialogue. We must imagine that speakers continued to shift direction in midsentence, use fragments, interrupt each other, and so on. Nevertheless, readers would have learned from dialogue a range of conversational strategies that could be internalized and reconstructed. This would be especially important for women, whose language use was so constrained by social norms. In reading fiction, in successively personating a range of characters, male and female, women were enabled to practice a range of possible identities.

Let us turn back to *Pride and Prejudice* and consider the range of speech strategies that it offers for the reader to practice. I do not make any claims about authorial intent here: one cannot know that Austen consciously planned for her novel to be a kind of conversation manual. But, as I argued above, it does seem clear that Austen did plan her novel to be read aloud. Given that and the arguments of the elocution and school texts about the effect of oral reading on the reader, we can legitimately ask what kind of reading a text like *Pride and Prejudice* invites, and what kinds of speech it offers to the reader to practice. In the following discussion, I focus on three categories of discourse competence that the reader may internalize from reading this text: norms of politeness, of authority, and of character.

PRACTICING POLITENESS

Pride and Prejudice, even more than the other Austen novels, hinges on modes of politeness or, as Austen generally calls it, "civility." Darcy, in particular, exemplifies the importance of civility as he learns it over the course of the novel. Darcy's pride expresses itself in his refusal to participate politely in conversation; his utter unwillingness to please others generates Elizabeth's original dislike of him. This unwillingness reaches its apogee in the heated scene at Hunsford parsonage: Darcy's failure to propose marriage in a way that Elizabeth might accept is in large part a failure in following the rule of conversation that instructs us not to offend (though Elizabeth explicitly denies that his manner of speaking mattered to her). And Darcy's reformation, when Elizabeth surprises him at Pemberley, is also conversational, depending crucially on small talk and polite gestures.

In thematizing politeness, *Pride and Prejudice* offers a number of direct examples of the kind of conversational advice we saw in Fielding's "Essay," often taught through negative examples. It begins (to repeat) with an example of what *not* to do in conversation, with Mr. Bennet's refusal to participate in the turn-taking cooperativeness we expect. Similarly, the "indelicacy

of putting himself forward" (207) exhibited by Mr. Wickham and his willingness—no, eagerness—to speak ill of another both violate polite norms, as
Elizabeth comes to realize. Earlier, formal modes of conversation are
ridiculed in the obsequious flattery of Mr. Collins, who not only constantly
spouts fawning phrases, but actually plans them out ahead of time. In so
doing, he follows the advice of early-eighteenth-century conversation manuals, one of whose functions was to provide the student with useful stock
phrases.[27]

Despite poking fun at the excesses of formal civility, though, Austen by
no means rejects the notion that conversation is governed by rules.
Developing skill in conversation is part of being socialized, being accomplished. Elizabeth gestures toward rules of conversation while dancing with
Mr. Darcy:

> [S]he made some slight observation on the dance. He replied, and was again
> silent. After a pause of some minutes she addressed him a second time with
> "It is *your* turn to say something now, Mr. Darcy.—*I* talked about the dance,
> and *you* ought to make some kind of remark on the size of the room, or the
> number of couples."
> He smiled, and assured her that whatever she wished him to say should be
> said. [91]

Darcy's willingness to take his turn, once he is reminded of his office, reveals
him to be somewhat more amiable than Elizabeth's father. But he still
doesn't understand that conversation is something that must be practiced;
Elizabeth explicitly tells him much later (at Rosings) that he should have
practiced his conversational skills as she practiced the piano.

In this, Elizabeth takes on a traditional role; in *Pride and Prejudice,* it is
often women who must "do the conversational work." Silence is nearly
always described as awkward in this text, something to be filled up with
chat. When Darcy visits unexpectedly, they "seemed in danger of sinking
into total silence. It was absolutely necessary, therefore, to think of something" (177). When Elizabeth visits Pemberley, there is "a pause, awkward
as such pauses must always be" until the conversation is bravely carried on
by Mrs. Annesley and Mrs. Gardiner, the most mature women present
(267). Another way of doing the conversational work is to shift the subject
away from anything that is potentially uncomfortable. When Elizabeth
reacts to Colonel Fitzwilliam's revelation that Darcy has separated his friend
Bingley from Elizabeth's sister Jane, "she would not trust herself with an
answer; and, therefore, abruptly changing the conversation, talked on
indifferent matters till they reached the parsonage" (186). Thus the polite
converser actively smoothes interactions and feelings.

And yet good conversation is not a reliable guide to character, as Wickham and Darcy demonstrate most clearly. Wickham's charm gives him entrée to places he doesn't belong; Darcy's taciturnity invites others to think more meanly of him than he deserves. In the case of Darcy's cousin Colonel Fitzwilliam, ease in conversation is the attribute of a true gentleman. But the link is very tenuous in *Pride and Prejudice*. Though both are important, conversational skill and moral worth are shown to be two separate qualities.

They are linked to some degree when civility is not just a matter of words, but marks real respect for another person. In modern terms (as we saw in Chapter 2), when politeness is theorized in terms of saving the other's face, it can be either positive (showing that you value the other) or negative (respecting the other's autonomy by not imposing). Both positive and negative politeness receive ample attention in this text. Most striking to the modern reader, perhaps, is the latter: we are accustomed to more forthright interactions and can experience the reticence of Austen's characters as quaint. Impertinence, on the other hand, remains the same: Lady Catherine's bossiness in advising Mrs. Collins about her poultry and her closets offends even a modern sensibility. Darcy is at first as unwilling to balance sincerity with tact as his aunt is; that he has learned the value of negative politeness by the time Elizabeth surprises him at Pemberley is apparent in his exaggerated avoidance of imposition: "Will you allow me, or do I ask too much, to introduce my sister to your acquaintance during your stay at Lambton?" (256).

Darcy must also practice positive politeness, those gestures that please the other and foster a sense of solidarity. Inviting Mr. Gardiner to fish is one of these, as is Darcy's repeated asking after Elizabeth's family. As always, Austen shows the dangers inherent in whatever she praises: Mr. Collins's empty flattery and even Sir William Lucas's studied courtliness take positive politeness to an extreme. But this does not reduce the value of politeness when practiced with wisdom and sincerity. The reader learns this proper degree of politeness by personating Darcy.

Darcy, however, has through the accident of birth a "natural" ethos that middle-class women did not. The question remains as to how women might be taught to negotiate the claims of sincerity and politeness so as to develop ethos without explicitly challenging their social role. Merely to please, to avoid offending, is to deny the full personhood that is characteristic of Austen's women. Politeness cannot be the only value in conversation. We saw in Chapter 2 that groups like the Quakers might favor sincerity over polite norms when the two conflict. For men, as well, there would be many occasions to practice norms other than politeness. But how would a middle-class woman who wants to forge an identity within the norms of polite behavior develop strategies for balancing politeness and sincerity?

To the extent that the reader personates Elizabeth and internalizes her speech, she may stretch the limits of conventional politeness. Elizabeth herself jokes that her behavior to Darcy "was at least always bordering on the uncivil," and she teases him that he fell in love with her precisely because he was "sick of civility, of deference, of officious attention" (380). Even when Elizabeth is not being witty, she adheres to norms other than polite ones, often preferring the mode of "manly" sincerity. Austen represents the conflict between sincerity and politeness in the scene in which Elizabeth rejects the proposal of the ridiculous Mr. Collins. While the proposal itself is long-winded enough, the scene is extended when Mr. Collins interprets Elizabeth's rejection as conventional and polite: "I am not now to learn [he says] . . . that it is usual with young ladies to reject the addresses of the man whom they secretly mean to accept, when he first applies for their favour" (107). In contrast to this polite indirectness, Elizabeth refers to her own "manly" directness in her refusal: "I am perfectly serious," she says (107), and later, "I do assure you, Sir, that I have no pretension whatever to that kind of elegance which consists in tormenting a respectable man. I would rather be paid the compliment of being believed sincere. . . . Can I speak plainer? Do not consider me now as an elegant female intending to plague you, but as a rational creature speaking the truth from her heart" (108–9). And he replies again in the language of courtship: "You are uniformly charming!" (109). Both Mr. Collins and Elizabeth recognize that plain sincerity is more associated with men. He cannot believe she is capable of it; and if he cannot, she plans to turn to her father, "whose negative might be uttered in such a manner as must be decisive, and whose behaviour at least could not be mistaken for the affectation and coquetry of an elegant female" (109).

If her sincerity is sometimes praiseworthy, Elizabeth's failing as a conversationalist is to be overly direct; she frequently makes statements that others more politely deflect. For example, when Miss Bingley says that Elizabeth enjoys nothing but reading, Elizabeth directly contradicts her, saying "I am *not* a great reader, and I have pleasure in many things." Mr. Bingley then turns the topic more politely: "In nursing your sister I am sure you have pleasure" (37). Several times, Elizabeth directly confronts Darcy, whether justly or not, and he deflects her attacks. While they are dancing, her accusation that he has mistreated Wickham is remarkably direct: "He has been so unlucky as to lose *your* friendship, . . . and in a manner which he is likely to suffer from all his life" (92); Darcy changes the subject. Later, at Hunsford, Elizabeth asks directly whether Darcy has seen Jane in London, knowing that he had not; she asked him only to embarrass him (171). Elizabeth's worst instance of overly direct speech, however, is in her reaction to her friend Charlotte's engagement: "Engaged to Mr. Collins! my dear Charlotte,—impossible!" (124). Elizabeth is repaid for this gaffe by her family's reaction to her own engagement: Jane echoes Elizabeth, saying, "You are joking, Lizzy. This cannot be!—engaged to Mr. Darcy! No, no, you shall not deceive me. I know it to be impossible" (372). Lizzy's tendency is to overly direct speech. When she does combine truth with tact, the narrator may explicitly mark the attempt: when Mr. Collins crows of his felicity with his bride, "Elizabeth could safely say that it was a great happiness where that was the case, and with equal sincerity could add that she firmly believed and rejoiced in his domestic comforts" (216).

Austen gives the reader practice in speech that deviates from the strict norms of the conduct books. Still, she stays just this side of incivility. Her model may perhaps be closest to the politeness defined by Hester Chapone in *Letters on the Improvement of the Mind*, which we glanced at in Chapter 2. Politeness, for Chapone, may have slightly different manifestations in different cultures, but it rests on universal principles:

> [T]he principles of politeness are the same in all places. Wherever there are human beings, it must be impolite to hurt the temper or to shock the passions of those you converse with. It must every where be good-breeding, to set your companions in the most advantageous point of light . . . ;—to exert your own endeavors to please, and to amuse, but not to outshine them;—to give each their due share of attention and notice . . . —In short, it is an universal duty in society to consider others more than yourself. (2:98–99)

For Chapone, doing the conversational work is more important than keeping a modest silence: "silence should only be enjoined, when it would be forward and impertinent to talk" (2:103). Rather, it is a duty to appear interested in the conversation, to ask questions, and when asked oneself, not to "draw back as unwilling to answer" but on the contrary to take "some share in the conversation" (2:104–5). As we saw above, Chapone even allows the kind of raillery on which Elizabeth Bennet prides herself, as long as it is delicate and good-natured. Even with gentlemen, "I wish you to behave with the same frankness and simplicity as if they were of your own sex. If you have natural modesty, you will never transgress its bounds, whilst you converse with a man, as one rational creature with another" (2:113).

Like Chapone, Austen invites her reader to practice a form of politeness that recognizes the duty to please but combines that with the need to utilize both reason and wit. Moreover, she recognizes that the norm she proposes is only grudgingly allowed to a middle-class woman. The Bingley sisters, with their fierce sense of what is appropriate in the "polite" world, consider Elizabeth pert. So did some real-life readers of *Pride and Prejudice*. Mary Russell Mitford wrote to a friend, "it is impossible not to feel in every line of *Pride and Prejudice,* in every word of 'Elizabeth,' the entire want of taste which could produce so pert, so worldly a heroine as the beloved of such a man as Darcy."[28] In a hierarchical society, to accuse someone of being "pert" is to accuse them of not knowing their place. Wit was more allowable for upper-class women; by personating and practicing Elizabeth's mediated form of politeness, the reader is indeed offered a sociolect that is not quite middle class.

PRACTICING AUTHORITY

Modern feminist linguists have often theorized authority in conversational interaction in terms of who directs the conversation: who proposes topics, whose topics are pursued, who "holds the floor." In the example of Mary Knowles (Introduction), we saw that authority could be represented in those terms in the eighteenth century as well. The representations that championed Knowles in her argument with Johnson gave her longer and more coherent speeches; Johnson himself became angry at the amount of "airtime" that Knowles was granted by the company.

However, the equation of "airtime" and authority is not a simple one for women, whose supposed volubility was a key feature of the stereotype of woman's language. Indeed, Austen is particularly mischievous with her voluble characters; it is generally the silliest people who speak the most. The opening dialogue of *Pride and Prejudice* reveals how Austen declines to link topic proposal and authority: Mrs. Bennet struggles mightily to propose a conversation on the tenant of Netherfield, while Mr. Bennet does all he can to prevent her. Her speech is, if anything, the signal of her power*less*ness.

In the case of Lady Catherine, however, authority *is* signaled by the choosing of topics and by lengthier speeches. When Elizabeth first encounters Lady Catherine, in Kent, we are told that "she was not rendered formidable by silence; but whatever she said, was spoken in so authoritative a tone, as marked her self-importance" (162). In the dialogue that follows, Lady Catherine asks questions to which Elizabeth gives very brief answers; Lady Catherine then comments on those and asks other questions, so that her speeches are always longer than Elizabeth's. For example:

> "Your father's estate is entailed on Mr. Collins, I think. For your sake," turning to Charlotte, "I am glad of it; but otherwise I see no occasion for entailing estates from the female line.—It was not thought necessary in Sir Lewis de Bourgh's family.—Do you play and sing, Miss Bennet?"

"A little."

"Oh! then—sometime or other we shall be happy to hear you. Our instrument is a capital one, probably superior to——You shall try it someday.—Do your sisters play and sing?"

"One of them does." (164)

When, after several such interchanges, Elizabeth does give a longer answer, she is rebuked by Lady Catherine: "Upon my word . . . you give your opinion very decidedly for so young a person.—Pray, what is your age?" (165–66). However, age is not the real issue here. Lady Catherine is allowed, and expected, to dominate the conversation because she is an aristocrat and Elizabeth is only a gentleman's daughter. Class is more salient here than either age or gender. Lady Catherine's birth grants her the privilege of conversational authority.

But what of our middle-class reader? She might well have enjoyed performing Lady Catherine's superciliousness, but she would have known that had she attempted that kind of speech in real life, she would probably suffer the fate of Mrs. Bennet. A woman's assumption of authority was not tolerated unless backed up by the claims of class position. Even Miss Bingley, whose wealth gives her some status, is consistently rebuffed by Darcy when she attempts to propose conversational topics. Among the lower-status speakers, Austen tends to represent the proposal of a conversational topic as rude. The narrator calls Lydia's bringing up Mr. Bingley's promise to have a ball a "sudden attack" (45). More seriously, Wickham directs his first conversation with Elizabeth toward Darcy's imputed unjust behavior. Again and again through this conversation, Wickham introduces topics and speaks at length, while Elizabeth merely responds to him. Only later does Elizabeth realize how improper Wickham's conversation was.

And no wonder, for Elizabeth's "pertness" consists in large part of her own tendency to introduce topics. Her reticence in speaking of Darcy with her aunt Gardiner is very much the exception; in that case, "They talked of his sister, his friends, his house, his fruit, of every thing but himself; yet Elizabeth was longing to know what Mrs. Gardiner thought of him, and Mrs. Gardiner would have been highly gratified by her niece's beginning the subject" (272). Elizabeth more frequently asserts herself exactly through the proposal of conversational topics. In her interactions with Darcy, her proposals often sound like attacks. When Elizabeth complains that Darcy is eavesdropping and Charlotte "defied her friend to mention such a subject" to Darcy (24), Elizabeth accepts the challenge immediately. Later in that scene, she brings up the subject of Wickham on purpose to provoke him. And at the end of the novel, it is her bringing up the subject of Lydia's elopement and thanking Darcy for his kindness to her that leads directly to his renewed proposal.

Elizabeth thus assumes the authority of a Lady Catherine in spite of her lower social class; no wonder some readers felt that she was "pert." Austen seems aware of this risk in her representation of Elizabeth's assertiveness: she represents Elizabeth's "attacks" on Darcy directly, but otherwise, she tends to introduce Elizabeth's topics indirectly, in narrative, before moving into dialogue. The narrator "covers" for Elizabeth in statements like "Elizabeth ventured to introduce the subject; and then, on her briefly expressing her sorrow for what he must have endured, [her father] replied, 'Say nothing of that'" (299). The reader thus is somewhat protected from the risk of internalizing such boldness.

If we think of *Pride and Prejudice* as a kind of conversation manual, with Elizabeth as the character whose personation matters most, the true climax of the novel is the splendid confrontation in which Lady Catherine tries to prevent Elizabeth from marrying Darcy and in which Elizabeth's verbal skill is best demonstrated. Both Lady Catherine and Elizabeth use language that differs markedly from the qualified, "feminine" speech of Mrs. Bennet. Mrs. Bennet's tentativeness is indicated by what linguists call hedges: "I believe," "I dare say," "may I take the liberty of asking," and so on. Lady Catherine imitates this style while in Mrs. Bennet's company: "Miss Bennet, there *seemed* to be a *prettyish kind of a little* wilderness on one side of your lawn. I *should be glad* to take a turn in it, *if you will favour me* with your company" (352, my italics). Once she is alone with Elizabeth, however, Lady Catherine asserts her allegiance to "manly" directness: "however insincere *you* may choose to be, you shall not find *me* so. My character has ever been celebrated for its sincerity and frankness" (353, italics original). Faced with such blunt language, Elizabeth stands her ground through the judicious use of indirectness. When asked outright whether there is cause for the rumor that she will marry Darcy, Elizabeth asserts, "I do not pretend to possess equal frankness with your ladyship. *You* may ask questions, which *I* shall not choose to answer." Asked again, if Darcy has proposed, she sidesteps: "Your ladyship has declared it to be impossible" (354). But Elizabeth changes her strategy in the middle of the scene, once Lady Catherine has forced her into a plain admission that she and Darcy are not engaged. After this point, Elizabeth becomes as direct as Lady Catherine, boldly asserting that she is "not to be intimidated," making her case, and stating flatly that Lady Catherine "can *now* have nothing farther to say" (357). In the end, she answers Lady Catherine's attacks only with a resistant silence.

This scene, like many others, demonstrates the complexity of linguistic competence, especially for women. In order for a woman to develop authority, or ethos, she must negotiate the conflicting claims of polite indirectness, the admonishment to silence, and the need for sincerity. By creating a character as powerful as Elizabeth Bennet, Austen invites her reader to practice strategies allowed by polite speech. This is not to say that listeners will always accept women's authoritative speech, nor to minimize the class hierarchies embedded in polite norms. Quite the opposite: performing a novel like *Pride and Prejudice* offers the reader the specificity and complexity that were beyond the range of conversation manuals and conduct books.

PRACTICING CHARACTER

Competent speakers learn to utilize a range of strategies to accomplish varied linguistic goals in a range of contexts in which they speak in varied roles or characters. We speak differently to achieve our goals when we speak "as" a professor, "as" a mom, "as" a customer with a complaint. In Chapter 1, I argued that one of the severest limitations of eighteenth-century language theorists was that they imagined that all women could have only one linguistic character, whereas men (as the example from *Tristram Shandy* indicated) had many.

In her representations of speech, Austen tends to be a conservative in this regard. She has often been praised for her representation of idiolect: individual characters are consistent and recognizable in the individuality of their voices. But Austen generally does not represent characters speaking in varied contexts; her women are individualized in utterly new and wonderful ways, but they do not speak outside of their traditional social roles. Woman's language is reserved for her lesser characters: Miss Bingley's "shockings" and "abominables," Lydia's bad grammar ("Mrs. Forster and me are *such* friends!" [221]), Mrs. Bennet's superlatives and misuse of *vast* (42) are all stereotypical. But although the more admirable characters speak sensibly, as full human beings, we don't see the range of their social identities. Nor do Austen's men speak in "such a variety of characters" as Tristram's father. For example, Elizabeth learns to respect Darcy for his goodness "as a brother, a landlord, a master" (250). The reader, though, does not see him speak in all those roles or personate them.

But the reader does practice speaking in different roles, by personating each of the characters. The very first, and the one with the most ethos, is the narrator (eighteenth-century critics would say the "author"). This is a narrator whose wit and confidence represent the very opposite of the conduct-book modest female, and one whose verbal skill any personating reader would welcome. As the (female) reader personates this female narrator, she takes on the ethos embedded in the text as surely as the schoolboy takes on that of Cicero as he performs an oration. If ethos is that quality in a verbal artifact that leads us to trust the speaker's intentions and judgment, ethos virtually defines third-person narration. In eighteenth-century fiction, there were unreliable narrators in other forms, like the deceiving letter writers of Laclos or the self-deceiving first-person narrators of Defoe. But the third-person narrator, Jane Austen's narrator in particular, spoke with absolute authority.

The personating reader, then, incorporates narrative ethos into her character as it is constructed in speech. But if the elocutionists taught this kind of ethos to future speakers of the senate, the pulpit, and the bar, it is not so certain that women would have occasions for the monologic speech that is the privilege of narration. As I argued above, Austen tends to conceive of ethos not as something constructed in a single utterance, but rather as embedded in an ongoing personal relationship, developed through conversation. The personating reader must learn not only the authoritative tone of the narrator, but also the conversational strategies that will enable her to construct a character.

And here again, a fiction like Austen's offers a richness to the reader that the conversation manuals did not. It must be said again that Austen presents many examples of what *not* to do in speech, from the silliness of woman's language to the many incivilities she represents. The reader, then, must personate the range of characters and experience their speech, but distinguish language to be imitated from that to be rejected. Edgeworth didn't trust a young child to make this distinction; personating a spoiled character might spoil the juvenile reader. Austen does expect her reader to be wise enough to try a character on and judge for herself whether or not it fits.

Listening to Persuasion

In *Pride and Prejudice,* Austen is optimistic about the possibilities of constructing a self through speech and implicitly teaches the reader to do so. She evinces less optimism in her last work, *Persuasion.* The heroine of *Persuasion,* Anne Elliot, has suffered for eight years because she broke off her engagement to a young naval officer at the urging of her older friend, Lady Russell. Like all the completed Austen novels, this one ends happily with a marriage, when Wentworth reappears and overcomes his bitterness toward Anne. But *Persuasion* is somber in tone. It is told almost entirely from Anne's point of view, and she has little hope of future happiness until very late in the novel. Even the narrator, who is well aware of the follies of those around

our heroine, reveals those follies without adopting the joyously ironi
stance of the narrator of *Pride and Prejudice*. Moreover, this novel has none
of the earlier work's repartee. Indeed, it is the Austen novel with the least
dialogue altogether. If *Pride and Prejudice* teaches the reader a range of speech
strategies, *Persuasion* explores the value of silence.

One of Austen's many gifts to us is the daring with which she experi-
ments with new ideas and points of view. While each of the six completed
novels has a plot that resolves with a marriage, each one sets up a different
kind of writing problem to give us a varied picture of the moral lives of
women (and men) of her period. Many critics claim *Persuasion* is the one
of Austen's novels that most anticipates nineteenth-century conceptions of
interiority. I would rather, however, adopt Claudia L. Johnson's suggestion
that we resist the temptation to impose a teleology on Austen's career.[29] Let
us appreciate the variety Austen gives us without creating a narrative
around it, and simply look at how, unlike *Pride and Prejudice* and its sense of
a self constructed in speech, *Persuasion* points toward a faith in an interiority that exists independently of speech, even in opposition to it.

Austen had often opposed feeling and speech in earlier works, criticizing characters whose speech was too polished or glib. In *Sense and Sensibility*,
one sign of sensibility is an unwillingness to utter civilities; *Emma's* Mr.
Knightley says, "If I loved you less, I might be able to talk about it more"
(*E* 430). And we are told that the cynical title character in *Lady Susan* "talks
vastly well, . . . talks *too* well to feel so very deeply" (267). Volubility is usually a negative characteristic in Austen, and skill in speech may be a sign of
manipulativeness. Yet, as we saw above, *Pride and Prejudice* fostered conversation that avoided awkward silences and framed politeness as a positive cooperative norm. In *Persuasion,* on the other hand, true communication is non-
verbal.

Words are often useless in *Persuasion*. Anne Elliot is presented to us as
one whose "word had no weight" (5). Her father and elder sister pointedly
ignore her and think she is nothing; "They had no inclination to listen to
her" (137). At the home of her younger sister, Anne is valued primarily as a
sounding board for the complaints of family members about each other.
Austen's representation exaggerates this, giving us verbatim Henrietta
Musgrove's long speeches, for example, but hiding Anne's in indirect discourse (102–3). At times, Anne feels herself muted; when she observes the
Musgrove girls acting foolishly toward Captain Wentworth, "Anne longed
for the power of representing to them all what they were about" (82). Yet
when she speaks even on a subject as trivial as their route while walking, we

are told, "nobody heard, or, at least, nobody answered her" (85). In the imagery that began this book, Anne Elliot has no voice.

But voice is not very positively presented in this novel. When the speaking characters are not complaining, they are often spouting empty civilities. Young Mr. Elliot, who wishes to ingratiate himself with Anne's family, resembles Mr. Wickham in his facility with words and his insincerity. And Anne mistrusts this instantly: "She felt that she could so much more depend upon the sincerity of those who sometimes looked or said a careless or a hasty thing, than of those whose presence of mind never varied, whose tongue never slipped" (161). Mrs. Clay, another character who schemes to marry well, was "a clever young woman, who understood the art of pleasing" (15).

Anne much prefers the warmth and informality of the naval community, which is explicitly contrasted with formal and aristocratic norms. The naval families at Lyme offer a hospitality without the reserve required by the polite world, and their conversation lacks any insincere gestures. Admiral and Mrs. Croft bridge the naval and the polite worlds to some extent, but even their speech is gruffer and more direct than is fashionable. Mrs. Croft, in particular, eschews feminine locutions and is "more conversant with business" than her husband (22).

But Anne is no Mrs. Croft, and her beloved Wentworth is certainly unlike the Admiral. Wentworth can hold the floor at a dinner party, even mesmerize his audience. But for Anne, his important communications are not through words, but through gestures. His increasing attentiveness is marked by indirect communication: by his silently relieving her of a clinging child, by his asking the Crofts to offer Anne a ride home. Wentworth's direct speech can be painful for Anne, especially when his words about her are reported to her or overheard. At times, such as at the concert, Anne tries and fails to engage him in polite small talk. But his silent gestures carry meaning that makes words superfluous.

Even in this novel's climactic scene, when Wentworth finally reveals his love for Anne, communication is indirect. Several scholars have praised this ending as one in which Anne Elliot finally gains a voice.[30] In an earlier draft of the novel, the Admiral has Wentworth ask Anne if she is to marry Mr. Elliot; Wentworth's query enables his own supplication. In the published version, Wentworth overhears Anne speaking to Captain Harville, defending women's constancy. Wentworth listens to their discussion, then declares his love in a note that he silently shows to Anne, writing that "a word, a look" will be enough to answer him. In view of this novel's skepticism about speakers and speaking, it seems probable that what is praised here is not Anne's speaking, but Wentworth's listening. The reader had already seen

Anne's attentiveness as a listener; what we needed to see to ensure our faith in a happy outcome is that Wentworth has also developed this quality.[31] This ending posits a gender-neutral norm unlike the binary systems proposed by most language theorists. Anne learns and grows as a character through her listening (to Mrs. Smith, for example); so must Wentworth.

To most modern readers, Elizabeth Bennet is the most appealing of Austen's heroines. Her wit makes her fun to spend time with; her ironic stance and assertiveness are comfortable for us. Elizabeth Bennet epitomizes the character constructed in speech. We know her good qualities only through the medium of her own words and those of the narrator; we do not see her performing virtuous actions or even (as we do hear of Darcy) performing an important social role conscientiously and well. Typically, when Darcy wishes to get to know Elizabeth better, he eavesdrops on her conversation; conversation is what Elizabeth is made of. Austen offers us a very different heroine in Anne Elliot, one who speaks very little and performs much. Anne's character consists in her actions: in the competence she displays during the emergency at Lyme, in the moral weight shown when she visits a needy friend despite her family's disapproval. Anne and Elizabeth thus personify the ambiguity about "character" discussed at the beginning of this chapter. Anne represents the sense of a "true" character, existing independent of and prior to speech; Elizabeth is constructed in speech.

In these two texts, Austen poses a challenge to the feminist binary of "having a voice" and "being silenced" with which this book began. Indeed, those metaphors do not adequately describe the position of women in an age in which their speech was likely to be ridiculed and their silence had strategic value. We saw in Chapters 2 and 3 that the stereotypical representations of women's voices decay when we examine the speech of any one woman, who may utilize a range of linguistic strategies to express different parts of her identity or to adapt to particular speech situations. In her fictional characters, Austen similarly utilizes "woman's language" as one linguistic possibility, but only one among the many strategies her characters invoke. Austen offers us good and bad speech, good and bad silence. Moreover, she offers her reader the opportunity to practice these strategies as she reads and personates the range of characters who inhabit Austen's novels.

Notes

Introduction

1. Cameron, "Gender, Language, and Discourse," 953; she is discussing Susan Gal, "Between Speech and Silence." Historians like Lawrence E. Klein, Michèle Cohen, and Leland E. Warren have done pioneering work on the discourses on women's speech in the eighteenth century but have not addressed individual usage. See Klein, "Gender, Conversation, and the Public Sphere"; Michèle Cohen, *Fashioning Masculinity;* Warren, "The Conscious Speakers"; and citations in Chapter 1.

2. Lanser, *Fictions of Authority,* 3.

3. See especially Ardener, "Belief and the Problem of Women."

4. Houston and Kramarae, "Speaking from Silence," 388–89. See also Spender, *Man Made Language,* and Lakoff, *Language and Woman's Place.* The French feminists, including Cixous, Kristéva, and Irigaray, make similar points, though their work comes out of a very different intellectual tradition.

5. Crawford, *Talking Difference,* 57.

6. The following paragraphs are indebted to Jaworski, *Power of Silence.*

7. Jaworski, *Power of Silence,* 53 and 24, describing the work of Keith H. Basso and Werner Enninger, respectively.

8. The next two paragraphs rely on Gal, "Between Speech and Silence."

9. On "dominance," in addition to Lakoff, see, for example, Zimmerman and West, "Sex Roles, Interruptions, and Silences," and Edelsky, "Who's Got the Floor?" In addition to her many scholarly publications, Tannen reached a popular audience in *You Just Don't Understand.* There are now several excellent overviews of

the development of feminist linguistics, including Cameron, *Feminism and Linguistic Theory*, and Coates, *Women, Men, and Language*.

10. Cameron, "Gender, Language, and Discourse," 953. She quotes Ochs from "Indexing Gender."

11. Tannen in *Gender and Discourse*, 71–74; Mills, "Discourse Competence," 11–12. See also West, "Women's Competence in Conversation," and Cameron, *Feminism and Linguistic Theory*, chapter 9.

12. See Bing and Bergvall, "The Question of Questions."

13. Meyerhoff, "Dealing with Gender Identity," 203. A similar argument is made in Eckert and McConnell-Ginet, "Think Practically and Look Locally."

14. On performativity and linguistics, see Cameron, "Theoretical Debates in Feminist Linguistics" and "Performing Gender Identity." The classic defense of concepts of character that predate the Romantic emphasis on authenticity is Sennett, *Fall of Public Man*.

15. Within British eighteenth-century studies, scholars have addressed the question of the accuracy of representations most directly in the disagreements about the reliability of Boswell's record of Samuel Johnson's conversations. More generally some, like Hess-Lüttich, "Maxims of Maliciousness," and Peter Burke, *Art of Conversation*, 22, argue that we can and must use literary dialogue as evidence for historical conversation analysis; others, like Davis, "Conversation and Dialogue," stress the huge gap between real-life and literary speech. Recent work by Johnsonians includes Korshin, "Johnson's Conversation in Boswell's *Life of Johnson*," and John J. Burke Jr., "Talk, Dialogue, Conversation"; the classic statement is Greene, " 'Tis a Pretty Book, Mr. Boswell, But—."

16. I am, of course, simplifying. For much more detail, see Biber, *Variation Across Speech and Writing*. Carey McIntosh has examined features within eighteenth-century prose that are characteristic of oral and written language in *Evolution of English Prose*, especially 34–38 and 117–41.

17. On the conventions of literary dialogue, see Page, *Speech in the English Novel*. On the ways that dialogue can be understood in terms of linguistic conversation analysis, see Toolan, "Analysing Fictional Dialogue," and Fowler, *Linguistic Criticism*, 130–59.

18. I quote from Salzmann, *Language, Culture, and Society*, 216; the standard handbook is Saville-Troike, *Ethnography of Communication*.

19. Johnson, *Works*, 4:310–11.

20. Fishman, "Interaction: The Work Women Do."

21. Seward, *Letters*, 1:100.

22. [Knowles?], "An Interesting Dialogue," 489.

23. Boswell, *Life of Johnson*, 3:298–99.

24. Quoted in Harriette Wilson, *Memoirs*, 37.

25. The critic most associated with reader-response criticism is undoubtedly Stanley Fish; see his essays collected in *Is There a Text in This Class?* More generally, see anthologies like Tompkins, *Reader-Response Criticism*. The interest in historical reading is evidenced, for example, in methodological essays like Darnton, "First

Steps Toward a History of Reading," Rose, "Rereading the English Common Reader," and Raven, "New Reading Histories"; in books like Machor, *Readers in History,* and Raven, Small, and Tadmor, *Practice and Representation of Reading in England;* and in the development of university programs in book history and of scholarly organizations like the Society for the History of Authorship, Readers, and Publishing (SHARP).

26. The phrase is from Finnegan, *Literacy and Orality,* 8; Ong's major study is *Orality and Literacy;* Eisenstein, *Printing Press as an Agent of Change.* On reading as a social practice, see, for example, Street, *Literacy in Theory and Practice,* or the essays in Boyarin, *Ethnography of Reading.*

27. For a linguistic approach to the interrelations, see the essays in Tannen, *Spoken and Written Language,* and especially the essay in that volume by Heath, "Protean Shapes in Literacy Events."

28. On Johnson, see Kernan, *Samuel Johnson and the Impact of Print,* and my discussion below (Chapter 1). On print culture more generally, see Siskin, *Work of Writing.*

29. The contrast between "intensive" and "extensive" reading derives from Engelsing, *Der Bürger als Leser;* Robert DeMaria Jr. makes more subtle distinctions in examining the practices of one reader in *Samuel Johnson and the Life of Reading.* On the link between silent solitary reading and the development of the novel, see, for example, Hunter, *Before Novels.* On women readers, see especially Pearson, *Women's Reading in Britain, 1750–1835,* and Kate Flint, *Woman Reader, 1837–1914;* additional references are given in Chapter 4.

30. When my first two articles on oral reading appeared, in 1989 and 1990, there had been almost no attention paid to oral reading in this period. Thankfully, this situation is changing. In addition to Pearson's valuable section on reading aloud in *Women's Reading,* three recent essays begin to address oral reading in the eighteenth century: Raven, "From Promotion to Proscription"; Brewer, "Reconstructing the Reader"; and Tadmor, " 'In the Even my Wife Read to Me.'" On oral reading in other periods, see Coleman, *Public Reading,,* and Kintgen, *Reading in Tudor England.*

31. For women's agency as resisting readers, see Pearson, *Women's Reading.*

Chapter 1. Women and Language in the Eighteenth Century

1. Richard Brinsley Sheridan, *Dramatic Works,* 1:86.

2. Inchbald, *Remarks for "The British Theater,"* 5 of "Remarks" on *The Rivals.*

3. Addison and Steele, *The Spectator,* 2:458. The essay is no. 247, dated December 13, 1711.

4. Jennifer Coates cites studies showing that men talk more than women do in settings as diverse as staff meetings, e-mail discussions, television panels, and spontaneous conversations between husbands and wives, in *Women, Men, and Language,* 115.

5. Davidoff and Hall, *Family Fortunes,* 13. See also Hill, *Women, Work, and Sexual Politics,* and McKeon, "Historicizing Patriarchy."

6. Vickery, "Golden Age to Separate Spheres?" 398 and 408. For other critiques of the metaphor, see Kerber, "Separate Spheres"; Klein, "Gender and the Public/Private Distinction in the Eighteenth Century"; and Shoemaker, *Gender in English Society.*

7. Quoted in Perrin, *Dr. Bowdler's Legacy,* xii. Perrin considers John Wesley "the first serious bowdlerizer of English literature" (35), with his 1744 verse anthology; by 1800, expurgation was quite common. See also Barker-Benfield, *Culture of Sensibility,* 55–65, "Campaign for the Reformation of Manners."

8. Coleridge, *Shakespearean Criticism,* 2:34–35. While the *Spectator* seems to us perfectly inoffensive, Coleridge is not the only commentator who found it a marker of the reformation of manners. Hester Thrale (Piozzi) wrote in 1782, "How great a Change has been wrought in Female Manners within these few Years in England! I was reading the Letter in the 3d Vol: of the Spectator 217. where the Man complains of his indelicate Mistress: I read it aloud to my little daughters of 11 & 12 Years old, & even the Maid who was dressing my Hair, burst out o' laughing at the Idea of *a Lady* saying her Stomach ach'd, or that something stuck between her Teeth. Sure if our Morals are as much mended as our Manners, we are grown a most virtuous Nation!" Piozzi, *Thraliana,* 1:547.

9. Morgan, *Manners, Morals, and Class in England,* 6.

10. *Persuasion,* 40. Austen's characters and her own family provide good examples of the continuum between what we call the middle class, the pseudo-gentry, and the gentry (occasionally reaching into the aristocracy). For convenience' sake, I will refer to this broad group as "the middle class," especially when its conservative ideology contrasts with its conception of a decadent aristocracy. It must be noted, however, that Austen's fictional world does not represent the ideology of separate spheres, and she never implies that women are morally more pure than men.

Quotations from Jane Austen's novels are cited in the text with abbreviations as follows: *E (Emma), MP (Mansfield Park), NA (Northanger Abbey), P (Persuasion), P&P (Pride and Prejudice),* and *S&S (Sense and Sensibility).*

11. Laqueur, *Making Sex,* 5.

12. Runge, *Gender and Language,* 26–27, 39.

13. Swift, "Proposal," 4:13.

14. In *Language in History,* Tony Crowley emphasizes this latter, arguing that the bourgeoisie claimed English as *their* language whereas the elite were learned in Latin. He relates the attacks on working-class forms of English to those against provincialism: "in the work of many eighteenth-century writers on language we see . . . the process of bourgeois self-identification, at the social, political and cultural levels, by means of language; a process which depends quite as much on the construction of social 'others' as it does upon the identification of who, or what, the bourgeoisie was" (74). Crowley discusses working-class and provincial speech on pp. 94–97 and women's speech on pp. 87–94. Like Crowley, Olivia Smith, in *Politics of Language,* sees standardization as generally repressive; Carey McIntosh defends it in *Evolution of English Prose.* See also Fitzmaurice, "Commerce of Language." On language and national identity, see Sorensen, *Grammar of Empire.*

15. Sklar, "So Male a Speech," 373. See also Michèle Cohen, *Fashioning Masculinity*.

16. Priestley, *Course of Lectures*, 72—73.

17. Bodine, "Androcentrism in Prescriptive Grammar."

18. More, *Complete Works*, 1:15.

19. More, *Essays on Various Subjects*, 40.

20. More, *Complete Works*, 1:373. The full title is *Strictures on the Modern System of Female Education; with a View of the Principles and Conduct Prevalent among Women of Rank and Fortune,* and the work is intended to urge "women of rank" to become examples of Christian behavior for women of other classes.

21. Sterne, *Tristram Shandy*, 1:55. John J. Richetti discusses this passage in "Voice and Gender."

22. Michèle Cohen, *Fashioning Masculinity*, 32.

23. Percy, "Easy Women," 322.

24. For a full discussion, see Sledd and Kolb, *Dr. Johnson's Dictionary*, especially chapter 3, "Lord Chesterfield and Dr. Johnson," and Reddick, *Making of Johnson's Dictionary*.

25. Jennifer Coates notes that in the early twentieth century, when linguistic innovation was valued, it was considered typical of men, while women were the conservative speakers. She posits "The Androcentric Rule: Men will be seen to behave linguistically in a way that fits the writer's view of what is desirable or admirable; women on the other hand will be blamed for any linguistic state or development which is regarded by the writer as negative or reprehensible" (*Women, Men, and Language*, 18, 16—17).

26. Hayley, *Essay on Old Maids*, 90—91. Hayley dedicated this three-volume account to the "bluestocking" Elizabeth Carter and explicitly intended it to be a defense of "ancient virgins," but Carter and other authors like Anna Seward found the work offensive. See Bishop, *Blake's Hayley*, 132—35.

27. Spacks, *Gossip*, 26. The book is in part a feminist defense of gossip as a community-building activity.

28. Edgeworth, *Letters for Literary Ladies*, "Essay," 5, 6—7. In "Satirizing Women's Speech in Eighteenth-Century England," Stephen H. Browne cites a number of early- to mid-century works that describe "the victimage of men compelled to listen to such talk. Typically, these narratives dramatize the unhappy plight of despairing men, captives of the female tongue" (24). For example, Browne cites "The Dumb Woman; a Tale from Rabelais" (1773), in which a mute woman has an operation that enables her to speak—much to her husband's regret.

29. Wells, *Letters*, xii. Carol [Elaine] Percy traces the connection between grammatical and moral correction in grammar books written by women, in "Paradigms for Their Sex?"

30. Nares, *General Rules*, vii. On the standardization of pronunciation and the rise of accent as social signifier, see Mugglestone, *"Talking Proper."*

31. For an overview of the elocution movement, see Bartine, *Early English Reading Theory*. In his magisterial survey, *Eighteenth-Century British Logic and Rhetoric,*

Wilbur Samuel Howell stresses the movement's continental origins. The falling-out between Johnson and Sheridan is discussed by Boswell in the *Life of Johnson*, 1:385–89; Boswell himself had studied with Sheridan to "correct" his Scottish accent (2:159). *Tristram Shandy*, 1:431, 3:355–56; as a clergyman, Sterne was a member of the elocutionists' target audience. Nicholas Hudson characterizes elocution as a dialectical antithesis to print culture in *Writing and European Thought*.

32. Gentleman, *Shakespeare's Plays*, 17.

33. Fliegelman, *Declaring Independence*, 2. On affective persuasion, see also Murray Cohen, *Sensible Words*.

34. Tucker, *Vocal Sounds;* Walker, *Melody of Speaking;* Steele, *Prosodia Rationalis* (I use the title of the second, 1779, edition).

35. Herries, *Elements of Speech*, 100.

36. In "Women in London Debating Societies," Mary Thale documents several women's and mixed-sex debating societies and the hostile reaction to them. As she points out, the "joke" of the women's parliament was a common trope during the period.

37. Richardson, *Familiar Letters*, 14–15; Grice, "Logic and Conversation." On Augustan models of conversation, see Henry Knight Miller, *Essays on Fielding's "Miscellanies"*, 164–89; Peter Burke, *Art of Conversation*; and articles by Warren cited below.

38. In *Shaftesbury and the Culture of Politeness*, Lawrence E. Klein prefers the term *gentlemanly* over *courtly*, both because it captures the "easiness" of eighteenth-century politeness and because it highlights the Whiggish distance from Tory royalism. I retain the term *courtly* only because *gentlemanly* is inevitably gendered male.

39. Fielding, *Miscellanies*, 145.

40. Klein, "Gender, Conversation, and the Public Sphere," 103. Michèle Cohen sees the seventeenth-century French tradition as defining two modes for women: "As 'conversation', women's talk was civilized and civilizing, polite and pleasing. . . . As 'tongue', women's talk was undisciplined and unregulated" (*Fashioning Masculinity*, 20). See also Georgia, "Joys of Social Intercourse," and McIntosh, *Evolution of English Prose*, chapter 9, "Politeness; feminization."

41. Warren, "Turning Reality Round Together." He develops the contrast with sensibility in "Conscious Speakers." See also Ann Cline Kelly, "Swift's *Polite Conversation*," in which Kelly contrasts the two kinds of conversation manuals: one promoting a humanistic model of truth-seeking through conversation and consensus, the other a "cookbook" approach of memorized proverbs and jokes.

42. See, for example, Broadhead, "Rhetoric of Conversation." While not fully comprehensive, Broadhead's bibliography demonstrates a historical shift: of seventy-three longer works listed, only six appeared after 1760.

43. See Cowper's own verse essay on "Conversation." On the historical shift toward sincerity over politeness, especially as that reflects a growing nationalism, see Newman, *Rise of English Nationalism*, 127–39, and Michèle Cohen, "Manliness, Effeminacy, and the French."

44. Michèle Cohen, *Fashioning Masculinity,* 35—41. Cohen also notes that foreign visitors to England were struck by how rarely the sexes conversed with each other, even at mixed gatherings (34).

45. Spacks, "Ambiguities of Pleasing," 82.

46. Gregory, *Father's Legacy,* 123.

47. Wollstonecraft, *Works,* 5:166—70.

48. Wollstonecraft, *Works,* 5:175. On Wollstonecraft's gendered rhetoric, see Barker-Benfield, "Mary Wollstonecraft," and Allen, "Uses and Problems."

49. Michèle Cohen, *Fashioning Masculinity.* On the plain style, see Brody, *Manly Writing.*

50. I paraphrase Thomas, *Honest Mind,* 67.

51. Godwin, *Enquirer,* 346. On Godwin's attitudes about sincerity, conversation, and writing, see Warren, "*Caleb Williams.*"

52. Wollstonecraft, *Works,* 5:7.

53. Duff, *Letters,* 243.

54. *E* 10, italics added. Claudia L. Johnson justifiably critiques the misogyny of mid-twentieth-century critics who dismissed Mr. Woodhouse as a "silly old woman" (quoting Edmund Wilson, in *Equivocal Beings,* 197). She reads *Emma* as redefining masculinity by rejecting the gallant Mr. Elton and Frank Churchill in favor of the landed but businesslike and uncourtly Mr. Knightley. My glance at the linguistic construction of identity in this novel both supports Johnson's interpretation and allows a reading of Mr. Woodhouse as "womanish."

Among the many excellent studies of dialogue in *Emma,* see especially Babb, *Jane Austen's Novels;* Dussinger, *Pride of the Moment;* Hough, "Narrative and Dialogue"; McMaster, "Secret Languages"; Sorensen, *Grammar of Empire;* and White, *When Words Lose Their Meaning.* Those paying especial attention to gendered speech include Armstrong, *Desire and Domestic Fiction,* and Meyersohn, "Jane Austen's Garrulous Speakers."

Chapter 2. Polite and Plain Language

1. Mitford, *Life,* 2:198—99.

2. Tave, *Amiable Humorist,* 3. The Quakers were unlike the Puritan rulers of the Commonwealth in *not* emphasizing the depravity of human nature, but as we will see, they were committed to an absolute truthfulness that left no room for wit. In *Arguments of Augustan Wit,* John Sitter contrasts the linguistic play of wit with the transparency of language that underlies Locke's concept of judgment; the Quakers would line up with Locke in imagining language as transparent. On how eighteenth-century theories of comedy are inflected by gender, see Bilger, *Laughing Feminism.*

3. I rely here on the literature review by Attardo, *Linguistic Theories of Humor,* chapters 9, "The Cooperative Nature of Humor," and 10, "Humor in Context."

4. Quoted in Clifford, *Hester Lynch Piozzi,* 446.

5. Fordyce, *Sermons to Young Women,* 86—88.

6. Kett, *Emily,* 1:277. Chapone, *Improvement of the Mind,* 2:108—11.

7. For a more negative reading of Henry's language and character, see Claudia L. Johnson, *Jane Austen,* 37–41.

8. Quoted in Brightwell, *Memorials,* 32. This "official" biography of Amelia Opie is the major source for all later ones.

9. Mack, *Visionary Women,* 166.

10. Wright, "Quakerism," 403–4.

11. Boswell, *Life of Johnson,* 1:463.

12. From a letter of 1777, quoted in Chilcote, *John Wesley,* 161–62. On Methodist women preachers, see also Krueger, *Reader's Repentance.*

13. On traveling ministry, see chapter 7, "The Propagation of Quakerism by Itinerant Ministry," in Jones, *Later Periods of Quakerism.*

14. Dudley, *Life,* 30–31.

15. For a non-Quaker account of these autobiographies, see Nussbaum, *Autobiographical Subject.*

16. Clarkson, *Portraiture of Quakerism,* 127–29.

17. *Observations on Plainness and Simplicity,* 2. In *Later Periods of Quakerism,* Rufus M. Jones includes linguistic practice as one of a number of Quaker practices whose function was to keep the sect separate from the world (1:171–77).

18. Richard Bauman describes similar phenomena in seventeenth-century Quaker language, in *Let Your Words Be Few.*

19. Lakoff, *Language and Woman's Place;* Tannen, *You Just Don't Understand;* Holmes, *Women, Men, and Politeness.*

20. Addison and Steele, *Spectator* No. 46 (1711), 1:198–99.

21. Introduction to vol. 48 of Barbauld, *British Novelists,* 48:ii–iii (Bage, *Hermsprong; or, Man as He Is Not*).

22. Shadwell, *Works,* 1:33.

23. Opie, *Adeline Mowbray,* in *Works,* 1:163.

24. Menzies-Wilson and Lloyd, *Amelia,* 1.

25. Thackeray, *Book of Sibyls,* 159. Opie's letters, some of which are printed in Brightwell's *Memorials,* provide better evidence than do her other writings of her wit and joy in life.

26. Mitford, *Life,* 3:294.

27. Brightwell, *Memorials,* 190. While she gave up writing novels, Opie did continue to write didactic fiction. The Quakers criticized her for this, and for authorizing a complete *Works.* She responded in a letter to Joseph John Gurney: "I never said, because I never thought that *works of fiction* were *never to be read,* on the contrary, I believe simple moral tales the very best mode of instructing the young and the poor, *else . . . why* did the blessed Saviour teach in Parables?" (Menzies-Wilson and Lloyd, *Amelia,* 263.)

28. Thackeray, *Book of Sibyls,* 192.

29. Robinson, *Diary, Reminiscences,* 2:9. Robert Southey writes, similarly, in 1826: Opie was "in stiffer garb and more primitive bonnet than when I saw her at Norwich, and corrupting the King's English with more malice prepense. She went

from hence to Lowther; but though she *thou'd* and *thee'd* them with great intrepidity, I am told that the sinful word Lady slipped not unfrequently from her lips; and that when Rogers, as if to put her young virtue to the proof, said things and told stories at which she ought not to have laughed, the temptation was sometimes so strong that she was obliged to stuff her handkerchief into her mouth, and still the struggling titter came forth, the old Eve prevailing in the context. I like her in spite of her Quakerism, nay, perhaps the better for it." Quoted in Curry, *Southey*, 108; I am grateful to Clive Jones for this reference.

30. Opie, *Works*, 3:414.

31. British Library Add. Mss 52451B/ff133–35. I am grateful to Shelley King for this reference.

Chapter 3. Acting, Text, and Correct Display

1. Ffrench, *Mrs. Siddons*, 78.

2. Boaden, *Mrs. Sarah Siddons*, 1:285. On the vocabulary used to describe Siddons, see Rogers, " 'Towering Beyond Her Sex.' "

3. Campbell, *Life of Mrs. Siddons*, 45–46. Campbell's was the biography "authorized" by Siddons.

4. Quoted in Campbell, *Life of Mrs. Siddons*, 124.

5. On the complex negotiations Siddons made between her role as actress and her gender role, see Backscheider, *Spectacular Politics*, 204–17; Donkin, "Mrs. Siddons Looks Back in Anger"; and Burroughs, *Closet Stages*, 51–58.

6. Straub, *Sexual Suspects*, 89.

7. Pascoe, *Romantic Theatricality*, 15. On the association of actresses with women aristocrats, see Crouch, "Public Life of Actresses." Julie A. Carlson considers how confounding Siddons was for contemporary male writers, in *Theatre of Romanticism*, 162–75.

8. Byng, *Torrington Diaries*, 3:149; Burney, *Diary & Letters*, 2:146.

9. Campbell, *Life of Mrs. Siddons*, 134–35.

10. Worthen, *Idea of the Actor*, 72–75.

11. John Hill's text was an adaptation of the French *Le Comédien* (1747), by Pierre Rémond de Sainte-Albine; a 1755 edition adds much material on English actors. Diderot knew a translation of the 1755 edition, Antonio Fabio Sticotti's *Garrick; ou, les acteurs Anglois* (1769). Diderot's *Paradoxe sur le Comédien* was written in the 1770s but was not published until 1830.

12. John Hill, *The Actor*, 16. Hill and Popple, *Prompter*, 127.

13. Wasserman, "Sympathetic Imagination," 268.

14. Worthen, *Idea of the Actor*, 90.

15. Diderot quoted in Worthen, *Idea of the Actor*, 90.

16. Worthen, *Idea of the Actor*, 92. Richard Sennett also connects Diderot's theory with the performativity of social interaction, in *Fall of Public Man*, 110–15.

17. Boswell, *Life of Johnson*, 4:243–44.

18. Boswell, *Life of Johnson*, 1:266.

19. Quoted in Taylor, " 'Just Delineation of the Passions,' " 56–57. Note that Garrick incorporates both of the more extreme positions by recognizing that acting may entail either imitating or assuming the passions.

20. Inchbald, *Remarks for "The British Theatre,"* preface to *Measure for Measure.* Johnson in Boswell, *Life of Johnson,* 4:243.

21. This paragraph is indebted to McKenzie, introduction to Le Brun, *Method to Learn.*

22. See Hughes, "Art and Eighteenth-Century Acting Style."

23. Hunt, *Essays (Selected),* 155. Boaden, *Memoirs,* 1:240–41.

24. Cooke, *Elements of Dramatic Criticism,* 183.

25. Quoted in Campbell, *Life of Mrs. Siddons,* 97–98. Siddons's sister also emphasized correctness in an advertisement for a school for girls she ran in Bath: "Mrs. Twiss . . . also teaches English Reading with the greatest attention to correct Pronunciation. Young ladies coming to Bath for a short time may receive Private Lessons in Pronunciation, and in reading the best English Poets." From the *Bath Herald,* 1815, quoted in Burney, *Journals and Letters,* 10:468.

26. Boaden, *Memoirs,* 2:546–47. Kemble's farewell address, on the other hand, was in prose.

27. Thomas Sheridan, *Lectures on the Art of Reading,* 1:207–12. Another author, John Trusler, printed an edition of the entire church service without commentary but marked for pronunciation with italics, dashes, exclamation points, and so on. His title bills his system as idiot-proof: *The Sublime Reader; or, The Morning and Evening Service of the Church so Pointed, and the Emphatical Words throughout so Marked, as to display all the Beauty and Sublimity of the Language, and render it, with the least Attention, impossible to be read by the most injudicious Reader, but with Propriety.*

28. Boaden, *Memoirs,* 2:522–23. Boaden analyzes Kemble's emphases in many works, for example, in *Hamlet,* 1:93–103.

29. Boaden, *Memoirs,* 2:520.

30. Quoted in Reynolds, *Life and Times,* 1:151. See also van Dijk, "Kembles and Vocal Technique."

31. Campbell, *Life of Mrs. Siddons,* 112, 114.

32. Boaden, *Memoirs,* 1:251.

33. Henry Angelo, quoted in Benzie, *Dublin Orator,* 63–64. Benzie discusses the earlier performances on 55–63. These readings were profitable not only to the performers but also to booksellers: "John Gilpin's Ride" had a second turn as a bestseller. And some years later, an anonymous author capitalized on their success in a book that gives advice on performing texts by Shakespeare, Milton, Gray, and others: *Sheridan's and Henderson's Practical Method of Reading and Reciting English Poetry.*

34. Boaden, *Memoirs,* 1:253.

35. Betsy Sheridan, *Journal,* 43. Edgeworth, *Belinda,* chapter 13.

36. Letter dated January 26, 1813, reprinted in Campbell, *Life of Mrs. Siddons,* 241–43.

37. Boaden, *Mrs. Sarah Siddons,* 2:318.

38. Campbell, *Life of Mrs. Siddons,* 260. Paula Backscheider points out that the mercer's ritualized speech was also a performance, which Siddons entered into, thereby exposing his hyperbole (letter to author).

39. Irving is quoted in Fitzgerald, *Kembles,* 2:228; Sydney Smith, *Wit and Wisdom,* 432.

40. Lockhart, *Memoirs,* 3:146.

41. Quoted in Fitzgerald, *Kembles,* 1:97–98.

42. Campbell, *Life of Mrs. Siddons,* 101–2.

43. Burney, *Diary & Letters,* 3:306.

44. Quoted in Manvell, *Sarah Siddons,* 305.

45. Quoted in Manvell, *Sarah Siddons,* 304–5.

46. Quoted in Brightwell, *Memorials,* 43.

47. Quoted in Manvell, *Sarah Siddons,* 133.

48. Burney, *Diary & Letters,* 2:146.

49. Campbell, *Life of Mrs. Siddons,* 98–99.

50. On the fear of upward mobility as part of the discourse on accomplishments, see P. J. Miller, "Women's Education."

51. Bermingham, "Aesthetics of Ignorance."

52. On these aristocratic theatricals, see Rosenfeld, *Temples of Thespis.*

53. Frederick Reynolds, *Life and Times,* 2:6–7.

54. Burney, *Early Diary,* 1:129, 1:170.

55. Burney, *Wanderer,* 115–16. On music as an accomplishment, see Leppert, *Music and Image,* and Rempel, "Complete Female." In an anthology for young women, *The Female Speaker,* Anna Laetitia Barbauld also defined reading as an accomplishment, parallel to music: "The greatest part of this Selection is calculated for *recital* as well as for reading; an exercise, the editor takes the liberty to say, which is too much neglected. Graceful reading is a most pleasing, and it is a scarce accomplishment. . . . Many English ladies profess to want courage to recite, or even to read aloud a copy of verses in a social party . . . : yet it is somewhat difficult to conceive, that a young lady shall have courage enough to stand up by the side of a professional singer, and entertain a large and mixed audience, for an hour together, and yet be too modest to read or recite, by her father's fireside, amidst a circle of his friends, a passage of twenty lines from Milton or Cowper" (v).

Heather MacFadyen describes another way in which reading could function as display. In "Lady Delacour's Library," she contrasts "fashionable reading," which one displays through allusions in one's conversation, with "domestic" (virtuous) reading and "female" (erotic) reading. In *Fashioning Masculinity,* Michèle Cohen argues that "accomplishments came to be valued or criticized depending not on what they were, but on whether they could be, or were meant to be, 'displayed'" (65); like MacFadyen, she stresses the opposition of domestic norms of virtue and the world of display.

56. Trilling, *Opposing Self,* 212. As is true of the other Austen novels, the secondary literature on *Mansfield Park* is too vast to cite adequately. On the "problem"

of the Mansfield theatricals, I have relied most on Rosenfeld, "Jane Austen and Private Theatricals"; Barish, *The Antitheatrical Prejudice,* especially 299–307; Marshall, "True Acting"; and Litvak, *Caught in the Act,* 1–26. On the larger question of whether Austen praises or critiques conduct-book norms in this novel, see especially Butler, *Jane Austen;* Poovey, *Proper Lady;* Claudia L. Johnson, *Jane Austen;* and Waldron, "Frailties of Fanny."

57. Gary Kelly also highlights this passage, though without relating it to the elocution movement, in "Reading Aloud in *Mansfield Park.*"

58. John Edwin, *Eccentricities* (1791), quoted in Rosenfeld, "Jane Austen and Private Theatricals," 47.

59. Quoted in Burroughs, *Closet Stages,* 151.

60. Gisborne, *Enquiry into the Duties of the Female Sex,* 173–75. Others who link Gisborne to *Mansfield Park* include Butler, *Jane Austen,* 231–32, and Litvak, *Caught in the Act,* 6–8.

61. From *The Search After Happiness,* in More, *Complete Works,* 1:111.

62. Wollstonecraft, *The Female Reader; or Miscellaneous Pieces in Prose and Verse* (1789), in *Works* 4:55–56.

63. *MP* 463. On the role of accomplishments in this novel, see Moler, *Jane Austen's Art of Allusion,* chapter 4.

Chapter 4. Reading and Domesticity

1. Burney, *Diary & Letters,* 1:21.

2. In the most thorough examination of eighteenth-century women readers to date, Jacqueline Pearson stresses both the ubiquity of the image of the woman reader in discourses of all kinds, and its "polyvalence": in its various permutations, it could be used to symbolize or to oppose domestic values (*Women's Reading,* 1). Pearson's appreciation for the complexities involved and her massive primary research make the book indispensable. Pearson's book appeared after this chapter had been written. Although I have tried to incorporate her findings and point the reader to passages relevant to my argument, I have chosen to leave in place material of mine that overlaps with Pearson's.

3. Brewer, "Reconstructing the Reader."

4. The classic text is Watt, *Rise of the Novel.* William B. Warner argues that the practice of reading as entertainment was a precondition for the development of the novel as we conceive it, in *Licensing Entertainment.* See also works on the novel and novel-reading cited in the Introduction, notes 29–30.

5. More, *Village Politics,* 3–4. *Strictures,* in *Complete Works* 1:345.

6. Lackington, *Memoirs,* 386–87. On working-class women readers, see Pearson, *Women's Reading,* 176–95.

7. Woolf, *A Room of One's Own,* 65.

8. For a summary of the historiography on the family in the eighteenth century and an argument for the importance of shifts in representations of the family, see Christopher Flint, *Family Fictions.* On the affective family, see, for example, Stone,

Family, Sex, and Marriage, and Davidoff and Hall, *Family Fortunes.* More skeptical of the ubiquity of domestic ideology are Vickery, "Golden Age to Separate Spheres?" Klein, "Gender and the Public/Private Distinction," and Shoemaker, *Gender in English Society*; for additional references, see my discussion of separate spheres, an important component of domestic ideology, in Chapter 1. For the connection of domestic ideology and fiction, in addition to Flint, see especially Poovey, *Proper Lady,* and Armstrong, *Desire and Domestic Fiction.*

9. See Bartine, *Early English Reading Theory.*

10. Mason, *Essay on Elocution,* 19.

11. Thomas Sheridan, *Lectures on the Art of Reading,* 1:ix.

12. Advertisements quoted in Wiles, "Relish for Reading," 109–10. Wiles says he has seen hundreds of advertisements relating reading and speaking.

13. Rice, *Introduction to the Art of Reading,* 4.

14. Buchanan, *Plan of an English Grammar-School Education,* 20. Much of Buchanan's text was plagiarized from Mason's *Essay on Elocution.*

15. Benedict, *Making the Modern Reader.*

16. Walker, *Rhetorical Grammar,* 29.

17. I use a version of this essay reprinted in Knox, *Elegant Extracts,* vii.

18. Blair himself was a Scot. On the role of Scottish writers in the linguistic construction of Englishness, see Sorensen, *Grammar of Empire.*

19. *Help to Elocution and Eloquence,* 1.

20. Piozzi, *Thraliana,* 2:828. *The Reader, or Reciter,* iii–iv. The author explicitly names "the late Mr. Sheridan" as a model "if the scholar's object be only that of rendering himself correct" (iv).

21. Knox, *Liberal Education,* 1:192; Walker, "On the Speaking of Speeches at Schools," reprinted in William Scott, *Lessons in Elocution,* 9–16.

22. Long, "Textual Interpretation as Collective Action," 182. Ferris, *Achievement of Literary Authority,* 37.

23. Several recent works carefully distinguish the trope of the woman reader from actual practice, while arguing that both are important. See Pearson, *Women's Reading,* and her essay " 'Books, my Greatest Joy' " and (for a later period, but one with some similar concerns) Kate Flint, *Woman Reader.* On earlier women readers, see Warner, *Licensing Entertainment.*

24. Samuel Johnson, *The Rambler* #4, dated March 31, 1750, in *Works,* 3:21.

25. *The Monthly Review* of July 1791, reprinted in Williams, *Novel and Romance,* 373.

26. Rousseau, *Julie,* 4.

27. Gallagher, *Nobody's Story,* 279. See also Pearson, *Women's Reading,* 82–86, and Richards, " 'Pleasures of Complicity.' "

28. Walter Scott, *Antiquary,* 221–22. Wollstonecraft, from the *Analytical Review* (1789), in *Works,* 7:192. Emphasis in original.

29. Mary Hays, *Letters and Essays, Moral and Miscellaneous* (1793), excerpted in a contemporary review and reprinted in Williams, *Novel and Romance,* 382–83.

30. Wollstonecraft, *A Vindication of the Rights of Woman,* in *Works,* 5:258.

31. From *An Essay on the Government of Children,* quoted in Gonda, *Reading Daughters' Fictions,* 31. Gonda's book examines the complexity of father-daughter relations in the period and their centrality to its fiction.

32. Burney, *Memoirs of Doctor Burney,* 1:26.

33. Charles Burney, *A General History of Music,* quoted in Lonsdale, *Dr. Charles Burney,* 12–13.

34. Burney, *Memoirs of Doctor Burney,* 1:108.

35. Burney, *Diary & Letters* 6:400–401.

36. Rizzo, "How (and How Not) to Explore the Burneys," 199–201. On Burney's relationship with her father and with patriarchy in general, see especially Hemlow, *History of Fanny Burney;* Doody, *Frances Burney;* Straub, *Divided Fictions;* Epstein, *Iron Pen;* Cutting-Gray, *Woman as "Nobody";* and Spacks, *Imagining a Self.* Pearson relates Burney's biography to her own and her characters' reading in *Women's Reading,* 127–37.

37. Quoted in Doody, *Frances Burney,* 92.

38. Burney, *Early Diary,* 1:252.

39. Burney, *Journals and Letters,* 6:801.

40. Burney, *Early Diary,* 2:224, 2:227, 2:223.

41. Burney, *Early Diary,* 2:238, 2:239, 2:242, 2:243, 2:244.

42. Dante, *Inferno,* 53.

43. Shelley, *Mary Shelley Reader,* 195. Pearson also discusses this scene in *Women's Reading,* 115–16.

44. Burney, *Journals and Letters,* 4:145.

45. Burney, *Journals and Letters,* 10:860.

46. Collier, *Essay on the Art of Ingeniously Tormenting,* 124–25. A happier example is provided by James Lackington, who tells of two virtues of his future bride: her goodness to her father and "that she was immoderately fond of books, and would frequently read until morning; this turn of mind in her was the greatest of all recommendations to me . . . ; so that I was in raptures with the bare thoughts of having a woman to read with, and also to read to me" (*Memoirs,* 249). Pearson provides many other examples of family reading (*Women's Reading,* 170–75).

47. Burney, *Journals and Letters,* 1:95–96.

48. Austen, *Letters,* 276–77.

49. Bell, *Hamwood Papers,* 58, 73.

50. Montagu, *Mrs. Montagu,* 2:273. Pearson discusses the pleasures and dangers of reading as they are figured in and about gothic fiction in *Women's Reading,* 100–121. In *Progress of Romance,* David H. Richter argues "that the Gothic novel sits astride a major shift in the response of readers to literature, . . . a shift from reading for information, and for the sake of entry into a verisimilar world otherwise inaccessible to the reader, toward reading as an escape from the world one inhabits into an inner site of fantasy" (112–13). One might then argue that the gothics were the first novels whose effect depended on silent reading.

51. Burney, *Journals and Letters*, 3:337.

52. Burney, *Diary & Letters*, 1:24, 1:26.

53. Burney, *Early Diary*, 2:219.

54. Burney, *Early Diary*, 2:225.

55. Burney, *Early Diary*, 2:229.

56. Burney, *Early Diary*, 2:226, 2:229.

57. Burney, *Diary & Letters*, 1:51.

58. Burney, *Early Diary*, 2:237. In anticipation of the concerns of Chapter 5, let me also note that according to Joyce Hemlow (*History of Fanny Burney*, 78–84), Burney revised the early drafts of *Evelina* to make the upper-class characters' speech more decorous and thus "concentrated the vulgar idiom in the speech of the lower classes" (79). This would mean that Burney "marked" good and vulgar speech, so that the reader would know which to imitate.

59. Caroline Austen, *My Aunt Jane Austen*, 10.

Chapter 5. Reading Austen, Practicing Speech

1. Babb, *Jane Austen's Novels*. Burrows, *Computation into Criticism*. There is, in addition, a bibliography on Austen's dialogue too vast to cite adequately, but see especially Page, *Language of Jane Austen*, and, on *Pride and Prejudice*, McMaster, "Talking About Talk," and Meyersohn, "Duets of *Pride and Prejudice*."

2. See, among many treatments, Hough, "Narrative and Dialogue"; Page, *Speech in the English Novel* and *Language of Jane Austen*; Pascal, *Dual Voice*; Dussinger, "'Language of Real Feeling'"; Flavin, "*Mansfield Park*" and "Austen's *Persuasion*"; Neumann, "Characterization and Comment."

3. For example, Finch and Bowen, "'Tittle-Tattle of Highbury'" and Meyersohn, "Jane Austen's Garrulous Speakers."

4. A young neighbor, Charlotte-Maria Middleton, made that comparison: "her keen sense of humour I quite remember, it oozed out very much in Mr. Bennett's [*sic*] Style. . . . We saw her often. She was a most kind & enjoyable person *to Children* but somewhat stiff & cold to strangers." More cruelly, Mary Russell Mitford quotes a friend who wrote, "till 'Pride and Prejudice' showed what a precious gem was hidden in that unbending case, she was no more regarded in society than a poker or a fire screen or any other thin, upright piece of wood or iron that fills its corner in peace and quiet. The case is very different now; she is still a poker but a poker of whom every one is afraid. It must be confessed that this silent observation from such an observer is rather formidable . . . a wit, a delineator of character, who does not talk, is terrific indeed!" Both quotations in Austen-Leigh and Austen-Leigh, *Family Record*, 178, 198–99.

5. This passage also receives attention in Claudia L. Johnson, *Jane Austen*, 85, and in Walzer, "Rhetoric and Gender."

6. I use the essay as reprinted as the introduction to Knox, *Elegant Extracts*, which incorporates the beginning of the next essay in Blair's original *Lectures*, "Means of Improving in Eloquence."

7. The next two paragraphs are indebted to Baumlin, "Positioning *Ethos.*" For reservations about this commonplace dichotomy, see Swearingen, *"Ethos."*

8. From the *Rhetoric* (II, 1, 6–18), quoted in Nan Johnson, "Ethos," 101.

9. Oakleaf, "Marks, Stamps, and Representations," 296. On eighteenth-century concepts of subjectivity as revealed in literature, see also Cox, *"Stranger Within Thee"*; Gelley, "Character and Person"; and Kraft, *Character and Consciousness.* Most studies in this vein rely on concepts developed by Goffman in *Presentation of Self in Everyday Life* and applied to the eighteenth century in Sennett, *Fall of Public Man.* For a different tradition, following Foucault, see, for example, Nussbaum, *Autobiographical Subject.*

10. Mason, *Essay on Elocution,* 5.

11. De Bolla, *Discourse of the Sublime,* 234.

12. Cockin, *Art of Delivering Written Language,* 1. Cockin goes on to say, "and I would particularly recommend [this] to the consideration of those readers, who think the common occurrences of a news-paper, &c. cannot be properly delivered without a good deal of elbow-room" (95). Murray, *English Reader,* vii.

13. Edgeworth and Edgeworth, *Practical Education,* 1:318–19.

14. Cited in Kinneavy and Warshauer, "From Aristotle to Madison Avenue," 175.

15. Enfield, *Speaker,* v.

16. Walker, *Rhetorical Grammar,* 29.

17. I summarize the chapter "Of Reading" in Austin, *Chironomia,* 187–206.

18. Rice, *Introduction to the Art of Reading,* 291.

19. Austen, *Novels,* 5:7.

20. Austen, *Letters,* 201, 203.

21. Lynch, *Economy of Character,* chapter 5: "Jane Austen and the Social Machine."

22. For Austen's use of free indirect discourse, see note 2 of this chapter. For more linguistic approaches, see McHale, "Free Indirect Discourse"; Banfield, *Unspeakable Sentences*; Neumann, "Free Indirect Discourse"; Fludernik, *Fictions of Language.* Claudia L. Johnson stresses the distinction between free indirect *speech* and free indirect *thought* in Austen's works: where many characters chatter, only a few rate the inwardness that is Austen's real gift to the novel (letter to author). Indeed, a tradition going back to Bakhtin conceives of free indirect discourse as articulating depth of character or interiority. For my purposes, what matters is not so much how free indirect discourse represents character as that it offers additional opportunities to the reader.

23. Caroline Austen, *My Aunt Jane Austen,* 10.

24. Page, *Language of Jane Austen,* 141, 161.

25. See especially Kaplan, *Jane Austen Among Women.*

26. Sacks, "Golden Birds and Dying Generations"; Susan Morgan, "Why There's No Sex in Jane Austen's Novels."

27. See Warren, "Turning Reality Round Together."

28. Mitford, *Life,* 1:300. The letter dates from December 1814.

29. Claudia L. Johnson, *Jane Austen,* 144–45.

30. See, for example, Swanson, "Rhetoric of Self"; also Giordano, "Word as Battleground." For an argument that gesture matters more than words, see Judy Van Sickle Johnson, "Bodily Frame."

31. Tave makes a similar point in *Some Words of Jane Austen,* 265–68. Others who examine the value of silence in this novel include Bander, "Uses of Silence"; Stout, *Strategies of Reticence;* and Thomsen, "Words 'Half-Dethroned.'" See also Laurence, *Reading of Silence.*

Bibliography

Primary Sources

Place of publication is London unless otherwise indicated. Where there are two dates, the first is of the first edition, the second of the edition I used. I omit lengthy subtitles unless they are pertinent to the argument of this book.

Addison, Joseph, and Richard Steele. *The Spectator.* Ed. Donald F. Bond. 1711–1714. 5 vols. Oxford: Clarendon, 1965.

Aikin, John, and Anna Laetitia Barbauld. *Evenings at Home; or, The Juvenile Budget Opened.* 6 vols. 1792–1796.

Austen, Caroline. *My Aunt Jane Austen: A Memoir.* London: Spottswood, Ballantyne, 1952.

Austen, Jane. *Jane Austen's Letters.* Ed. Deirdre Le Faye. 3d ed. Oxford: Oxford University Press, 1995.

Austen, Jane. *Lady Susan.* In vol. 6, *Minor Works,* of R. W. Chapman, ed., *The Works of Jane Austen.* London: Oxford University Press, 1954.

Austen, Jane. *The Novels of Jane Austen.* Ed. R. W. Chapman. 3d ed. 5 vols. Oxford: Clarendon, 1932–1934. Novels are cited in the text by their initials: *E* (*Emma*), *MP* (*Mansfield Park*), *NA* (*Northanger Abbey*), *P* (*Persuasion*), *P&P* (*Pride and Prejudice*), *S&S* (*Sense and Sensibility*).

Austen-Leigh, William, and Richard Arthur Austen-Leigh. *Jane Austen: A Family Record.* Revised and enlarged by Deirdre Le Faye. Boston: G. K. Hall, 1989.

Austin, Gilbert. *Chironomia; or, a Treatise on Rhetorical Delivery.* 1806.

Bage, Robert. *Man As He Is.* 4 vols. 1792.

Barbauld, Anna Laetitia, ed. *The British Novelists.* 50 vols. 1810.

Barbauld, Anna Laetitia. *The Female Speaker; or, Miscellaneous Pieces, in Prose and Verse, Selected from the Best Writers, and Adapted to the Use of Young Women.* 1811; 1816.

Beattie, James. *The Theory of Language.* In *Dissertations, Moral and Critical.* 2 vols. Dublin: 1783.

Bell, Eva Mary Hamilton. *The Hamwood Papers of the Ladies of Llangollen and Caroline Hamilton.* London: Macmillan, 1930.

Beresford, James. *The Miseries of Human Life.* 1806. 6th ed., 1807.

Blair, Hugh. "Pronunciation, or Delivery." In *Lectures on Rhetoric and Belles Lettres.* 1783. Reprinted in Vicesimus Knox, ed., *Elegant Extracts.* 1784.

Boaden, James. *Memoirs of the Life of John Philip Kemble, Esq.* 2 vols. 1825.

Boaden, James. *Mrs. Sarah Siddons.* 1827; original title *Memoirs of Mrs. Siddons.* 2 vols. London: Grolier, n.d.

Boswell, James. *Life of Johnson.* Ed. George Birkbeck Hill and L. F. Powell. 6 vols. Oxford: Clarendon, 1934.

Boswell, James. "On the Profession of a Player." 1770. London: Elkin Mathews & Marrot, 1929.

Brunton, Alexander. "Memoir." In Mary Brunton, *Emmeline, with Some Other Pieces.* Edinburgh: 1819.

Buchanan, James. *A Plan of an English Grammar-School Education.* Edinburgh: 1770.

Burgh, James. *The Art of Speaking.* 1761; 1768.

Burgh, James. *The Dignity of Human Nature.* 1754; 1794.

Burney, Frances. *Diary & Letters of Madame d'Arblay.* Ed. Charlotte Barrett. 1842–46. 6 vols. London: Macmillan, 1904–1905.

Burney, Frances. *The Early Diary of Frances Burney, 1768–1778.* Ed. Annie Raine Ellis. 2 vols. London: Bell, 1907.

Burney, Frances. *Evelina; or, The History of a Young Lady's Entrance into the World.* 1778. Ed. Edward A. Bloom. London: Oxford University Press, 1968.

Burney, Frances. *The Journals and Letters of Fanny Burney (Madame d'Arblay).* Ed. Joyce Hemlow et al. 10 vols. Oxford: Clarendon, 1972–82.

Burney, Frances (Madame d'Arblay). *Memoirs of Doctor Burney.* 3 vols. 1832.

Burney, Frances. *The Wanderer; or, Female Difficulties.* 1814. Ed. Margaret Anne Doody, Robert L. Mack, and Peter Sabor. Oxford: Oxford University Press, 1991.

Byng, John. *The Torrington Diaries.* Ed. C. Bruyn Andrews. 4 vols. New York: Holt, 1935–38.

Campbell, Thomas. *Life of Mrs. Siddons.* New York: 1834.

Chapone, Hester. *A Letter to a New-Married Lady.* 1777.

Chapone, Hester. *Letters on the Improvement of the Mind, Addressed to a Young Lady.* 1773. 2 vols. 1774.

Clarkson, Thomas. *A Portraiture of Quakerism.* 1806. Indianapolis: Merrill & Field, 1870.

Cobb, James. *English Readings.* 1787.

Cockin, William. *The Art of Delivering Written Language; or, an Essay on Reading.* 1775.

Coleridge, Samuel Taylor. *Shakespearean Criticism.* Ed. Thomas Middleton Raysor. 2 vols. London: Dent, 1960.

Collier, Jane. *An Essay on the Art of Ingeniously Tormenting, with Proper Rules for the Exercise of that Pleasant Art.* 1753.

Colman, George (the elder). *Polly Honeycombe, A Dramatick Novel of One Act.* 1760.

Cooke, William. *The Elements of Dramatic Criticism.* 1775.

Corp, Harriet. *An Antidote to the Miseries of Human Life, in the History of the Widow Placid, and her Daughter Rachel.* 1807; 1808.

Corp, Harriet. *A Sequel to the Antidote to the Miseries of Human Life, Containing a Further Account of Mrs. Placid and her Daughter Rachel.* 1809.

Cowper, William. "Conversation." In John D. Baird and Charles Ryskamp, eds., *The Poems of William Cowper.* 2 vols. Oxford: Clarendon, 1980.

Cumberland, Richard. *The Observer.* 1785.

Dana, Joseph. *A New American Selection of Lessons, in Reading and Speaking.* Boston: 1792.

Dante. *The Inferno of Dante.* Trans. Robert Pinsky. New York: Farrar, Straus and Giroux, 1994.

Darwin, Erasmus. *A Plan for the Conduct of Female Education in Boarding Schools.* Derby: 1797.

Defoe, Daniel. *Roxana, the Fortunate Mistress.* 1724. Ed. David Blewett. London: Penguin, 1982.

Dudley, Mary. *The Life of Mary Dudley.* 1825.

Duff, William. *Letters on the Intellectual and Moral Character of Women.* Aberdeen: 1807.

Edgeworth, Maria. *Belinda.* 1801. Ed. Kathryn J. Kirkpatrick. Oxford: Oxford University Press, 1994.

Edgeworth, Maria. *Letters for Literary Ladies; To which is added, An Essay on the Noble Science of Self-Justification.* 1795. Facs. with an introduction by Gina Luria. New York: Garland, 1974.

Edgeworth, Maria, and Richard Lovell Edgeworth. *Practical Education.* 2 vols. 1798.

Enfield, William. *Exercises in Elocution, Selected from Various Authors and Arranged under Proper Heads.* Warrington: 1780.

Enfield, William. *The Speaker; or, Miscellaneous Pieces, Selected from the Best English Writers, and Disposed under Proper Heads, with a View to Facilitate the Improvement of Youth in Reading and Speaking.* 1774.

Fell, Margaret. *Womens [sic] Speaking Justified, Proved and Allowed of by the Scriptures.* 1666. Amherst: New England Yearly Meeting of Friends, 1980.

Fielding, Henry. *Miscellanies by Henry Fielding, Esq.; Volume One.* 1743. Ed. Henry Knight Miller. Oxford: Wesleyan University Press, 1972.

Fordyce, James. *Sermons to Young Women.* 1766. Dublin: 1796.

Gentleman, Francis. *Introduction to Shakespeare's Plays, containing an Essay on Oratory.* 1774.

Gisborne, Thomas. *An Enquiry into the Duties of the Female Sex.* 1797.

Godwin, William. *The Enquirer: Reflections on Education, Manners, and Literature, in a Series of Essays.* 1797.

Godwin, William. *Enquiry Concerning Political Justice and its Influence on Morals and Happiness.* 1793. Ed. F. E. L. Priestley. 3 vols. Toronto: University of Toronto Press, 1946.

Gregory, John. *A Father's Legacy to His Daughters.* 1774.

Gurney, Joseph John. *Observations on the Distinguishing Views and Practices of the Society of Friends.* 1824; original title *Observations on the Religious Peculiarities of the Society of Friends.* New York: Wood, 1854.

Half an Hour after Supper; an Interlude, in One Act. 1789.

Hanway, Jonas. *Advice from Father Trueman to his Daughter Mary upon her Going into Service.* Edinburgh: 1789.

Harris, James. *Hermes; or, a Philosophical Inquiry Concerning Language and Universal Grammar.* 1751.

Hayley, William. *A Philosophical, Historical, and Moral Essay on Old Maids.* 1785; 1786.

A Help to Elocution and Eloquence, . . . Designed to Form the Minds of Youth to a True Taste in Reading. 1770.

Herries, John. *The Elements of Speech.* 1773.

Hill, Aaron, and William Popple. *The Prompter: A Theatrical Paper (1734–1736).* Ed. William W. Appleton and Kalman A. Burnim. New York: Benjamin Blom, 1966.

Hill, John. *The Actor: A Treatise on the Art of Playing.* 1750.

Hunt, Leigh. *Essays (Selected).* Ed. J. B. Priestley. London: Dent, 1929.

Inchbald, Elizabeth. *Remarks for "The British Theatre" (1806–1809).* Delmar, N.Y.: Scholars' Facsimiles & Reprints, 1990.

Johnson, Samuel. *The Yale Edition of the Works of Samuel Johnson.* Ed. Walter Jackson Bate and Albrecht B. Straus. 15 vols. New Haven, Conn.: Yale University Press, 1958–1985.

Kett, Henry. *Emily: A Moral Tale, including Letters from a Father to his Daughter, upon the Most Important Subjects.* 2 vols. 1809. 2d ed., 1809.

[Knowles, Mary?] "An Interesting Dialogue between the late Dr. Johnson, and Mrs. Knowles the Quaker." *The Lady's Magazine* 22 (1791): 489–91.

Knox, Vicesimus. *Elegant Extracts; or, Useful and Entertaining Passages in Prose, Selected for the Improvement of Scholars at Classical and Other Schools in the Art of Speaking, in Reading, Thinking, Composing; and in the Conduct of Life.* 1784.

Knox, Vicesimus. *Liberal Education; or, A Practical Treatise in the Methods of Acquiring a Useful and Polite Learning.* 1781. 2 vols. 1785.

Lackington, James. *Memoirs of the First Forty-Five Years of the Life of James Lackington.* 1791; 1792.

Le Brun, Charles. *A Method to Learn to Design the Passions.* 1734. French original, 1698. Edited with an introduction by Alan T. McKenzie. Los Angeles: Augustan Reprint Society, 1980.

Lewis, Matthew G. *The Monk: A Romance.* 1796. Ed. Howard Anderson. London: Oxford University Press, 1973.

Lockhart, John Gibson. *Memoirs of the Life of Sir Walter Scott, Bart.* 1837–38. 10 vols. Toronto: Morang, 1901.

Lowth, Robert. *A Short Introduction to English Grammar.* 1762.

Mason, John. *An Essay on Elocution; or, Pronunciation.* 1748.

Mitford, Mary Russell. *The Life of Mary Russell Mitford.* Ed. A. G. L'Estrange. 3 vols. London: Bentley, 1870.

Montagu, Elizabeth. *Mrs. Montagu: Queen of the Blues.* Ed. Reginald Blunt. 2 vols. London: Constable, 1923.

More, Hannah. *The Complete Works of Hannah More.* 2 vols. New York: Harper, 1855.

More, Hannah. *Essays on Various Subjects, Principally Designed for Young Ladies.* 1777.

More, Hannah. *Village Politics, by Will Chip, a Country Carpenter.* 1792. 2d ed., 1792.

Morse, Samuel B. *School Dialogues . . . Calculated to Promote an Early and Elegant Mode of Conversation Among the Young Masters and Misses of the United States.* Boston: 1797.

Murray, Lindley. *English Grammar.* York: 1795.

Murray, Lindley. *The English Reader; or, Pieces in Prose and Poetry, Selected from the Best Writers, Designed to Assist Young Persons to Read with Propriety and Effect.* York: 1799.

Murry, Ann. *Mentoria; or, The Young Ladies Instructor.* 1778; 1791.

Nares, Robert. *General Rules for the Pronunciation of the English Language.* 1784; original title *Elements of Orthoepy.* 1792.

Observations on Plainness and Simplicity in Conduct and Conversation in Accordance with the Principles of the Society of Friends. Stockport: Claye, n.d.

O'Keefe, John. *The Young Quaker.* 1784.

Opie, Amelia. *The Works of Mrs. Amelia Opie.* 3 vols. Philadelphia: Crissy & Markley, 1848.

Piozzi, Hester Lynch (Thrale). *Thraliana. The Diary of Mrs. Hester Lynch Thrale (later Mrs. Piozzi), 1776–1809.* Ed. Katharine C. Balderston. 2 vols. Oxford: Clarendon, 1942.

The Polite Lady; or, a Course of Female Education, in a Series of Letters from a Mother to her Daughter. 1760.

Priestley, Joseph. *A Course of Lectures on the Theory of Language, and Universal Grammar.* Warrington: 1762.

Radcliffe, Ann. *The Mysteries of Udolpho.* 1794. Ed. Bonamy Dobrée. Oxford: Oxford University Press, 1966.

The Reader, or Reciter: By the Assistance of which Any Person may Teach Himself to Read or Recite English Prose with the Utmost Elegance and Effect. 1799.

Reynolds, Frederick. *The Life and Times of Frederick Reynolds.* 2 vols. 1826.

Rice, John. *An Introduction to the Art of Reading with Energy and Propriety.* 1765.

Richardson, Samuel. *Familiar Letters on Important Occasions.* 1741. New York: Dodd, Mead, 1928.

Robinson, Henry Crabb. *Diary, Reminiscences, and Correspondence of Henry Crabb Robinson.* 1869. Ed. Thomas Sadler. 2 vols. Boston: Osgood, 1871.

Rousseau, Jean-Jacques. *Julie, ou La nouvelle Héloïse*. 1761. Paris: Garnier, 1960.

Scott, Walter. *The Antiquary*. Vol. 5 of *The Works of Sir Walter Scott*. 50 vols. Boston: Houghton Mifflin, 1912–13.

Scott, William. *Beauties of Eminent Writers, Selected and Arranged for the Instruction of Youth in the Proper Reading and Reciting of the English Language*. Edinburgh: 1793.

Scott, William. *Lessons in Elocution; or, A Selection of Pieces, in Prose and Verse, for the Improvement of Youth in Reading and Speaking*. 1779. Boston: 1820.

Seward, Anna. *Letters of Anna Seward*. 6 vols. Edinburgh: 1811.

Shadwell, Charles. *The Fair Quaker of Deal; or, The Humours of the Navy*. 1710. In *The Works of Mr. Charles Shadwell*. 2 vols. Dublin: 1720.

Shelley, Mary. *Mathilda*. In Betty T. Bennett and Charles E. Robinson, eds., *The Mary Shelley Reader*. New York: Oxford University Press, 1990.

Sheridan, Betsy. *Betsy Sheridan's Journal: Letters from Sheridan's Sister, 1784–1786 and 1788–1790*. Ed. William LeFanu. London: Eyre & Spottiswoode, 1960.

Sheridan, Richard Brinsley. *The Dramatic Works of Richard Brinsley Sheridan*. Ed. Cecil Price. 2 vols. Oxford: Clarendon, 1973.

Sheridan, Thomas. *British Education; or, The Source of the Disorders of Great Britain*. 1756.

Sheridan, Thomas. *A Course of Lectures on Elocution*. 1762.

Sheridan, Thomas. *Lectures on the Art of Reading*. 2 vols. 1775.

Sheridan's and Henderson's Practical Method of Reading and Reciting English Poetry. 1796.

Short, C. *Dramas for the Use of Young Ladies*. Birmingham: 1792.

Smellie, William. *The Philosophy of Natural History*. 2 vols. Edinburgh: 1790/1799.

Smith, Sydney. *Wit and Wisdom of the Rev. Sydney Smith*. New York: Redfield, 1856.

Steele, Joshua. *Prosodia Rationalis; or, An Essay Towards Establishing the Melody and Measure of Speech, to be Expressed and Perpetuated by Peculiar Symbols*. 1775.

Sterne, Laurence. *The Life and Opinions of Tristram Shandy, Gentleman*. 1759–67. Ed. Melvyn New and Joan New. 3 vols. Gainesville: University Presses of Florida, 1978–84.

Swift, Jonathan. "A Proposal for Correcting, Improving, and Ascertaining the English Tongue." 1712. In vol. 4 of *The Prose Works of Jonathan Swift*. Edited by Herbert Davis. 13 vols. Oxford: Basil Blackwell, 1939–1959.

The Thespian Oracle; or, A New Key to Theatrical Amusements. 1791.

Thompson, Edward. *The Fair Quaker; or, The Humours of the Navy. Formerly written by Mr. Charles Shadwell, and now alter'd with great additions and a new character*. 1773.

Tooke, John Horne. *Divisions of Purley*. 1786. London: Tegg, 1857.

Trusler, John. *Principles of Politeness, and of Knowing the World. Part II. Addressed to Young Ladies*. 1775.

Trusler, John. *The Sublime Reader; or, The Morning and Evening Service of the Church so Pointed, and the Emphatical Words throughout so Marked, as to display all the Beauty and Sublimity of the Language, and render it, with the least Attention, impossible to be read by the most injudicious Reader, but with Propriety*. 1782; 1784.

Tucker, Abraham. *Vocal Sounds*. 1773.

"The Turf, and Reading Made Easy." Monaghan: 1788.

Walker, John. *The Melody of Speaking Delineated; or, Elocution Taught Like Music, by Visible Signs, Adapted to the Tones, Inflexions, and Variations of Voice in Reading and Speaking.* 1787.

Walker, John. *A Rhetorical Grammar, or Course of Lessons in Elocution.* 1785.

Waring, Mary. *A Diary of the Religious Experience of Mary Waring.* 1809; 1810.

Wells, Helena. *Letters on Subjects of Importance to the Happiness of Young Females, Addressed by a Governess to her Pupils.* 1799.

West, Jane. *Letters to a Young Lady; in which the Duties and Character of Women are Considered.* 3 vols. 1806.

Wilson, Harriette. *Memoirs.* 1825. Reprinted as *The Game of Hearts: Harriette Wilson's Memoirs, Interspersed with Excerpts from the Confessions of Julia Johnstone, Her Rival.* Ed. Lesley Blanch. New York: Simon and Schuster, 1955.

Wilson, John. *Principles of Elocution, and Suitable Exercises; or, Elegant Extracts, in Prose and Verse.* Edinburgh: 1798.

Wilson, Rachel. "A Discourse, Delivered on Saturday, the 10th Day of August, 1769, in the Friends Meeting-House, in Beekman's Precinct, Dutches County, In the Province of New-York." Newport: 1769.

Wollstonecraft, Mary. *The Works of Mary Wollstonecraft.* Ed. Janet Todd and Marilyn Butler. 7 vols. London: Pickering, 1989.

The World. Ed. Edward Moore. 1753–56. 4 vols. 1761.

Secondary Sources

Allen, Julia. "The Uses and Problems of a 'Manly' Rhetoric: Mary Wollstonecraft's Adaptation of Hugh Blair's *Lectures* in Her Two *Vindications*." In Molly Meijer Wertheimer, ed., *Listening to Their Voices: The Rhetorical Activities of Historical Women.* Columbia: University of South Carolina Press, 1997.

Ardener, Edwin. "Belief and the Problem of Women." In Shirley Ardener, ed., *Perceiving Women.* New York: Wiley, 1975.

Armstrong, Nancy. *Desire and Domestic Fiction: A Political History of the Novel.* New York: Oxford University Press, 1987.

Attardo, Salvatore. *Linguistic Theories of Humor.* Berlin: Mouton de Gruyter, 1994.

Babb, Howard S. *Jane Austen's Novels: The Fabric of Dialogue.* Columbus: Ohio State University Press, 1962.

Backscheider, Paula R. *Spectacular Politics: Theatrical Power and Mass Culture in Early Modern England.* Baltimore: Johns Hopkins University Press, 1993.

Bander, Elaine. "Jane Austen and the Uses of Silence." In Gary Wihl and David Williams, eds., *Literature and Ethics: Essays Presented to A. E. Malloch.* Kingston, Canada: McGill-Queen's University Press, 1988.

Banfield, Ann. *Unspeakable Sentences: Narration and Representation in the Language of Fiction.* Boston: Routledge & Kegan Paul, 1982.

Barish, Jonas. *The Antitheatrical Prejudice.* Berkeley and Los Angeles: University of California Press, 1981.

Barker-Benfield, G. J. *The Culture of Sensibility: Sex and Society in Eighteenth-Century Britain.* Chicago: University of Chicago Press, 1992.

Barker-Benfield, G. J. "Mary Wollstonecraft: Eighteenth-Century Commonwealth-woman." *Journal of the History of Ideas* 50 (1989): 95–115.

Bartine, David. *Early English Reading Theory: Origins of Current Debates.* Columbia: University of South Carolina Press, 1989.

Bauman, Richard. *Let Your Words Be Few: Symbolism of Speaking and Silence Among Seventeenth-Century Quakers.* Cambridge: Cambridge University Press, 1983.

Baumlin, James S. "Introduction: Positioning *Ethos* in Historical and Contemporary Theory." In James S. Baumlin and Tita French Baumlin, eds., *Ethos: New Essays in Rhetorical and Critical Theory.* Dallas: Southern Methodist University Press, 1994.

Belenky, Mary Field, Blythe McVicker Clinchy, Nancy Rule Goldberger, Jill Mattuck Tarule. *Women's Ways of Knowing: The Development of Self, Voice, and Mind.* New York: Basic Books, 1986.

Benedict, Barbara M. *Making the Modern Reader: Cultural Mediation in Early Modern Literary Anthologies.* Princeton, N.J.: Princeton University Press, 1996.

Benzie, W. *The Dublin Orator: Thomas Sheridan's Influence on Eighteenth-Century Rhetoric and Belles Lettres.* Menston, England: Scolar Press, 1972.

Bermingham, Ann. "The Aesthetics of Ignorance: The Accomplished Woman in the Culture of Connoisseurship." *The Oxford Art Journal* 16, no. 2 (1993): 3–20.

Biber, Douglas. *Variation Across Speech and Writing.* Cambridge: Cambridge University Press, 1988.

Bilger, Audrey. *Laughing Feminism: Subversive Comedy in Frances Burney, Maria Edgeworth, and Jane Austen.* Detroit, Mich.: Wayne State University Press, 1998.

Bing, Janet M., and Victoria L. Bergvall. "The Question of Questions: Beyond Binary Thinking." In Victoria L. Bergvall, Janet M. Bing, and Alice F. Freeds, eds., *Rethinking Language and Gender Research: Theory and Practice.* London: Longman, 1996.

Bishop, Morchard. *Blake's Hayley: The Life, Works, and Friendships of William Hayley.* London: Victor Gollancz, 1951.

Bodine, Ann. "Androcentrism in Prescriptive Grammar: Singular 'They,' Sex-Indefinite 'He,' and 'He or She.'" *Language in Society* 4 (1975): 129–46.

Boyarin, Jonathan, ed. *The Ethnography of Reading.* Berkeley and Los Angeles: University of California Press, 1993.

Brewer, John. "Reconstructing the Reader: Prescriptions, Texts and Strategies in Anna Larpent's Reading." In James Raven, Helen Small, and Naomi Tadmor, eds., *The Practice and Representation of Reading in England.* Cambridge: Cambridge University Press, 1996.

Brightwell, Cecilia Lucy. *Memorials of the Life of Amelia Opie.* Norwich, England: Fletcher and Alexander, 1854.

Broadhead, Glenn J. "A Bibliography of the Rhetoric of Conversation in England, 1660–1800." *Rhetoric Society Quarterly* 10 (1980): 43–48.

Brody, Miriam. *Manly Writing: Gender, Rhetoric, and the Rise of Composition.* Carbondale: Southern Illinois University Press, 1993.

Brown, Penelope, and Stephen C. Levinson. *Politeness: Some Universals in Language Usage.* 2d ed. Cambridge: Cambridge University Press, 1987.

Browne, Stephen H. "Satirizing Women's Speech in Eighteenth-Century England." *Rhetoric Society Quarterly* 22, no. 3 (1992): 20–29.

Burke, John J., Jr. "Talk, Dialogue, Conversation, and Other Kinds of Speech Acts in Boswell's *Life of Samuel Johnson.*" In Kevin L. Cope, ed., *Compendious Conversations: The Method of Dialogue in the Early Enlightenment.* Frankfurt: Peter Lang, 1992.

Burke, Peter. *The Art of Conversation.* Ithaca, N.Y.: Cornell University Press, 1993.

Burroughs, Catherine B. *Closet Stages: Joanna Baillie and the Theater Theory of British Romantic Women Writers.* Philadelphia: University of Pennsylvania Press, 1997.

Burrows, J. F. *Computation into Criticism: A Study of Jane Austen's Novels and an Experiment in Method.* Oxford: Clarendon, 1987.

Butler, Marilyn. *Jane Austen and the War of Ideas.* Oxford: Clarendon, 1975.

Cameron, Deborah. *Feminism and Linguistic Theory.* 2d ed. London: Macmillan, 1992.

Cameron, Deborah. "Gender, Language, and Discourse: A Review Essay." *Signs* 23 (1998): 945–73.

Cameron, Deborah. "Performing Gender Identity: Young Men's Talk and the Construction of Heterosexual Masculinity." In Sally Johnson and Ulrike Hanna Meinhof, eds., *Language and Masculinity.* Oxford: Blackwell, 1997.

Cameron, Deborah. "Theoretical Debates in Feminist Linguistics: Questions of Sex and Gender." In Ruth Wodak, ed., *Gender and Discourse.* London: Sage, 1997.

Carlson, Julie A. *In the Theatre of Romanticism: Coleridge, Nationalism, Women.* Cambridge: Cambridge University Press, 1994.

Chilcote, Paul Wesley. *John Wesley and the Women Preachers of Early Methodism.* Metuchen, N.J.: Scarecrow Press, 1991.

Clifford, James L. *Hester Lynch Piozzi (Mrs. Thrale).* Oxford: Clarendon, 1941.

Coates, Jennifer. *Women, Men, and Language: A Sociolinguistic Account of Gender Differences in Language.* 2d ed. London: Longman, 1993.

Cohen, Michèle. *Fashioning Masculinity: National Identity and Language in the Eighteenth Century.* London: Routledge, 1996.

Cohen, Michèle. "Manliness, Effeminacy, and the French: Gender and the Construction of National Character in Eighteenth-Century England." In Tim Hitchcock and Michèle Cohen, eds., *English Masculinities, 1660–1800.* London: Longman, 1999.

Cohen, Murray. *Sensible Words: Linguistic Practice in England, 1640–1785.* Baltimore: Johns Hopkins University Press, 1977.

Coleman, Joyce. *Public Reading and the Reading Public in Late Medieval England and France.* Cambridge: Cambridge University Press, 1996.

Cox, Stephen D. *"The Stranger Within Thee": Concepts of the Self in Late-Eighteenth-Century Literature.* Pittsburgh: University of Pittsburgh Press, 1980.

Crawford, Mary. *Talking Difference: On Gender and Language.* London: Sage, 1995.

Crouch, Kimberly. "The Public Life of Actresses: Prostitutes or Ladies?" In Hannah

Barker and Elaine Chalus, eds., *Gender in Eighteenth-Century England: Roles, Representations, and Responsibilities.* London: Longman, 1997.

Crowley, Tony. *Language in History: Theories and Texts.* London: Routledge, 1996.

Curry, Kenneth. *Southey.* London: Routledge & Kegan Paul, 1975.

Cutting-Gray, Joanne. *Woman as "Nobody" and the Novels of Fanny Burney.* Gainesville: University Press of Florida, 1992.

Darnton, Robert. "First Steps Toward a History of Reading." *Australian Journal of French Studies* 23 (1986): 5–30.

Davidoff, Leonore, and Catherine Hall. *Family Fortunes: Men and Women of the English Middle Class, 1780–1850.* Chicago: University of Chicago Press, 1987.

Davis, Lennard J. "Conversation and Dialogue." *The Age of Johnson* 1 (1987): 347–73.

De Bolla, Peter. *The Discourse of the Sublime: Readings in History, Aesthetics, and the Subject.* Oxford: Basil Blackwell, 1989.

DeMaria, Robert, Jr. *Samuel Johnson and the Life of Reading.* Baltimore: Johns Hopkins University Press, 1997.

Donkin, Ellen. "Mrs. Siddons Looks Back in Anger: Feminist Historiography for Eighteenth-Century British Theater." In Janelle G. Reinelt and Joseph R. Roach, eds., *Critical Theory and Performance.* Ann Arbor: University of Michigan Press, 1992.

Doody, Margaret Anne. *Frances Burney: The Life in the Works.* New Brunswick, N.J.: Rutgers University Press, 1988.

Dussinger, John A. *In the Pride of the Moment: Encounters in Jane Austen's World.* Columbus: Ohio State University Press, 1990.

Dussinger, John A. "'The Language of Real Feeling': Internal Speech in the Jane Austen Novel." In Robert W. Uphaus, ed., *The Idea of the Novel in the Eighteenth Century.* Lansing, Mich.: Colleagues Press, 1988.

Eckert, Penelope, and Sally McConnell-Ginet. "Think Practically and Look Locally: Language and Gender as Community-Based Practice." *Annual Review of Anthropology* 21 (1992): 461–90.

Edelsky, Carol. "Who's Got the Floor?" *Language in Society* 10 (1981): 383–421.

Eisenstein, Elizabeth L. *The Printing Press as an Agent of Change: Communications and Cultural Transformations in Early-Modern Europe.* 2 vols. Cambridge: Cambridge University Press, 1979.

Engelsing, Rolf. *Der Bürger als Leser: Lesergeschichte in Deutschland, 1500–1800.* Stuttgart: Metzler, 1974.

Epstein, Julia. *The Iron Pen: Frances Burney and the Politics of Women's Writing.* Madison: University of Wisconsin Press, 1989.

Ferris, Ina. *The Achievement of Literary Authority: Gender, History, and the Waverley Novels.* Ithaca, N.Y.: Cornell University Press, 1991.

Ffrench, Yvonne. *Mrs. Siddons: Tragic Actress.* London: Cobden-Sanderson, 1936.

Finch, Casey, and Peter Bowen. "'The Tittle-Tattle of Highbury': Gossip and the Free Indirect Style in *Emma.*" *Representations* 31 (summer 1990): 1–18.

Finnegan, Ruth. *Literacy and Orality: Studies in the Technology of Communication.* Oxford: Blackwell, 1988.

Fish, Stanley. *Is There a Text in This Class? The Authority of Interpretive Communities.* Cambridge: Harvard University Press, 1980.

Fishman, Pamela M. "Interaction: The Work Women Do." *Social Problems* 25 (1978): 397–406.

Fitzgerald, Percy. *The Kembles.* 2 vols. London: Tinsley, 1871.

Fitzmaurice, Susan M. "The Commerce of Language in the Pursuit of Politeness in Eighteenth-Century England." *English Studies* 79 (1998): 309–28.

Flavin, Louise. "Austen's *Persuasion.*" *The Explicator* 47, no. 4 (1989): 20–23.

Flavin, Louise. "*Mansfield Park:* Free Indirect Discourse and the Psychological Novel." *Studies in the Novel* 19 (1987): 137–59. .

Fliegelman, Jay. *Declaring Independence: Jefferson, Natural Language, and the Culture of Performance.* Stanford, Calif.: Stanford University Press, 1993.

Flint, Christopher. *Family Fictions: Narrative and Domestic Relations in Britain, 1688–1798.* Stanford, Calif.: Stanford University Press, 1998.

Flint, Kate. *The Woman Reader, 1837–1914.* Oxford: Clarendon, 1993.

Fludernik, Monika. *The Fictions of Language and the Languages of Fiction: The Linguistic Representation of Speech and Consciousness.* London: Routledge, 1993.

Fowler, Roger. *Linguistic Criticism.* 2d ed. Oxford: Oxford University Press, 1996.

Gal, Susan. "Between Speech and Silence: The Problematics of Research on Language and Gender." In Micaela di Leonardo, ed., *Gender at the Crossroads of Knowledge: Feminist Anthropology in the Postmodern Era.* Berkeley and Los Angeles: University of California Press, 1991.

Gallagher, Catherine. *Nobody's Story: The Vanishing Acts of Women Writers in the Marketplace, 1670–1820.* Berkeley and Los Angeles: University of California Press, 1994.

Gelley, Alexander. "Character and Person: On the Presentation of Self in Some Eighteenth-Century Novels." *The Eighteenth Century* 24 (1980): 109–27.

Georgia, Jennifer. "The Joys of Social Intercourse: Men, Women, and Conversation in the Eighteenth Century." In Kevin L. Cope, ed., *Compendious Conversations: The Method of Dialogue in the Early Enlightenment.* Frankfurt: Peter Lang, 1992.

Gilligan, Carol. *In a Different Voice: Psychological Theory and Women's Development.* 2d ed. Cambridge: Harvard University Press, 1993.

Giordano, Julia. "The Word as Battleground in Jane Austen's *Persuasion.*" In Carol J. Singley and Susan Elizabeth Sweeney, eds., *Anxious Power: Reading, Writing, and Ambivalence in Narrative by Women.* Albany: State University of New York Press, 1993.

Goffman, Erving. *The Presentation of Self in Everyday Life.* Garden City, N.Y.: Doubleday, 1959.

Gonda, Caroline. *Reading Daughters' Fictions, 1709–1834: Novels and Society from Manley to Edgeworth.* Cambridge: Cambridge University Press, 1996.

Greene, Donald. "'Tis a Pretty Book, Mr. Boswell, But—" *Georgia Review* 32 (1978): 17–43.

Grice, H. P. "Logic and Conversation." In Peter Cole and Jerry L. Morgan, eds., *Speech Acts.* Vol. 3 of *Syntax and Semantics.* New York: Academic Press, 1975.

Heath, Shirley Brice. "Protean Shapes in Literacy Events: Ever-Shifting Oral and Literate Traditions." In Deborah Tannen, ed., *Spoken and Written Language: Exploring Orality and Literacy.* Norwood, N.J.: Ablex, 1982.

Hemlow, Joyce. *The History of Fanny Burney.* Oxford: Clarendon, 1958.

Hess-Lüttich, Ernest W. B. "Maxims of Maliciousness: Sheridan's School for Conversation." *Poetics* 12 (1982): 419–37.

Hill, Bridget. *Women, Work, and Sexual Politics in Eighteenth-Century England.* Oxford: Blackwell, 1989.

Holmes, Janet. *Women, Men, and Politeness.* London: Longman, 1995.

Hough, Graham. "Narrative and Dialogue in Jane Austen." *Critical Quarterly* 12 (1970): 201–29.

Houston, Marsha, and Cheris Kramarae. "Speaking from Silence: Methods of Silencing and of Resistance." *Discourse and Society* 2 (1991): 387–99.

Howell, Wilbur Samuel. *Eighteenth-Century British Logic and Rhetoric.* Princeton, N.J.: Princeton University Press, 1971.

Hudson, Nicholas. *Writing and European Thought, 1600–1830.* Cambridge: Cambridge University Press, 1994.

Hughes, Alan. "Art and Eighteenth-Century Acting Style. Part III: Passions." *Theatre Notebook* 41 (1987): 128–39.

Hunter, J. Paul. *Before Novels: The Cultural Contexts of Eighteenth-Century English Fiction.* New York: Norton, 1990.

Jaworski, Adam. *The Power of Silence: Social and Pragmatic Perspectives.* Newbury Park, Calif.: Sage, 1993.

Johnson, Claudia L. *Equivocal Beings: Politics, Gender, and Sentimentality in the 1790's; Wollstonecraft, Radcliffe, Burney, Austen.* Chicago: University of Chicago Press, 1995.

Johnson, Claudia L. *Jane Austen: Women, Politics, and the Novel.* Chicago: University of Chicago Press, 1988.

Johnson, Judy Van Sickle. "The Bodily Frame: Learning Romance in *Persuasion.*" *Nineteenth-Century Fiction* 38 (1983): 43–61.

Johnson, Nan. "Ethos and the Aims of Rhetoric." In Robert J. Connors, Lisa S. Ede, and Andrea A. Lunsford, eds., *Essays on Classical Rhetoric and Modern Discourse.* Carbondale: Southern Illinois University Press, 1984.

Jones, Rufus M. *The Later Periods of Quakerism.* 2 vols. London: Macmillan, 1921.

Kaplan, Deborah. *Jane Austen Among Women.* Baltimore: Johns Hopkins University Press, 1992.

Kelly, Ann Cline. "Swift's *Polite Conversation:* An Eschatological Vision." *Studies in Philology* 73 (1976): 204–24.

Kelly, Gary. "Reading Aloud in *Mansfield Park.*" *Nineteenth-Century Fiction* 37 (1982): 29–49.

Kerber, Linda K. "Separate Spheres, Female Worlds, Woman's Place: The Rhetoric of Women's History." *Journal of American History* 75 (1988): 9–39.

Kernan, Alvin. *Samuel Johnson and the Impact of Print.* Princeton, N.J.: Princeton University Press, 1989.

Kinneavy, James L., and Susan C. Warshauer. "From Aristotle to Madison Avenue: *Ethos* and the Ethics of Argument." In James S. Baumlin and Tita French Baumlin, eds., *Ethos: New Essays in Rhetorical and Critical Theory*. Dallas: Southern Methodist University Press, 1994.

Kintgen, Eugene R. *Reading in Tudor England*. Pittsburgh: University of Pittsburgh Press, 1996.

Klein, Lawrence E. "Gender and the Public/Private Distinction in the Eighteenth Century: Some Questions about Evidence and Analytic Procedure." *Eighteenth-Century Studies* 29 (1995): 97–109.

Klein, Lawrence E. "Gender, Conversation, and the Public Sphere in Early Eighteenth-Century England." In Judith Still and Michael Worton, eds., *Textuality and Sexuality: Reading Theories and Practices*. Manchester: Manchester University Press, 1993.

Klein, Lawrence E. *Shaftesbury and the Culture of Politeness: Moral Discourse and Cultural Politics in Early Eighteenth-Century England*. Cambridge: Cambridge University Press, 1994.

Korshin, Paul J. "Johnson's Conversation in Boswell's *Life of Johnson*." In Greg Clingham, ed., *New Light on Boswell*. Cambridge: Cambridge University Press, 1991.

Kraft, Elizabeth. *Character and Consciousness in Eighteenth-Century Comic Fiction*. Athens: University of Georgia Press, 1992.

Krueger, Christine L. *The Reader's Repentance: Women Preachers, Women Writers, and Nineteenth-Century Social Discourse*. Chicago: University of Chicago Press, 1992.

Lakoff, Robin. *Language and Woman's Place*. New York: Harper & Row, 1975.

Lanser, Susan Sniader. *Fictions of Authority: Women Writers and Narrative Voice*. Ithaca, N.Y.: Cornell University Press, 1992.

Laqueur, Thomas. *Making Sex: Body and Gender from the Greeks to Freud*. Cambridge: Harvard University Press, 1990.

Laurence, Patricia Ondek. *The Reading of Silence: Virginia Woolf in the English Tradition*. Stanford, Calif.: Stanford University Press, 1991.

Leppert, Richard. *Music and Image: Domesticity, Ideology, and Socio-cultural Formation in Eighteenth-Century England*. Cambridge: Cambridge University Press, 1988.

Litvak, Joseph. *Caught in the Act: Theatricality in the Nineteenth-Century English Novel*. Berkeley and Los Angeles: University of California Press, 1992.

Long, Elizabeth. "Textual Interpretation as Collective Action." In Jonathan Boyarin, ed., *The Ethnography of Reading*. Berkeley and Los Angeles: University of California Press, 1993.

Lonsdale, Roger. *Dr. Charles Burney: A Literary Biography*. Oxford: Clarendon, 1965.

Lorde, Audre. "The Transformation of Silence into Language and Action." In *Sister Outsider: Essays and Speeches*. Trumansburg, N.Y.: The Crossing Press, 1984.

Lynch, Deidre Shauna. *The Economy of Character: Novels, Market Culture, and the Business of Inner Meaning*. Chicago: University of Chicago Press, 1998.

MacFadyen, Heather. "Lady Delacour's Library: Maria Edgeworth's *Belinda* and Fashionable Reading." *Nineteenth-Century Literature* 48 (1994): 423–39.

Machor, James L., ed. *Readers in History: Nineteenth-Century American Literature and the Contexts of Response*. Baltimore: Johns Hopkins University Press, 1993.

Mack, Phyllis. *Visionary Women: Ecstatic Prophecy in Seventeenth-Century England*. Berkeley and Los Angeles: University of California Press, 1992.

Manvell, Roger. *Sarah Siddons: Portrait of an Artist*. New York: Putnam, 1970.

Marshall, David. "True Acting and the Language of Real Feeling: *Mansfield Park*." *Yale Journal of Criticism* 3 (1989): 87–106.

McHale, Brian. "Free Indirect Discourse: A Survey of Recent Accounts." *PTL* 3 (1978): 249–87.

McIntosh, Carey. *The Evolution of English Prose, 1700–1800: Style, Politeness, and Print Culture*. Cambridge: Cambridge University Press, 1998.

McKeon, Michael. "Historicizing Patriarchy: The Emergence of Gender Difference in England, 1660–1760." *Eighteenth-Century Studies* 28 (1995): 295–322.

McMaster, Juliet. "The Secret Languages of *Emma*." In *Jane Austen the Novelist: Essays Past and Present*. London: Macmillan, 1996.

McMaster, Juliet. "Talking About Talk in *Pride and Prejudice*." In Juliet McMaster and Bruce Stovel, eds., *Jane Austen's Business: Her World and Her Profession*. Basingstoke, England: Macmillan, 1996.

Menzies-Wilson, Jacobine, and Helen Lloyd. *Amelia: The Tale of a Plain Friend*. London: Oxford University Press, 1940.

Meyerhoff, Miriam. "Dealing with Gender Identity as a Sociolinguistic Variable." In Victoria L. Bergvall, Janet M. Bing, and Alice F. Freed, eds., *Rethinking Language and Gender Research: Theory and Practice*. London: Longman, 1996.

Meyersohn, Marylea. "The Duets of *Pride and Prejudice*." In Marcia McClintock Folsom, ed., *Approaches to Teaching Austen's "Pride and Prejudice."* New York: Modern Language Association, 1993.

Meyersohn, Marylea. "Jane Austen's Garrulous Speakers: Social Criticism in *Sense and Sensibility, Emma,* and *Persuasion*." In Bege K. Bowers and Barbara Brothers, eds., *Reading and Writing Women's Lives: A Study of the Novel of Manners*. Ann Arbor, Mich.: University of Michigan Research Press, 1990.

Miller, Henry Knight. *Essays on Fieldings's "Miscellanies"; A Commentary on Volume One*. Princeton, N.J.: Princeton University Press, 1961.

Miller, P. J. "Women's Education, 'Self-Improvement,' and Social Mobility: A Late Eighteenth Century Debate." *British Journal of Educational Studies* 20 (1972): 302–14.

Mills, Sara. "Discourse Competence: Or How to Theorize Strong Women Speakers." *Hypatia* 7, no. 2 (1992): 4–17.

Moler, Kenneth L. *Jane Austen's Art of Allusion*. Lincoln: University of Nebraska Press, 1968.

Morgan, Marjorie. *Manners, Morals, and Class in England, 1774–1858*. New York: St. Martin's, 1994.

Morgan, Susan. "Why There's No Sex in Jane Austen's Novels." *Studies in the Novel* 19 (1987): 346–56.

Mugglestone, Lydia. *"Talking Proper": The Rise of Accent as Social Symbol*. Oxford: Clarendon, 1995.

Neumann, Anne Waldron. "Characterization and Comment in *Pride and Prejudice: Free Indirect Discourse* and 'Double-Voiced' Verbs of Speaking, Thinking, and Feeling." *Style* 20 (1986): 364–94.

Neumann, Anne Waldron. "Free Indirect Discourse in the Eighteenth-Century English Novel: Speakable or Unspeakable? The Example of *Sir Charles Grandison*." In Michael Toolan, ed., *Language, Text and Context: Essays in Stylistics*. New York: Routledge, 1993.

Newman, Gerald. *The Rise of English Nationalism: A Cultural History, 1740–1830*. New York: St. Martin's, 1987.

Nussbaum, Felicity A. *The Autobiographical Subject: Gender and Ideology in Eighteenth-Century England*. Baltimore: Johns Hopkins University Press, 1989.

Oakleaf, David. "Marks, Stamps, and Representations: Character in Eighteenth-Century Fiction." *Studies in the Novel* 23 (1991): 295–311.

Ochs, Elinor. "Indexing Gender." In Alessandro Duranti and Charles Goodwin, eds., *Rethinking Context: Language as an Interactive Phenomenon*. Cambridge: Cambridge University Press, 1992.

Olsen, Tillie. "Silences in Literature." In *Silences*. New York: Dell, 1978.

Ong, Walter J. *Orality and Literacy: The Technologizing of the Word*. London: Methuen, 1982.

Ong, Walter J. "Writing Is a Technology That Restructures Thought." In Pamela Downing, Susan D. Lima, and Michael Noonan, eds., *The Linguistics of Literacy*. Amsterdam: Benjamins, 1992.

Page, Norman. *The Language of Jane Austen*. New York: Barnes and Noble, 1972.

Page, Norman. *Speech in the English Novel*. 2d ed. Atlantic Highlands, N.J.: Humanities Press International, 1988.

Pascal, Roy. *The Dual Voice: Free Indirect Speech and Its Functioning in the Nineteenth-Century European Novel*. Manchester, England: Manchester University Press, 1977.

Pascoe, Judith. *Romantic Theatricality: Gender, Poetry, and Spectatorship*. Ithaca, N.Y.: Cornell University Press, 1997.

Pearson, Jacqueline. "'Books, My Greatest Joy': Constructing the Female Reader in *The Lady's Magazine*." *Women's Writing* 3 (1996): 3–15.

Pearson, Jacqueline. *Women's Reading in Britain, 1750–1835: A Dangerous Recreation*. Cambridge: Cambridge University Press, 1999.

Percy, Carol Elaine. "'Easy Women': Defining and Confining the 'Feminine' Style in Eighteenth-Century Print Culture." *Language Sciences* 22 (2000): 315–37.

Percy, Carol [Elaine]. "Paradigms for Their Sex? Women's Grammars in Late Eighteenth-Century England." *Histoire Epistémologie Langage* 16, no. 2 (1994): 121–41.

Perrin, Noel. *Dr. Bowdler's Legacy: A History of Expurgated Books in England and America*. New York: Atheneum, 1969.

Poovey, Mary. *The Proper Lady and the Woman Writer: Ideology as Style in the Works of Mary Wollstonecraft, Mary Shelley, and Jane Austen*. Chicago: University of Chicago Press, 1984.

Raven, James. "From Promotion to Proscription: Arrangements for Reading and Eighteenth-Century Libraries." In James Raven, Helen Small, and Naomi Tadmor, eds., *The Practice and Representation of Reading in England*. Cambridge: Cambridge University Press, 1996.

Raven, James. "New Reading Histories, Print Culture and the Identification of Change: The Case of Eighteenth-Century England." *Social History* 23 (1998): 268–87.

Raven, James, Helen Small, and Naomi Tadmor, eds. *The Practice and Representation of Reading in England*. Cambridge: Cambridge University Press, 1996.

Reddick, Allen. *The Making of Johnson's Dictionary, 1746–1773*. Cambridge: Cambridge University Press, 1990.

Rempel, Ursula M. "The Complete Female: Musical 'Accomplishment' in the Late Eighteenth Century." *Man and Nature* 8 (1989): 39–48.

Rich, Adrienne. *On Lies, Secrets, and Silence: Selected Prose, 1966–1978*. New York: Norton, 1979.

Richards, Cynthia. "'The Pleasures of Complicity': Sympathetic Identification and the Female Reader in Early Eighteenth-Century Women's Amatory Fiction." *The Eighteenth Century* 36 (1995): 220–33.

Richetti, John J. "Voice and Gender in Eighteenth-Century Fiction: Haywood to Burney." *Studies in the Novel* 19 (1987): 263–72.

Richter, David H. *The Progress of Romance: Literary Historiography and the Gothic Novel*. Columbus: Ohio State University Press, 1996.

Rizzo, Betty. "How (and How Not) to Explore the Burneys: Questions of Decorum." *Review* 11 (1989): 197–218.

Rogers, Pat. "'Towering Beyond Her Sex': Stature and Sublimity in the Achievement of Sarah Siddons." In Mary Anne Schofield and Cecilia Macheski, eds., *Curtain Calls: British and American Women and the Theater, 1660–1820*. Athens: Ohio University Press, 1991.

Rose, Jonathan. "Rereading the English Common Reader: A Preface to a History of Audiences." *Journal of the History of Ideas* 53 (1992): 47–70.

Rosenfeld, Sybil. "Jane Austen and Private Theatricals." *Essays and Studies* n.s. 15 (1962): 40–51.

Rosenfeld, Sybil. *Temples of Thespis: Some Private Theatres and Theatricals in England and Wales, 1700–1820*. London: Society for Theatre Research, 1978.

Runge, Laura L. *Gender and Language in British Literary Criticism, 1660–1790*. Cambridge: Cambridge University Press, 1997.

Sacks, Sheldon. "Golden Birds and Dying Generations." *Comparative Literature Studies* 6 (1969): 274–91.

Salzmann, Zdenek. *Language, Culture, and Society: An Introduction to Linguistic Anthropology*. 2d ed. Boulder, Colo.: Westview Press, 1998.

Saville-Troike, Muriel. *The Ethnography of Communication: An Introduction.* 2d ed. Oxford: Blackwell, 1989.

Sennett, Richard. *The Fall of Public Man.* New York: Norton, 1974.

Shoemaker, Robert B. *Gender in English Society, 1650–1850: The Emergence of Separate Spheres?* London: Longman, 1998.

Siskin, Clifford. *The Work of Writing: Literature and Social Change in Britain, 1700–1830.* Baltimore: Johns Hopkins University Press, 1998.

Sitter, John. *Arguments of Augustan Wit.* Cambridge: Cambridge University Press, 1991.

Sklar, Elizabeth S. "So Male a Speech: Linguistic Adequacy in Eighteenth-Century England." *American Speech* 64 (1989): 372–79.

Sledd, James H., and Gwin J. Kolb. *Dr. Johnson's Dictionary: Essays in the Biography of a Book.* Chicago: University of Chicago Press, 1955.

Smith, Olivia. *The Politics of Language, 1791–1819.* Oxford: Clarendon, 1984.

Sorensen, Janet. *The Grammar of Empire in Eighteenth-Century British Writing.* Cambridge: Cambridge University Press, 2000.

Spacks, Patricia Meyer. "Ambiguities of Pleasing." *Eighteenth-Century Life* 10, no. 3 (1986): 74–85.

Spacks, Patricia Meyer. *Gossip.* Chicago: University of Chicago Press, 1986.

Spacks, Patricia Meyer. *Imagining a Self: Autobiography and Novel in Eighteenth-Century England.* Cambridge: Harvard University Press, 1976.

Spender, Dale. *Man Made Language.* 2d ed. London: Routledge & Kegan Paul, 1985.

Stone, Lawrence. *The Family, Sex, and Marriage in England, 1500–1800.* New York: Harper & Row, 1977.

Stout, Janis P. *Strategies of Reticence: Silence and Meaning in the Works of Jane Austen, Willa Cather, Katherine Anne Porter, and Joan Didion.* Charlottesville: University Press of Virginia, 1990.

Straub, Kristina. *Divided Fictions: Fanny Burney and Feminine Strategy.* Lexington: University Press of Kentucky, 1987.

Straub, Kristina. *Sexual Suspects: Eighteenth-Century Players and Sexual Ideology.* Princeton, N.J.: Princeton University Press, 1992.

Street, Brian V. *Literacy in Theory and Practice.* Cambridge: Cambridge University Press, 1984.

Swanson, Janice Bowman. "Towards a Rhetoric of Self: The Art of *Persuasion.*" *Nineteenth-Century Fiction* 36 (1981): 1–21.

Swearingen, C. Jan. "*Ethos:* Imitation, Impersonation, and Voice." In James S. Baumlin and Tita French Baumlin, eds., *Ethos: New Essays in Rhetorical and Critical Theory.* Dallas: Southern Methodist University Press, 1994.

Tadmor, Naomi. "'In the Even my Wife Read to Me': Women, Reading, and Household Life in the Eighteenth Century." In James Raven, Helen Small, and Naomi Tadmor, eds., *The Practice and Representation of Reading in England.* Cambridge: Cambridge University Press, 1996.

Tannen, Deborah. *Gender and Discourse.* New York: Oxford University Press, 1994.

Tannen, Deborah, ed. *Spoken and Written Language: Exploring Orality and Literacy.* Norwood, N.J.: Ablex, 1982.

Tannen, Deborah. *You Just Don't Understand: Women and Men in Conversation.* New York: Morrow, 1990.

Tave, Stuart M. *The Amiable Humorist: A Study in the Comic Theory and Criticism of the Eighteenth and Early Nineteenth Centuries.* Chicago: University of Chicago Press, 1960.

Tave, Stuart M. *Some Words of Jane Austen.* Chicago: University of Chicago Press, 1973.

Taylor, George. "'The Just Delineation of the Passions': Theories of Acting in the Age of Garrick." In Kenneth Richards and Peter Thomson, eds., *Essays on the Eighteenth-Century English Stage.* London: Methuen, 1972.

Thackeray, Anna Isabella. *A Book of Sibyls: Mrs. Barbauld, Miss Edgeworth, Mrs. Opie, Miss Austen.* London: Smith, Elder, & Co., 1883.

Thale, Mary. "Women in London Debating Societies in 1780." *Gender and History* 7 (1995): 5–24.

Thomas, D. O. *The Honest Mind: The Thought and Work of Richard Price.* Oxford: Clarendon, 1977.

Thomsen, Inger Sigrun. "Words 'Half-Dethroned': Jane Austen's Art of the Unspoken." In Juliet McMaster and Bruce Stovel, eds., *Jane Austen's Business: Her World and Her Profession.* Basingstoke, England: Macmillan, 1996.

Tompkins, Jane P., ed. *Reader-Response Criticism: From Formalism to Post-Structuralism.* Baltimore: Johns Hopkins University Press, 1980.

Toolan, Michael. "Analysing Fictional Dialogue." *Language and Communication* 5, no. 3 (1985): 193–206.

Trilling, Lionel. *The Opposing Self: Nine Essays in Criticism.* New York: Viking, 1955.

van Dijk, Maarten. "The Kembles and Vocal Technique." *Theatre Research International* 8 (1983): 23–42.

Vickery, Amanda. "Golden Age to Separate Spheres? A Review of the Categories and Chronology of English Women's History." *Historical Journal* 36 (1993): 383–414.

Waldron, Mary. "The Frailties of Fanny: *Mansfield Park* and the Evangelical Movement." *Eighteenth-Century Fiction* 6 (1994): 259–81.

Walzer, Arthur E. "Rhetoric and Gender in Jane Austen's *Persuasion*." *College English* 57 (1995): 688–707.

Warner, William B. *Licensing Entertainment: The Elevation of Novel Reading in Britain, 1684–1750.* Berkeley and Los Angeles: University of California Press, 1998.

Warren, Leland E. "*Caleb Williams* and the 'Fall' into Writing." *Mosaic* 20 (1987): 57–69.

Warren, Leland E. "The Conscious Speakers: Sensibility and the Art of Conversation Considered." In Syndy McMillen Conger, ed., *Sensibility in Transformation: Creative Resistance to Sentiment from the Augustans to the Romantics.* Rutherford, N.J.: Fairleigh Dickinson University Press, 1990.

Warren, Leland E. "Turning Reality Round Together: Guides to Conversation in Eighteenth-Century England." *Eighteenth-Century Life* 8, no. 3 (1983): 65–87.

Wasserman, Earl R. "The Sympathetic Imagination in Eighteenth-Century Theories of Acting." *Journal of English and Germanic Philology* 46 (1947): 264–72.

Watt, Ian. *The Rise of the Novel: Studies in Defoe, Richardson, and Fielding.* Berkeley and Los Angeles: University of California Press, 1957.

West, Candace. "Women's Competence in Conversation." *Discourse and Society* 6 (1995): 107–31.

White, James Boyd. *When Words Lose Their Meaning: Constitutions and Reconstitutions of Language, Character, and Community.* Chicago: University of Chicago Press, 1984.

Wiles, Roy McKeen. "The Relish for Reading in Provincial England Two Centuries Ago." In Paul J. Korshin, ed., *The Widening Circle: Essays on the Circulation of Literature in Eighteenth-Century Europe.* Philadelphia: University of Pennsylvania Press, 1976.

Williams, Ioan, ed. *Novel and Romance, 1700–1800: A Documentary Record.* London: Routledge & Kegan Paul, 1970.

Woolf, Virginia. *A Room of One's Own.* San Diego: Harcourt Brace Jovanovich, 1989.

Worthen, William B. *The Idea of the Actor: Drama and the Ethics of Performance.* Princeton, N.J.: Princeton University Press, 1984.

Wright, Sheila. "Quakerism and Its Implications for Quaker Women: The Women Itinerant Ministers of York Meeting, 1780–1840." In W. J. Sheils and Diana Wood, eds., *Women in the Church.* Oxford: Blackwell, 1990.

Zimmerman, Donald H., and Candace West. "Sex Roles, Interruptions, and Silences in Conversation." In Barrie Thorne and Nancy Henley, eds., *Language and Sex: Difference and Dominance.* Rowley, Mass.: Newbury House, 1975.

Index